Steps to Academic Reading 5

Between the Lines

Jean Zukowski/Faust
Susan S. Johnston

THOMSON
™
HEINLE

Australia • Canada • Mexico • Singapore • Spain • United Kingdom • United States

THOMSON
™
HEINLE

Steps to Academic Reading 5
Between the Lines
Jean Zukowski/Faust
Susan S. Johnston

Developmental Editor: *Phyllis Dobbins*
Production Editor: *Angela Williams Urquhart*
Marketing Manager: *Katrina Byrd*
Manufacturing Coordinator: *Holly Mason*
Production/Composition: *Real Media Solutions*

Copy Editor: WordPlayers
Cover Designer: *Bill Brammer Design*
Printer: *Webcom*

Printed in Canada.
5 6 7 8 9 10 06

For more information contact Heinle, 25 Thomson Place, Boston, Massachusetts 02210 USA, or you can visit our Internet site at http://www.heinle.com

For permission to use material from this text or product, contact us:
Tel   1-800-730-2214
Fax   1-800-730-2215
Web http://www.thomsonrights.com

Library of Congress Control Number:
2001095322
ISBN: 0-03-033994-4

Photo Credits: Page 1: Comstock; Page 31: Andrew Ward/Life File/PhotoDisc; Page 59: Adalberto Rios Lanz/SextoSol/PhotoDisc; Page 69: Phillip Spears/PhotoDisc; Page 94: Javier Pierini/PhotoDisc; Page 105: Don Farral/PhotoDisc; Page 107: John Wang/PhotoDisc; Page 118: Jason Reed/PhotoDisc; Page 137: Sami Sarkis/PhotoDisc; Page 139: Dr. Ronald Blakey, Dept. of Geology, Northern Arizona University; Page 149: D. Falconer/PhotoLink/PhotoDisc; Page 175: Kim Steele/PhotoDisc; Page 175: Hisham F. Ibrahim/PhotoDisc; Page 198: Ryan McVay/PhotoDisc; Page 215: Steve Cole/PhotoDisc; Page 217: photo provided by Jean Zukowski/Faust; Page 227: Alan Pappe/PhotoDisc; Page 249: Hisham F. Ibrahim/PhotoDisc; Page 252: Neil Beer/PhotoDisc; Page 255: 1996–1998 N.A.F. McNally; Page 260: Andrew Ward/Life File/PhotoDisc; Page 265: Kim Steele/PhotoDisc; Page 266: Akira Kaede/PhotoDisc; Page 289: Chad Baker/PhotoDisc

Contents

Preface

Reading is a complex interactive process involving the mind, experiences, knowledge, and intention of the reader, and the meaning, organization, structure, and purpose of the text. While the printed text remains fixed in time and space, the reader's understanding and interpretation of the text changes with each reading and over time. When second language learners approach a text in the target language, the reading process becomes even more complex as they work additionally to decode meaning with new language and unfamiliar cultural contexts. Each learner's reading of a text is therefore unique, variable, and creative. When readers are second language learners, they can use practice in explicit reading strategies to assist with the reading process.

Steps to Academic Reading 5, Between the Lines is a collection of readings with academic content designed to meet the interests and needs of high-intermediate English language learners. Each of the eight main Units contains a cluster of high-interest readings related to an academic field: **Ecology, Business, Biotechnology, Geology, Sociology, Psychology, Film, History,** and **Archaeology**. Each reading has an accompanying series of activities focusing on reading strategies that naturally emerge from the text. These strategies encourage learners to use what they already know about reading in their first language. The text also introduces new strategies to support learners in becoming effective academic readers in English. Some of the strategies introduced include strategies for:

- anticipating ideas
- analyzing cause and effect
- increasing reading speed
- learning new words
- looking for meaning in context
- making questions
- organizing information for writing
- reading critically
- restating main ideas
- scanning for key ideas
- understanding definitions
- understanding sequence
- understanding the audience

Unit Structure

Each unit begins with a Preparation section with specific strategies for anticipating the ideas in the unit. These strategies give learners practice in activating their prior knowledge so they can better synthesize the content of the various theme-based readings. The Main Reading and activities follow, setting the context for the unit. Two to four readings related in topic to the main reading follow, also with strategy-focused activities. Each unit has writing activities, strategies for maintaining a personal vocabulary journal, and a 400-word timed reading. The activity types are dependent upon textual features of each reading, so each unit has a variety of activities types.

A sample of strategy-focused activities in *Steps to Academic Reading 5, Between the Lines*

Strategy Focus	Purpose
Analyzing the Sequence	to become aware of pronoun references, transitions, and time progressions
Discussing the Ideas	to push the use of concepts and domain-specific vocabulary in meaningful spoken contexts (*pushed-output*)
Finding Main Ideas	to practice reading consciously; to generalize and synopsize
Learning about Word Families	to apply knowledge of word stems, prefixes, and suffixes for vocabulary extension
Learning Vocabulary in Context	to reduce dictionary dependence and to analyze the relationship between context, coherence, and meaning
Making Inferences	to practice determining facts, opinions, and implications and to become aware of a writer's intentions
Scanning for Details	to read rapidly in search of particular types of information
Understanding Internal Structure	to become aware of English rhetorical patterns and their uses

An effort has been made to include both contrast and multiple points of view. For example in Unit 3, "Biotechnology: Feeding the Billions," the main article has two points of view, one advocating biotechnology, the other arguing against it.

Approaches to using the text

Steps to Academic Reading 5, Between the Lines can be used as a classroom text for intensive reading practice in a general English program or in an English-for-academic-purposes program. One of the most important features of the text is the variety of **choices** available to both the teacher and students. The text is arranged in a flexible manner, so that once the instructor establishes that learners understand the basic strategies presented in the Preliminary Unit, the instructor can work with the learners to decide which thematic units to cover. Within each unit there are choices as well—learners can be polled to decide which related readings are the most interesting or relevant for them. Research indicates that when learners have real choices relating directly to their learning, they perform better.

Units can be presented in the following manner:

1. Introduce the general theme of a unit by doing the **Preparation** section. The Strategy for Anticipation activity presents strategies for helping learners activate prior knowledge. Introducing the theme can mean surveying the unit, noting the titles, and generating vocabulary words. The concepts behind these activities are that
   - adult learners can use their own world knowledge and experience actively in predicting what will form the ideas of a reading.
   - vocabulary associated with a topic awakens the awareness of the topic in the students.

2. The **Main Reading** is essential reading for each unit because it introduces the theme with the greatest depth. Activities associated with each reading can be selected by the instructor, but it is recommended that they be followed as presented. Decide with the learners—or, of course, you as instructor can decide—which of the **Related Readings** are most interesting or relevant for the learners. Of course, it is best to read as much as possible, but depending on the level of the group of participants and the time constraints, it may not be possible to present every reading in a unit.

3. Engage the class in **critical thinking** about the readings whenever possible. The activities that require critical thinking skills (Making Inferences, Analyzing Evidence, Distinguishing Fact from Non-Fact, for example) quickly bring out differences of opinion that underscore cultural differences. Point of view might be an important concept to present. The critical reading exercises in which students are distinguishing facts from opinions and judgments, for this reason, might be the most challenging for an instructor, who must remain flexible and ask for clear thinking from the learners. If a disagreement develops, a clearly stated rationale from each participant forces the learners to use their full language abilities.

4. **Evaluate** what you have been teaching in multiple ways. If you are emphasizing strategies, are the students aware of the strategies and how to use them? If you are working on vocabulary acquisition, are the students using their vocabulary journals to expand their active vocabulary knowledge? Do the students understand the content of the unit? Do their writing products reflect their comprehension and application of the unit theme, structures, and vocabulary?

Acknowledgments

We thank all those who helped us—and had the patience and good will to wait for us—to finish this revision of *Steps to Academic Reading 5, Between the Lines*. We wish particularly to acknowledge Michael Aslett, Robert Bovasso, Elizabeth Geary, and Constance Wynn-Smith of Real Media Solutions; Jacqueline Flamm and Dina Forbes of WordPlayers; Adele Young; and Phyllis Dobbins, Matt Drapeau, Sherrise Roehr, and Charlotte Sturdy of Heinle.

Jean Zukowski/Faust
Susan S. Johnston

Introducing the Authors

Jean Zukowski/Faust, Ph.D., is an ESL/EFL methodologist, specializing in teaching reading and writing, a teacher, and a teacher educator. She has taught English to students in the United States, Turkey, and Poland and worked with teachers in many other places around the world. She has authored or co-authored four other texts in the Steps to Academic Reading series published by Heinle: *Steps to Academic Reading 1, Steps and Plateaus; Steps to Academic Reading 2, Out of the Ordinary; Steps to Academic Reading 3, Across the Board; Steps to Academic Reading 4, In Context.* She is a professor at Northern Arizona University.

Susan S. Johnston, Ed.D., has taught and directed ESL programs in American universities in the United States and Japan for more than twenty years. Her interests include the use of technology in language instruction, content-based language instruction, qualitative program analysis, reading education, and second language curriculum development. Dr. Johnston has co-authored a number of ESL/EFL texts, including *Steps to Academic Reading 4, In Context; Keys to Composition*; and the *Holt-Cassell Foundation English Series*.

PRELIMINARY
UNIT

Using Reading Strategies

Strategies for Anticipation ⸺⸺⸺⸺⸺⸺⸺⸺⸺⸺⸺⸺

Before you begin to read anything, anticipate; think about the background. Think about your own knowledge of the topic. Survey the reading: look at it, front to back. Check out the titles, subtitles, and headings, and then look at the pictures. Then you will know what to expect as you read. You'll be looking for some specific ideas.

1. Look at the different parts of this unit. Make a list of the five additional main parts. The first and last ones are done for you.

    a. _Strategies for Anticipation_____

    b. _____

    c. _____

    d. _____

    e. _____

    f. _____

    g. _Practice Reading_____

2. The first part of this unit is (a) Strategies for Anticipation, the first one in the list above in number 1. This part helps you to understand what the topic is and to explore the ideas before you read. What will the second part (b) help you with? Circle your choice.

    a. preparing to read

    b. learning new vocabulary

    c. reading for details

    d. organizing facts

    e. finding the main ideas

3. What will the third part (c) of this unit (from item 1 above) help you learn about? Circle your choice.

    a. preparing to read

    b. learning new vocabulary

    c. critical reading

    d. finding the main ideas

    e. reading for details

4. What is the purpose of the fourth part (d) of this unit? Circle your choice.

    a. to help you get ready to read quickly

    b. to help you learn new vocabulary

    c. to help you do a better job of critical reading

    d. to help you find the details in a reading

    e. to help you understand grammar

5. What will the fifth part (e) of this unit help you learn to do? Circle your choice.

    a. read critically

    b. learn to find word meanings in context

    c. be a more critical reader

    d. prepare you to read

    e. determine what the main ideas are in a reading

6. What is the sixth main part (f) of this unit? Circle your choice.

    a. practice in finding main ideas

    b. learning to guess at word meanings in context

    c. anticipating the topic

    d. learning to read critically

    e. asking questions about the topic

7. What is the last main section (g)? Circle your choice.

    a. sample exercises

    b. a timed reading with some examples of exercises

    c. a sample unit for the rest of the book

    d. a list of ways to learn new words quickly

    e. vocabulary practice

Before you read, survey the material first. To read well, every reader needs some idea about the structure or form of the reading. It is also important to have some ideas about the topic. You will read more efficiently if you know what to expect—the content and the form of a book, a chapter, a unit, an essay, or even a paragraph.

Strategies for Understanding New Words

How do you figure out the meanings of new words? As you read, you suddenly see a new word. What should you do? You could reach for your dictionary and look it up. If you use your dictionary for every new word, you become very good at using the dictionary. However, your reading process is stopped. Every time you look up a word, you forget some of the ideas in the reading. You have to go back and read some of the sentences again.

Another way to discover the meaning of a new word is to find clues to its meaning *in context*. Look at the sentences around the new word and try to find hints or ideas about the meaning. The meaning can come from these sources:

- a word with an opposite meaning (an *antonym*)
- an *appositive*, a group of words that follows a new word and gives its definition
- a *relative clause*, which is a sentence-like expression of explanation
- a whole paragraph or even a whole page of information about the topic

The following reading and exercises contain practice with learning new words in context.

Strategy Focus: Finding Meanings in Context

To find the meanings of words using context clues, remember these four important points:

1. If a word is important, the writer has probably used it more than once in the article. So if you cannot find a clue at first, read on. If the word is not repeated and you still think that you understand the article, you can safely skip the word.

2. If you learn to find clues to meanings (instead of depending on the dictionary for meanings), you will become a much better reader. Looking for context clues helps you pay attention to the full meaning of sentences. You will also read more naturally if you do not depend on a dictionary. Nothing will interrupt your reading process.

3. If you learn a new word in context, you learn it in a meaningful situation. The word is related to other words, and it is used with them. A dictionary meaning is a "cold" definition; the word is not being used in a real context, even though the word is sometimes given in a sample sentence.

4. When reading a second language, you should read the same way you read in your first language. Do you need a dictionary to read your hometown newspaper? Think about the ways you read in your mother tongue and use the same strategies in reading English.

As you read "Monuments of the Old West," use these four points to help you understand new words. The new words are in *italic* type.

 ## Reading

Monuments of the Old West

1   At the turn of the 20th *century*, the broad *plains* of North America were quiet. In the 1800s, approximately 70 million *bison* roamed the *grasslands* between northern Mexico and the wide-open lands of Canada. Huge herds of the cattle-like animals wandered freely. They went wherever they liked and lived on the native vegetation. They were the perfect inhabitants of the North American *prairies*.

2   When European settlers came, the number of bison (or American buffalo) began to fall. The newcomers made farms on the richest lands, which were places with water. The bison moved to drier, less desirable lands. Their numbers naturally *decreased* by 30%.

3   Then came the buffalo hunter. There was a market for buffalo robes. Buffalo *hide*, or skin, made fine quality leather, and the skins with thick buffalo hair made warm blankets. By 1900, more than 50 million buffalo had been killed. Only 500 buffalo *survived*.

4   Charles J. Jones, called Buffalo Jones, was one famous hunter. He watched as the herds got smaller and smaller. He noticed that bison were disappearing fast, too fast, and worried that they might disappear forever. He rounded up 87 young bison and kept them on a farm in Kansas. Theodore Roosevelt, the American president at that time, heard about Jones. Roosevelt recognized that this hunter had a special quality about him. He noticed that Jones had changed from being a hunter to being a keeper of bison.

5   Roosevelt hired Buffalo Jones to run the first U.S. national park, Yellowstone Park in Montana. In 1915, he also asked Jones to go to Arizona to see the Grand Canyon. Roosevelt was considering the Grand Canyon as another national park. Jones went *to check it out*, and he reported favorably. Jones also found a place for his buffalo near the Grand Canyon. He brought 87 bison from his Kansas herd to Grand Canyon country.

6   Today the descendants of the 500 bison (the survivors in 1900) number 350,000. They live in 30 public herds. Two such herds live in northern Arizona where Buffalo Jones first looked for suitable lands for them. John and Susan Kohler manage one of these buffalo ranches. Like Buffalo Jones a hundred years ago, the Kohlers work to keep the grasslands and water supply healthy. Their bison now *wander* free over 65,000 acres of *open range*. These animals are living monuments of the Old West.

Strategies for Learning Vocabulary from Context

Write or choose the meaning that best fits the context of the reading.

1. The word *bison* (paragraphs 1 and 2) is defined directly: "In the 1800s, approximately 70 million *bison* roamed the grasslands between northern Mexico and the wide-open lands of Canada. Huge herds of the cattle-like animals wandered freely. They went wherever they liked and lived on the native vegetation. They were the perfect inhabitants of the North American *prairies*."

   When European settlers came, the number of bison (or American buffalo) began to fall.

   Bison are ___animals___. They are similar to ___buffalo___.
   Another name for *bison* is ___cattle___.

2. You can find the meanings of *plains*, *grasslands*, and *prairies* in sentences in the same paragraph (paragraph 1): "…"the broad plains of North America were quiet. In the 1800s approximately 70 million bison roamed the *grasslands* between northern Mexico and the wide-open lands of Canada…They lived on the native vegetation. They were the perfect inhabitants of the North American *prairies*."

The sentences give clear synonyms—words with the same meaning—and supporting information: the open lands between Mexico and Canada, a place where there were plants (vegetation) for animals to eat.

A *prairie* is land that ____synonyms a place where animals live____

Grasslands are places where ____between northern Mexico and Canada____

Plains are lands that are _____.

3. The meaning of *decrease* (paragraph 3) can be found in sentences around the sentence in which it is used. "When European settlers came, the number of bison (or American buffalo) <u>began to fall</u>. The newcomers made farms on the richest lands, places with water. The bison moved to drier, less desirable lands. Their numbers naturally *decreased* by 30%."

To *decrease* can mean…

a. to start a farm.

b. to fall in number.

c. to move to another place.

4. The meaning of *hide* (paragraph 3) comes from a parallel structure: "Buffalo *hide*, or <u>skin</u>, made <u>fine quality</u> leather, and the skins with thick buffalo hair made <u>warm blankets</u>."

In this sentence, buffalo *hide* refers to…

a. the leather.

b. the skin of the animal , with or without the hide.

c. secret buffalo.

5. The word <u>*survive*</u> is defined as the opposite of the verb in the sentence before it (paragraph 3): "By 1900, more than 50 million buffalo had been killed. Only 500 buffalo *survived*."

To *survive* is not to be ____not to be killed____.

6. To *roam* and to *wander* mean almost the same thing. The meaning is in the following sentence from paragraph 1: They went wherever they liked and lived on the native vegetation.

   To *roam* and to *wander* both mean...

   a. to stay in one place.

   b. to go wherever one wants to go.

7. To *check* something *out* is defined in a preceding sentence, a sentence that comes before the word is used (paragraph 6): "...he also asked Jones to go to Arizona to see the Grand Canyon. Roosevelt was considering the Grand Canyon as another national park. Jones went *to check it out*, and he reported favorably."

   To *check* something *out* is...

   a. to go to see something with a special purpose.

   b. to report one's opinion.

8. The word century is found in paragraph 1. Sentences throughout the reading all point to the meaning: "At the turn of the 20th century, the broad plains of North America were quiet. In the 1800s...Like Buffalo Jones a hundred years ago..."

   A century is _____ 100 _____ years.

Strategy Focus: Reading for Details

When you do research, you might only be looking for a small piece of information. You do not have to read everything in an article to get the necessary information. At the library, for example, you might be looking in an encyclopedia for a name or a date. You will look for capital letters or for numbers. You just move your eyes quickly over the reading to find facts, names, dates, and titles. Punctuation is also a clue for finding specific information. Quotation marks [" "], commas [,], parentheses [( )], and dashes [–] all separate special information. Also look for words in **bold** or *italic* type. Practice this skill as you read.

Use the ideas about this reading strategy as you look for the key facts in the reading "Monuments of the Old West." Begin by scanning the whole reading, looking for capital letters, numbers, and different kinds of punctuation.

Strategy Focus: Making Inferences

What made Buffalo Jones an unusual person? Circle all the correct answers. (Hint: Which statements about him are not true of many other people? There are several possible answers.)

a. He was one of a thousand buffalo hunters.

b. He observed the decreasing buffalo herds and decided to do something about the loss of the animal.

c. He looked for solutions to problems of all kinds.

d. He traveled widely and learned about nature in his travels.

e. He knew President Theodore Roosevelt.

f. He went to Yellowstone Park.

Strategies for Finding Answers to Detail Questions

 Reading    9–607 Thursday

Using Science to Fill a Pothole

1   Every winter makes spring headaches for highway repair crews. Freezing water in road cracks expands and makes more cracks in concrete and asphalt. For years, highway departments have had to guess the right mixture of asphalt to repair roads—but now there is a scientific answer. It is called Superpave.

2   Superpave is the result of a five-year study by the Strategic Highway Research Program (SHRP). It is a system of technologies that include asphalt tests and specifications that gives repair crews a much better idea of what to use and when to use it. For example, according to program director Damian Kulash, by adding a substance such as *polyurethane*—a synthetic substance—to asphalt, repair crews can get a tougher road surface. This road surface will not melt in the sun when the road temperature reaches 180 degrees Fahrenheit. The mixture will not crack at 10 degrees below zero in the winter.

Furthermore, it can extend the life of a road by a full 5%. More than $10 billion is spent on road repairs each year in the United States. Therefore, Superpave could save $500 million a year in the United States alone; that's a savings of 5%.

3   The materials for road building are better now too. For example, great improvements have been made in concrete. Vincent Janoo of the Cold Regions Research and Engineering Laboratory in Hanover, New Hampshire, reported that his laboratory had poured an "antifreeze concrete" in temperatures as cold as 10 degrees Fahrenheit. Charles H. Korhonen, a research civil engineer at the Cold Regions Lab, says, "We can make concrete think it's…in Florida instead of Alaska."

4   For years, many highway crews have used the cheap "dump and run" technique: The crew sweeps out a hole and throws in some asphalt. But those potholes need to be fixed again and again. Science has made a difference. With Superpave, there are formulas to follow, and the results are sure. Superpave can show repair crews exactly what to use for repairs, and although the high-quality materials are 300% of the cost of the ordinary ones, the repairs last five times longer. ■

Look carefully in the reading to find the details. Write them in the blanks.

1. What are the names of two researchers at the Cold Regions Research and Engineering Laboratory? (Look for capital letters.)
   <u>vincent Janoo</u> and <u>charles H. korhonen.</u>

2. Where is the Cold Regions Research and Engineering Laboratory? (Look for capital letters.) <u>Hanover, New Hampshire.</u>

3. How much more do high-quality materials for road repair cost compared to ordinary asphalt? (Look for numbers, percentage signs, or dollar signs.) <u>300%</u>

4. What is SHRP? <u>Strategic highway Research Program</u>

5. How long was the SHRP study? (Look for numbers of years.)

   _____ five years.

6. What is polyurethane? (Look for italic type.) a synthetic substance.

7. What is the "dump and run" technique of pothole repair? (Look for quotation marks.) _The crew sweeps out a hole and throws in some asphalt._

8. How much is spent in the United States on road repair each year? (Look for a dollar sign and a number.) _$10 billion._

9. How hot does a road surface get in the summer? (Look for a number.)

   _____ 180 °C _.

10. What did Charles H. Korhonen say about antifreeze concrete? (Look for quotation marks.) _you will think it's in Florida instead of Alaska._

11. Who is Damian Kulash? (Look for capital letters.)

    _____ SHRP _.

12. How much money could Superpave save in road repairs in one country in one year? (Look for dollar signs.) _$500 million_

Strategies for Critical Reading to Identify Facts, Implications, and Judgments

Read

Do you believe something just because it's in print? It is important to make up your own mind (that is, form your own opinions) by learning how to read critically. Critical reading combines the skills of understanding:

- what the writer wrote
- what evidence he or she used to form the ideas
- whether or not the writer's argument is strong
- what the information can be used for

Critical reading means thinking about what is on the page and what it means to you after you have read it. Critical reading is more than agreeing or disagreeing with a writer. It involves the skill of telling the difference between a fact and an *opinion* or a *judgment*. It also means looking carefully to tell whether something can be proved to be true or whether it only seems to be so. Think about what the writer does to present his or her perspective.

Remember, it is natural for a writer to choose the tools of writing that will result in convincing readers that the writer is right! Every article includes many kinds of ideas. Here are some of a writer's important tools and techniques:

- **Word choice:** A writer chooses words carefully in order to give readers a feeling about his or her attitude toward the subject.

- **Organization:** A writer organizes ideas so that readers are likely to agree with his or her viewpoint.

- **Examples:** A writer chooses examples that prove his or her point.

- **Selection of ideas:** A writer omits ideas that will weaken his or her argument.

- **Supporting facts:** A writer uses facts, statements that can be proved, whenever possible. Examples of facts are statistics (numbers from research studies), proper names, dates, true stories, and experimental results.

- **Implementations:** A writer uses implications, ideas that are not quite facts. The author guides the reader to use the facts (the already-known ideas) to form new ideas about the unknown. In other words, the writer tries to lead the reader to the same conclusion that he or she has already made. Changing the reader's mind is the writer's purpose for writing. An implication results in inferences, conclusions, and deductions.

- **Judgments:** A writer uses his or her own judgments, and a critical reader must learn to recognize them. Judgments are the writer's conclusions; the reader may or may not agree with them. The attitude of the writer—whether the writer approves or disapproves, whether the writer thinks something is right or wrong—is in the article as part of the judgments. The writer's choice of words can alert a critical reader about that writer's judgments. The critical reader understands the writer's point of view and balances his or her own information with the writer's.

What are your opinions? Readers also need to think about their own personal opinions. You, as a reader, bring your knowledge and your background to the reading. Your ideas, therefore, are added to the ideas of the writer. Your ideas may also be inferences, conclusions, deductions, and, of course, your own opinions.

As you read the following paragraph, think about which parts of the information are **facts**, which parts are **implications**, and which parts are clearly **judgments** that the writer has made. Please remember, however, that your experience and the experiences of other students in your class are not the same. What is a fact should always be a fact because it is definite and unchanging. However, each person's interpretation is unique (different from all others). What is a fact to you may not seem factual to another person. What is a judgment to you may be a fact or an inference to someone else. Your purpose in thinking about this reading is to practice critical reading—to figure out what you think.

Take a Poll

Take a poll and find out what people think. For example, in politics, every week someone asks people for their opinions. The Gallup Poll is one of the most famous poll-taking companies. Every week, Gallup pollsters decide on a group of questions and pick up their telephones. They call telephone numbers at random (that is, they do not choose the numbers according to any plan) and simply ask people for their feelings: "What is your favorite television show?" "What do you think of the government's latest program?" "Who will you vote for?" In a recent poll, a group of people were asked about their preferences in music. The results were startling: 37% said they preferred modern soft rock music, 28% liked classical music, 19% liked folk music, especially country western music, and the rest liked new music and hard rock. The results were surprisingly striking because of a sharp decrease in the popularity of rock and roll music. Just ten years ago, nearly 30% of people listened to new music. It seems people are becoming more conservative in their tastes in music.

Fact

Some of the statements that can be made about the paragraph are facts. A fact is an idea that everyone agrees on because it is true. These sample statements are marked as if they were in an exercise (*F* stands for fact).

1. __F__ A company named Gallup takes polls.

2. __F__ Gallup pollsters use telephones.

3. __F__ Random numbers are not selected according to any plan.

4. __F__ Ten years ago, 30% of people listened to new music.

Non-Fact

Some of the statements that can be made about the paragraph are not facts. The reader needs to add together ideas to be able to say whether a statement is true or not (inferences), or the reader needs to make a judgment. Here are some non-facts, which may or may not be true. These sample statements are marked as if they were in an exercise (*NF* stands for non-fact).

1. _NF_ People change their opinions over a period of time.

2. _NF_ There is a greater variety of kinds of music these days.

3. _NF_ It is surprising that 19% of the people in the poll like folk or country western music.

4. _NF_ The pollsters must have talked to more men than women.

Word Choice

Sometimes a reader is led to believe ideas because of the words that the writer used. Look at these sentences for words that can influence a person's opinion:

1. They call telephone numbers at random and simply ask people for their feelings.
2. The results were startling.
3. The difference was striking because of a sharp decrease in the popularity of new music.

In the first statement, the word *simply* gives the reader a feeling that the poll is OK. The pollsters are not asking personal questions; they are not being impolite. What they are doing is simple. In the second statement, the writer wants the reader to agree with her that the poll results were more than surprising: they were startling. In the third statement, the author uses the word *sharp*—another word to change the minds of the readers.

Critical readers must be aware of writers' attempts to influence them, to change their minds. By the way, did you figure out the meaning of poll without your dictionary?

Practice with Facts and Non-Facts

Now read the following paragraphs and the numbered statements that follow each one. Indicate which statements are facts by writing *F* in the blank and which ones are inferences or judgments (your own or the writer's) by writing *NF* in the blank.

Hidden Persuader   *Read*

   In 1957, James Vicary, an American market researcher, thought of using a special movie projector, a *tachistoscope* [ta-KISS-ta-SCOPE], as an advertising instrument. He knew that the tachistoscope can flash a message on a movie screen at 1/3,000 of a second. He also knew that people were able to read such a fast message, but they did not know it—they didn't even know that the message was there. Vicary arranged a six-week study. During those six weeks, messages suggesting that people buy popcorn and soft drinks were flashed on the screen while the movie was going on. Sales for that period showed a 60 percent increase in popcorn sales and a 20 percent increase in soft drink sales. Vicary proved that the tachistoscope could influence people in a theater. No one complained about the messages on the screen until the results of the study were published.

What do you think about the following statements? Do they seem to be facts? Are some of them opinions? Are some the writer's judgments? Decide for yourself, and be aware that your classmates might not all agree with you. Write *F* or *NF* in the blank.

1. __NF__ One three-thousandth of a second is a very short time.

2. __NF__ James Vicary was interested in advertising as part of his job.

3. __F__ The tachistoscope was invented before 1958.

4. __F__ Popcorn and soft drinks are sold in movie theaters.

5. __F__ People can read a message that is flashed on a movie screen for 1/3,000 of a second.

6. __F__ The people in the movie theater did not know that the tachistoscope was being used.

7. __NF__ Because people are influenced without knowing it, the tachistoscope is a bad machine.

8. __F__ People respond to suggestions.

9. __N F__   Movie-theater owners should not have allowed the use of the tachistoscope.

10. __F__   The tachistoscope increased sales of popcorn more than sales of soft drinks.

11. __N F__   People prefer popcorn to soft drinks.

12. __N F__   People do not like to be tricked.

حدود الانهيار

The Wonderful Worm

Some people use them for fishing, but what other uses does an earthworm have? Well, according to Mary Appelhof in her book, *Worms Eat My Garbage*, worms can turn garbage into a valuable resource. Nearly everyone knows that some garbage (the peelings of vegetables, grass cuttings, leftover food) decays. It gets fungus, it rots, it turns into a stinking mess. Millions of people (those who have yards and maybe even gardens) compost all organic material. But what do people who live in cities do? Appelhof suggests *vermicomposting*. First, Appelhof says, you need a large plastic bin, like a garbage can, and a lot of worms. She recommends the cute little red worms that are common on farms. Then you dump in food waste like banana skins, bread crusts, apple cores, vegetable peelings, and teabags. The food decays, and the worms eat it. They transform the garbage into rich compost—good stuff for gardens or houseplants. Appelhof calls it "on-site recycling." In a local school, the kitchen staff decided to try vermicomposting. They wanted to know whether it would work, and how well it would work, so they kept careful records. They bought five pounds of worms and three bins. They set them up outside the kitchen and started throwing in food scraps. The five pounds of industrious little worms in those three bins ate more than two tons of garbage in one year! That was eight percent of the total weight of waste for the whole school. That eight percent equals a great savings because each bag of garbage costs $2.75—that's the haul-away fee. And it costs nothing to maintain the worm bins. Besides being almost free, the vermicomposting process is odorless, and most important, the worms cannot get out of the bins.

Write *F* or *NF* in the blank.

1. __F__ Worms eat garbage.
2. __NF__ It's expensive to have someone take away your garbage.
3. __NF__ Little red worms are cute.
4. __NF__ Worms will eat grass cuttings.
5. __NF__ Vermicomposting is odorless and safe.
6. __NF__ There are lots of worms in the soil of a farm.
7. __NF__ Rotting food smells bad.
8. __NF__ "On-site recycling" is a good idea.
9. __NF__ Five pounds of worms is a lot of worms.
10. __NF__ People should put compost on their houseplants.

A Sweet Taste of Spring

Quebec is famous for its maple forests, and also for maple *syrup*. This natural sweet, much sweeter than cane or beet sugar, is almost unknown to most of the world, but for the people of North America, it is the perfect topping for pancakes. Making maple syrup is an interesting process. Each of the sugar maple trees in Quebec's maple forests produces a watery sap each spring, when there is still lots of snow on the ground. To take the sap out of a tree, a farmer makes a slit in the bark with a special knife and puts a "tap" on the tree. Then the farmer hangs a bucket from the tap, and the sap drips into it. That sap is collected and boiled until a sweet syrup remains—forty gallons of maple tree "water" make one gallon of syrup. That's a lot of buckets, a lot of steam, and a lot of work. Even so, Quebec has about 11,000 maple syrup producers, most of them family farmers who collect the buckets by hand and boil the sap into syrup themselves. In any case, making maple syrup is big, sweet business in Quebec.

Write *F* or *NF* in the blank.

1. _____ Forty gallons of maple sap make one gallon of maple syrup.
2. _____ Carrying buckets of maple sap is hard work.
3. _____ Canadians enjoy maple syrup on pancakes.
4. _____ There are about 11,000 maple sugar producers in Quebec.
5. _____ Quebec has a lot of maple trees.

6. _____ Maple sugar farmers have to work hard in the early spring.

7. _____ The tree that produces sap is a sugar maple.

8. _____ A slit is a cut in a tree.

9. _____ A fire is needed to make syrup out of maple sap.

10. _____ Maple syrup is sweeter than regular sugar.

Strategies for Finding Main Ideas

The main idea of an article or paragraph is its purpose—the reason for which it was written. To find the main idea, ask yourself these questions:

- Why did the author write the article?
- What ideas do most of the sentences support?

Note that most of the ideas are supporting information. That is, they are specific examples, reasons, or details about the main idea. The main idea is something like a cover over all the smaller supporting ideas. Try to find the main idea in the following paragraph.

Who Will Feed Africa?

Who will feed Africa? If you ask Musu Kegba Drahmmeh of The Gambia, she'll tell you, "We will." With money from the country of Norway to help them get started, Musu and her neighbors are learning how to make the desert yield cabbage and squash. These women of Africa all have gardens to feed their families. They do "intensive farming." They grow vegetables on dry land by carrying water to each plant. They use bottomless pots to hold the water close to the growing vegetables. These women are successful gardeners. They can also produce more than their own families need, so they can sell their extra produce. Each woman alone, however, would find the whole job of farming and marketing too much. They need to take care of their families as well as their gardens. So they cannot spend time trying to sell small amounts of extra food. In addition, if each woman went to the market to sell, the competition to sell would hurt every one of them. The solution was to form a *cooperative*. Now more than 500 women work together. Their cooperative bought two trucks. They have a contract with one trusted seller. The women are also learning how to read, write, and keep records. At the same time, perhaps, they are learning how to feed the hungry, growing continent.

Sample Questions and Answers

What is the main idea of the paragraph? Choose the best answer and circle it.

The main idea of this paragraph is that...

   a. Musu Kegba Drahmmeh is a good gardener.
   b. The Gambia has land that can grow good food if people are willing to carry water.
   c. Africans need to do intensive farming to produce food to feed the people.
   d. A cooperative in The Gambia made a group of small gardeners into one large business.

Analysis

   a. The first choice is too narrow. The information is about one specific idea in the whole paragraph, and for this reason, it cannot be the main idea.
   b. The second idea is very broad. It contains ideas beyond the paragraph. We don't know how much good farmland The Gambia has.
   c. The third idea is implied by the article, but it is not a main idea. It is a conclusion that you make when you think about the situation in the article. However, a main idea must be within the paragraph. You cannot take an inference as the main idea.
   d. The fourth idea is the correct answer because it is general enough to include all the supporting information in the paragraph.

Strategy Focus: Finding the Main Idea

Read the three paragraphs that follow. For each one, think about the main idea. Underline the idea that is closest to the main idea you thought about as you read.

   A. Cooking with the sun is cheap (it's really free), and it's not messy (no smoke and everything stays clean). The food keeps all the vitamins because cooking with the sun's heat (solar cooking) is slow and steady. The food actually tastes better because all the natural juices stay in the food. In addition, food cannot burn in a solar cooker because most days there isn't enough heat to burn it. Of course, the

— made w/ simple materials.

— don't need to plan ahead.

cook needs a solar oven (which can be made at home with simple materials) and also needs to plan ahead. Solar cooking takes more time, and you have to do it outside on a sunny day. Even so, you might wonder why more people don't use solar cookers.

1. The main idea of this paragraph is that...

   a. a solar cooker is easy to make from simple materials.

   b. it is puzzling that more people don't cook in a solar cooker.

   c. food cannot burn in a solar cooker.

   d. solar cooking requires a great deal of planning.

2. Give the paragraph a title:

   _____

B. Three hundred sixty million years ago, the horseshoe crab lived and looked much as it does today. It is one of the few animal species that has remained unchanged since its prehistoric beginnings. The cockroach and a rare Indian Ocean fish are the only two living creatures that are as old as the horseshoe crab. When the Earth was still forming and mountains were rising, horseshoe crabs were already swimming in the oceans. As they are not good to eat and because they have few natural enemies, they are probably strong enough to survive as a species for millions of years more.

1. The main idea of this paragraph is that...

   a. the horseshoe crab is one of the world's oldest and strongest creatures.

   b. there were horseshoe crabs 360 million years ago.

   c. the cockroach and a rare Indian Ocean fish are the only two creatures as old as the horseshoe crab.

   d. there will be horseshoe crabs for many years more.

2. Give the paragraph a title: The history of horseshoe crab-

   _____

C. The idea of renting rooms for travelers developed from the custom of gift-giving. In the days when most travelers rode on horses or in small carriages that were pulled by horses, there were few places along the roads for travelers to spend the night. A tired traveler would be welcomed into a private home. There, after a meal, the homeowners would offer a place to sleep and shelter and food for the animals. The traveler, in exchange, was expected to have news from the outside world and stories to tell. When the guest left, he would leave something of value for the family. It was only a matter of time before keeping a hotel, with rooms to rent and food to buy, became common as a kind of business.

1. The main idea of this paragraph is…

   a. travelers needed to pay for room and food.

   b. why travelers became storytellers.

   c. how the hotel business got started.

   d. why it is a custom to give a hotel keeper a gift.

2. Give the paragraph a title: _____

   _____

Practice Reading

This next section is a sample of the work you'll be doing in the units to come. Most of the book is made of content-centered reading practice. This section will help you learn how to do the exercises in Units 1–8.

Strategies for Anticipation

Answer these questions.

1. What do you think the next reading is about? _____

   _____

2. What gave you your ideas? _____

3. How long is the reading? _____

4. What kinds of exercises follow the reading? _____

   _____

5. What is the best way to read this reading? Slowly and carefully? Or quickly? Why? _____

   _____

Reading

Under the Surface

1   The planet Earth is like a cracked egg. Its shell (or crust) is broken into about a dozen pieces (plates). These surface pieces seem to "float" on melted rock (called *magma*), like wood on water. The planet's plates, however, are huge, hard, and thick. They also move, bumping into one another, breaking at the edges. When they move, the surface of the planet changes where they have moved. Volcanoes erupt, and earthquakes rumble. Sometimes valleys form and mountains rise. The land mass of India is an example of a small plate that ran into a larger plate. When the Indian subcontinent hit the Asian plate, the pressure formed the highest mountains in the world, the Himalayas. Most of these changes happened slowly, but the results are there on the surface for all to see.

2   Some plates abut (touch each other) under the oceans and seas. In some of these places (like where the North American plate meets the Caribbean plate), there is less danger. Most of the time, the two plates move quietly, one sliding smoothly under the other. Does the water have anything to do with it? In the Pacific Northwest, from British Columbia to northern California, the under-ocean plate movement meets land at the coast. Plate movement here causes volcano eruptions and earthquakes. There are several actively changing mountain ranges from Canada, along the western coast into Mexico. A number of these mountains along the coast, for example, are active volcanoes. Mountains like Mount St. Helens and Mount Rainier have the potential (the possibility) of exploding. However, there are few such mountains in the Caribbean region, with the dangerous volcano on the small island of Montserrat the major exception. What is the difference? Why is the Caribbean plate so much quieter? The only way to find out may be to drill deep into the earth's underwater crust to find out what the differences are.

3   There is a great deal to learn from the study of the ocean floor. The mountain ranges and breaks or cracks in the planet's surface are easy to see under the water from the satellites above the planet. For example, there are 40,000 miles of mountain ranges under water. One such mountain range stretches from the northern areas of the Atlantic Ocean south, nearly to Antarctica. The tops of some mountains are visible as islands. Satellites above the Earth can record even the smallest details about the oceans and the ocean bottoms. New maps with these details are helping geologists study the changes in the planet's crust (surface) and how it works.

4   Scientists know that all parts of the Earth interact. The surface of the Earth is solid. They believe that underground, like water boiling in a pot, molten (hot liquid rock) magma rolls toward the surface. These circular movements carry the plates with them. The circular currents (convection currents) also perform an earth-cleaning function. The carbon dioxide in the air on the surface of the earth dissolves into water in the ocean. The waves reach into the air and "catch" the carbon dioxide. The carbon dioxide forms a solid carbonate (CO_3) in the water and falls to the ocean bottom. There it forms a kind of rock. As the plate on the ocean floor slips down under the continent plates, the carbonate rock melts into the magma. Thus some of the CO_2 that could cause global warming is recycled.

5   Scientists have learned about the interactions of the Earth from some aspects of ocean study. Figuring out the meaning of these surprising facts is part of the geologists' job. For example, there is evidence that ocean waves today are 3 feet higher than waves 50 years ago. Scientists are wondering why. Could it be because more fossil fuels are burned, because the world is getting warmer, because everything in the world is connected? These cause-and-effect questions give geologists plenty to think about.

Strategy Focus: Learning Vocabulary in Context

Here are some words from the reading that may be new to you. They are used in context in the following sentences. Decide on their meanings and fill in the blanks.

abut	major	dissolve
shell	molten	land mass
crust	current	convection

1. A **land mass** is defined in the next sentence: "The **land mass** of India is an example of a small plate that ran into a larger plate. When the Indian subcontinent hit the Asian plate, the pressure formed the highest mountains in the world, the Himalayas." From this context, we can tell that a **land mass** is _____ .

2. **Crust** is defined in several places. It is defined in the next sentence after the first use of **crust**: "The planet Earth is like a cracked egg. Its shell (or crust) is broken into about a dozen pieces (plates). These surface pieces seem to 'float' on melted rock (called magma), like wood on water." Thus we know that **crust** means

   _____ .

3. **Molten** is defined by an opposite meaning, telling what it is not: "Scientists know that the surface of the Earth is solid. They believe that underground, like water boiling in a pot, **molten** magma (hot liquid rock) rolls toward the surface. **Molten** rock is not

   _____ .

4. **Abut** is something that one body does in relation to another. Think about what it means for two boxes or two boards to touch each other on the edges. Look at the sentence in which **abut** first occurs: "Some plates abut (touch each other) under the oceans and seas." **Abut** must mean _____ .

5. A **convection current** is a movement of some kind: "They believe that underground, like water boiling in a pot, molten magma (hot liquid rock) rolls toward the surface. These circular movements carry the plates with them. The circular currents (**convection currents**) also perform an earth-cleaning function." It is clear that a **convection current** is _____ .

6. The meaning of **dissolve** occurs in context: "The carbon dioxide in the air on the surface of the earth **dissolves** into water in the ocean. The waves reach into the air and 'catch' the carbon dioxide. The carbon dioxide forms a solid carbonate (CO_3) in the water and falls to the ocean bottom." Where does the carbon dioxide go? Why does it become a carbonate? It is clear that to **dissolve** means to

   _____ .

7. An egg has a **shell**, and it can crack. The Earth has a **shell**, and it is cracked. We can see the shell. A **shell** is _____ .

8. The meaning of **major** must be guessed or inferred from the context: "However, there are few such mountains in the Caribbean region, with the dangerous volcano on the small island of Montserrat the **major** exception." Note that only one Caribbean volcano is important enough to mention. Therefore, **major** must mean _____ .

Stragegy Focus: Finding the Main Idea

First look at each paragraph and think about the main idea. Then read the four choices for each paragraph. Circle *a, b, c,* or *d*—whichever answer best states the main idea of that paragraph.

1. The main idea of paragraph 1 is that...

   a. where two places touch, there can be volcanoes and earthquakes.

   b. plates float on magma.

   c. India is a land mass that bumped into Asia and made high mountains.

   d. The Earth is cracked, like an egg.

2. The main idea of paragraph 2 is that...

   a. Montserrat is an island in the Caribbean that has an active and dangerous volcano on it.

   b. Mount St. Helens has the potential of erupting.

   c. water may be the reason for the quiet where the North American and Caribbean plates meet.

   d. there are active volcanoes along the western coast of North America, from Canada to Mexico.

3. The main idea of paragraph 3 is that...

   a. we should study underwater mountain ranges.

   b. the Atlantic Ocean covers a long mountain range.

   c. satellites can help geologists.

   d. there is a lot to learn from the study of the ocean floor.

4. The main idea of paragraph 4 is that...

   a. carbon dioxide from the air gets into the magma through the oceans.

   b. there are convection waves in oceans.

   c. we can recycle carbon dioxide through the oceans.

   d. magma is boiling rock.

5. The main idea of paragraph 5 is that...

   a. the ocean waves are getting bigger at a fast rate.

   b. we are burning more fossil fuels.

   c. ocean study can show us how parts of the world are connected.

   d. geologists need something to work on.

Stragegy Focus: Reading for Details

Skim and scan to find these details. Write them in the blanks.

1. Find the name of a kind of an island in the Caribbean. (Look for a capital letter.) _____

2. How much higher have waves become in the last 50 years? (Look for numbers.) _____

3. What is another phrase for melted rock? (Look for parentheses.)

   _____

4. How many miles of underwater mountain ranges are there? (Look for numbers.) _____

Stragegy Focus: Making Inferences

Indicate that a statement is a fact by writing *F* in the blank after the sentence, or that a statement is an inference, opinion, or judgment by writing *NF* in the blank.

1. _____ Ocean waves are getting higher.

2. _____ There are satellites that can note small changes in the oceans.

3. _____ Convection currents are circular in nature.

4. _____ Geologists need something new to study.

5. _____ India has some very high mountains.

6. _____ India is a separate plate.

7. _____ Islands in the ocean are mountaintops that show above the water surface.

8. _____ The Earth must be old because it is cracked.

9. _____ Montserrat is a Caribbean island.

10. _____ There is more volcanic activity along the western North American coast than along the Caribbean coast.

Strategy Focus: Keeping a Vocabulary Journal

As you go through each unit of *Steps to Academic Reading 5, Between the Lines*, you will learn many new words. You can learn to use them well by keeping a vocabulary journal.

Find a notebook with about 50 pages to use for your vocabulary journal. You will use this notebook for your own vocabulary journal. Give it a title, write your name in it, and carry it with you to class every day.

Your personal vocabulary journal will be a record of the words that you want to learn. Each day, ask yourself the following questions:

- What are the new words in this unit?
- How many do I already know?
- Which words are useful new words for me?

Then follow these directions every day:

- Choose five new words for your vocabulary journal. (These are your target words.)
- Find your target words in the Main Reading or get them from other sources (such as your teacher).

- Copy the five sentences in which your target words appear.
- For each new word, you will need several lines, perhaps half a page in a small notebook.
- On the first line, write the target word.
- On the second line, copy the sentence (or, if you like, the sentences) in which your target word appears.
- On the next line, write a definition.
  Is the target word a noun?
  Is it a verb?
  Is it an adjective or an adverb?
  It might even be a word that is more than one type of word!
  What does it mean?
  What are the singular and plural forms?
- Then write a sentence or two of your own with the target word. If you are not sure of the new word, ask your teacher. It's also a good idea to look the target word up in a dictionary.

You are on your way to improving your vocabulary! You can learn twenty-five new words every week, and use them every day!

    Example: A useful new word in this unit is shell.

    For shell, the vocabulary journal will look something like this:

> shell (noun)
>
> Its shell (or crust) is broken into
> about a dozen pieces (plates).
> A turtle has a hard shell.
> An egg has a hard outside shell and
> a watery inside with white and yolk.
> A writer has to have a hard shell
> because everyone will criticize what
> she has written.
> They could not afford a whole new
> house, so they bought the shell of
> a house and finished the inside of
> it themselves.

Looking Ahead to the Eight Units

As you read through the rest of *Steps to Academic Reading 5, Between the Lines*, you will find topics that are important in today's world. Each unit has a broad theme with several readings about different aspects of that topic. There are exercises to help you learn to read better. Some exercises (like the samples in "Under the Surface") will help you learn to recognize main ideas more quickly; others will help you understand what conclusions you are drawing or how word families work in English. At the end of every unit there is also a 400-word timed reading to help you increase your reading speed.

CLEANING UP
THE MESS

Preparation

Strategies for Anticipation

When you look over this book, you will get a general idea of what is going to be the focus for each of the lessons. Each unit is one complete chapter, or section, of the book. Look over this unit. You will be scanning and surveying it—that is, you will be forming a general idea of the topic in your own mind.

Is a general idea useful to you? How does it help you to have a general idea about a unit that you are going to read? The answer is simple. Every person who is reading this book has some knowledge about the topics before beginning to read about them. The reader gets some ideas first from the title of a unit. The title of this unit is "Cleaning Up the Mess." You will look a little deeper at the readings, and you will see that they are about the Earth, our planet. You already know that it is unlikely to be about sports like soccer or swimming. It is unlikely to be about making paper, nor is it likely to be about taking care of sick people in hospitals. The unit is going to be about making some changes that affect our environment, which is something you already know a lot about. What you know will help you understand new ideas.

1. First check the unit title. Then look at the titles of other sections in the unit. Also look at the pictures and graphics. Do they give you information about the content of the unit? What can you learn about this unit before you begin reading? What concepts are already familiar to you?

_____

2. Consider this idea: A Native American leader, Chief Seattle, allegedly wrote the following in 1854 upon the surrender of his land to the U.S. government:

   > This we know: The Earth does not belong to man; man belongs to the Earth.
   > This we know: All things are connected, like the blood that unites one family.
   > And whatever befalls the Earth, befalls the sons of the Earth.
   > Man did not weave the web of life. He is merely a strand in it.
   > Whatever he does to the web, he does to himself.

If all humankind can learn to love the Earth, perhaps the
Earth of our children and grandchildren will still contain
diversity of life. However, time is running out. Many
indigenous (native) tribes are disappearing; many animal
species and hundreds of plant species are becoming
extinct (disappearing). Some people compare the situation
with illness: our planet is getting sick, and all nations need
to work together to treat the disease before it becomes
incurable. Others think of the situation in another way:
that we people have made our own home dirty. We need
to clean up our mess.

[handwritten annotation: may kind, city]

[handwritten annotation: curable = can be treated healed.]

1. Which descriptions do you prefer, sickness or dirtiness?
2. What is your opinion? Can we clean up the mess?
3. What do you think needs cleaning first? Why?

[handwritten annotation: missile, Cars.]

Strategy: Learning New Words

This book contains many exercises for learning new words and practicing
them. In fact, the first reading in every unit gives you the new vocabulary
in context. In other words, the new words that you might not know are used
in sentences. Clues within the main reading help you learn the new words
in a natural way. As you go through the reading, you will be able to figure
out the meaning of the new words from the *context*, the surrounding ideas.

As you read the main reading, also titled "Cleaning Up the Mess," you will
find new words and concepts. However, do not use your dictionary to look up
the new words until you have worked at understanding these new words
from the ways that they are used in the reading. Read past a word. Notice the
other words around it. Note how the word is used. There are probably clues
to the word's meaning all around it. Look for those hints!

Strategy: Learning Meanings in Context

Try to understand the reading without using a dictionary the first time you
read it. Using a dictionary interrupts your thinking about the ideas in the
reading. If you can read it once without using a dictionary and understand
many of the important ideas, you are strengthening your reading ability.

The first word in "Cleaning Up the Mess" is *perceptions*. It might be a new word for you. You could stop and look up this word in your dictionary, or you could read on and find the meaning in the paragraph that follows it. Look at the first three sentences of the reading:

> *Perceptions* are relative. A single oak tree may *seem* large compared to a person. If you compare it to an average redwood tree, however, the large oak tree *seems* small.

The word *seem* gives a clue that a *perception* is a thought, the way things seem. Of course, you might not know what an oak tree or a redwood tree looks like. But how much do you need to know? You can guess that they are two types of trees. Furthermore, you can guess that oak trees are rather large and that redwood trees are much, much larger.

The word *relative* in the first sentence might also be a new one for you. Can you find its meaning in the two sentences that follow it? The word *relative* modifies *perceptions*. And the sentence about the two kinds of trees involves a comparison. It seems that one large tree is small *relative to, related to,* or *compared to* another kind of tree. The word *compared* is the clue.

Now try your skill with the whole reading.

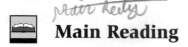

Main Reading

Cleaning Up the Mess

1   Perceptions are <u>relative</u>. A single oak tree may seem large compared to a person. If you compare it to an average redwood tree, however, the large oak tree seems small. In other words, things in nature are large or small, new or old, according to the measure and the comparisons involved.

2   It is easy to understand why time is relative. We think in human terms. We live day by day, but in the great scheme of things, the time of days and weeks is so small that a day is insignificant. Time means billions of years. During one human lifetime, not many things change. Even trees live longer than people, and the Earth itself is very old.

In human terms of years, the Earth was formed from a swirling cloud of gas and dust about five billion years ago. The turning slowed, and the planet cooled and became able to support life. Again in human terms, it probably took a billion years for this cooling to occur. As the planet cooled, water and air separated from the solid masses of heavier elements. The great land masses—the continents—and the great bodies of water were formed.

3   Then, about a billion years ago, another great change occurred. An enormous ecosystem of oceans and continents began to develop with many diverse forms of life, all dependent on one another. The first animals on the living sphere, the Earth, were tiny *marine* animals, and then these sea animals developed shells. Seventy million years later, the first animals with backbones—fish—appeared. Next, insects developed, about 400 million years ago. After another 200 million years, dinosaurs and the first mammals walked the Earth. Then warm-blooded animals took to the air—the first birds. Fifty million years later, both birds and mammals were well established as Earth-dwellers. About three million years ago, scientists believe, the first human beings walked the Earth. Life was now widespread.

4   In comparison to fish, insects, and birds, human beings have just arrived. In a geologic sense, people are newcomers. Despite their short time on Earth, however, they have brought about enormous changes to the surface of the planet—changes far out of proportion to the length of time they have occupied it. In many ways, humans have made a mess.

People Try to Control Resources

5   People have more control over their surroundings than any other species on Earth. With the combination of intelligence and *manual dexterity* (the ability to make and use tools), people have found ways to make much of the land on Earth usable, ways to use plant and animal resources, and ways to use minerals, fuels, and other Earth materials and resources.

6   As the number of people on the Earth increases, it becomes increasingly difficult for the population to survive on the resources of the land. The amount of land is limited. It can produce only so much food and no more. As the human population grows, people *consume* more. In fact, the increase in population is phenomenal. In 1900, there were 1.2 billion people on the Earth. In 1950, there were 2.5 billion. By 2000, there were more than 6 billion people, and this number is likely to increase to 8 billion by 2030. Clearly, some locations on Earth are already overpopulated; in many of these areas, future increases will surely bring about more poverty and suffering for the people who live there. Yet people in rich nations use more of the available resources than people in poorer nations. As they consume these resources, they also waste (use carelessly or squander) large amounts of them. This waste of resources pollutes the air, the land, and the water. Pollution is a human-caused mess.

7   There is a direct connection between overpopulation and the problems in our ecosystem. A direct influence also exists between human behavior and the state of the ecosystem. People are only one part of the whole planet. Yet their numbers create a drain on *nonrenewable* resources. For example, the amount of water on Earth is limited; this water is cleaned through natural processes. However, the natural processes for filtering water can clean, or renew, only a limited amount of water by removing the contamination.

8   If billions of people pollute trillions of tons of water, Earth might not be able to renew its water supply. Therefore, much of our water would not be clean and safe. Water pollution is a mess that someone must clean up. Likewise, a limited amount of petroleum can be found under the Earth's surface. Petroleum is a valuable resource. Should some people use it up by running automobiles? As people strive to control the planet and make life comfortable, are they using up resources that are needed for the survival of all? How can we understand the human impact on the Earth's general ecosystem?

What Is an Ecosystem?

9　　An *ecosystem* is a balance of plants, animals, and even micro-organisms that interact with one another and their environments. In an ecosystem, cycles of life are continued through the use and reuse of renewable resources. Oxygen, nitrogen, carbon, and other elements, in combination with the energy that flows through ecosystems, supply the life support system for more than six billion people and countless numbers of animals and plants. People are part of an ecosystem, and an ecosystem controls itself. If too many bears live in a forest for the amount of food in that forest, some of the bears die. If there are too many of one kind of fish, another kind of ocean animal eats them. This kind of balance is a natural phenomenon. If people can live in balance with the Earth, they will have enough food. But when the balance is upset, some people die. People are trying to control the balance of nature by creating more food so that they can survive. However, it is not possible for people to control all of nature.

10　　Ecosystems regulate the climate, determine the composition of the atmosphere, make new soil, control diseases, pollinate crops, and provide food from the sea. Ecosystems provide nutrition for life and dispose of waste. When a plant or animal dies, the dead parts decompose and enrich the soil. The soil then uses the nutrients to create more food for living plants and animals. Planet Earth is one major ecosystem. All parts balance with all other parts. Sections of the planet can also be considered minor ecosystems.

11　　*Tropical rain forests* are a classic example of one type of ecosystem. These rain-rich regions of vegetation support an amazing diversity of species for the planet. They simultaneously absorb carbon dioxide and create oxygen. The CO_2 is used by trees and plants in the process of *photosynthesis* (process in which green plants utilize the energy of sunlight, carbon dioxide, and water to manufacture carbohydrates in the presence of chlorophyll). This function of rain forests is important because, for people, carbon dioxide can affect the climate.

In a sense, rain forests clean the air. People need oxygen to live, and plants—especially in the tropical rain forests—provide it.

12   Unfortunately, however, the rain forests of the equatorial lands are disappearing. People who want to use the land or the trees are cutting the forests down. There is a market for the heavy hardwoods of the rain forest—teak, ebony, and mahogany—for furniture. Because customers will pay a lot of money for the hardwoods, the people who live in or near the forests are glad to sell it to them. Some rain-forest dwellers also cut the trees to clear land for farms in order to grow food. It doesn't matter what the reason is. Cutting down the trees destroys the ecosystem of the rain forest. Furthermore, most rain forest soil is poor; it does not support good farms. Some parts of the world, like the Bragantina of Brazil, were cleared for farms only a few years ago. Now the land is a desert because the soil was not rich enough to hold water. Farming took away the few natural nutrients, and now the land is useless.

The Balance of Nature

13   Human beings have upset the balance of nature. All natural systems, like ecosystems, tend toward balance, or *equilibrium*, among opposing factors or forces. Human activities can cause or accelerate permanent changes in natural systems. The smoke of one campfire causes no harm to the environment. Natural cleaning systems can clean the smoke from the air. However, the collective smoke from thousands of factories, through more than two centuries of industrialization, has caused enormous increases in air pollution levels worldwide. Cleaning this smoke has exceeded the ability of natural processes. The rain forests cannot clean the air fast enough. People will have to find ways to stop new pollution and to clean up this mess.

14   Rapid population increases and industrial growth notwithstanding, some groups of people have been able to live in harmony with the planet. These people have not changed their ways of living from the ways of their *ancestors*. Called *indigenous peoples*, they continue the

ways of life of their parents, grandparents, and great-grandparents, who lived on the land. Many of their cultural values and ways of life include practices that return resources to the Earth. Some people believe that indigenous peoples can teach the rest of the world important lessons for the survival of the planet and its people. Indigenous peoples live with the Earth. They do not use the Earth and its resources for power over other people.

15   Human population growth is creating food shortages, problems of air quality, and changes in weather patterns. The rain forests are disappearing, and land and seas are changing. Acid rain forms from water passing through polluted air. There is the threat of global warming. All these problems come from the overuse of resources and the human struggle to control the environment.

16   The twentieth century began with powerful countries competing to take advantage of the resources of Earth. As an outcome of their hunger for power, the Earth was *abused*, treated badly. Now in the third millennium, people all over the world are living with the problems caused by this greed. As they realize the causes of the sickness of our planet, they seek ways to enrich the Earth, to give back what they take away. Global opportunism meant using the Earth. Now people must practice global protectionism. Everyone must protect and nurture the ecosystem of planet Earth. In other words, we have to clean up the mess.

Strategy Focus: Discussing the Concepts

Review the main reading for words and ideas that you consider important. Write them here:

_____ _____ _____

_____ _____ _____

Then compare and discuss your list with a group of classmates. Note: In the next sections of this unit, you will find questions on key words and ideas.

Strategy: Figuring Out What "X" Means

Were you able to read the main reading without a dictionary? If you understood the main ideas (the gist of the reading), then you made good use of context clues. Of course, there are times when getting the exact meaning of a word is important and you have to use a dictionary. You need only a <u>working definition</u>. That is the reason a dictionary isn't always necessary. You can learn to use context clues to get an idea of a word's meaning. Let's look at some clues for figuring out a working definition of X—any unknown word.

First, ask yourself this question: *What kind of word is "X"?* To find the meaning of a word and make a definition, you must understand how words work in sentences. You do not need to know the exact grammatical label for the kind of word. You need only an example of the word in a context. Then you can see how the word is used. For example, let's figure out the term *solid masses* in paragraph 2 of the main reading:

As the planet cooled, water and air separated from the <u>*solid masses*</u> of heavier elements. The great land masses—the continents—and the great bodies of water were formed.

Perhaps your first reaction at seeing this expression is to reach for your dictionary. But wait. In the sentences around the word, there are clues to its meaning:

- *Masses* has the regular -(*e*)s ending that shows either 1. plural for a noun, or 2. third-person singular for a verb.

- The word *the* comes before *solid masses,* so *solid masses* must be a noun, like the *apples* or the *automobiles.*

From this evidence, you know that *solid masses* is a plural noun. Therefore, you could start your definition this way: *Solid masses are things that…*

As you read, you can learn more about the relationships between words. For example, you can find clues that tell you what *solid masses* are not. Look at the sentence that contains the word *separated: solid masses* are <u>not</u> like water and air because they "separated" from water and air. Also, the last part of this sentence tells you that the *solid masses* are "heavier elements" than water and air. Therefore, you can guess that *solid masses* are not air or water but something else. You know also that air and water are simple, basic things. *Solid masses* are also simple and basic.

You probably already know that air is an invisible gas; water and the other substances that you can pour like water are liquids. Things that are not liquid or gas are *solids.* (There are three common states of matter: gas, liquid, and solid.) The context shows that the word *masses* has some connection to things that are not gas and not liquid. The next sentence gives you more information: the *solid mass* is the same as land, and the land is a continent. Thus, the meaning becomes clear from the context. Perhaps now you can make a definition of the word. But remember that understanding the meaning of a word is more important than having a definition—although a working definition like the following can come out of this meaning: *Solid masses are not gas and not liquid. They are things like land.* Note that a working definition gives only the meaning that is necessary to understand the main idea. For example, look at this sentence:

The boy picked a large *persimmon* from the tree.

A working definition of *persimmon is a thing that a person can pick from a tree.* At some later time, you might need to know more about persimmons, but for now your working definition is enough.

Strategy Focus: Figuring Out How to Identify Nouns

The definition of a noun should start with the information that the word means a person, place, thing, or idea.

The example of *solid masses* shows you two important processes:

1. how to find the meaning of X by looking at what X is like, what it is not like, and what it is an example of
2. how to form a working definition of X

Let's apply these processes to a few more words in the reading. In paragraph 3, the Earth is called a *living sphere*:

The first animals on the *living sphere*, the Earth, were tiny marine animals, and then these sea animals developed shells.

The word *sphere*, it seems, describes our *planet*. It might be another term for planet. You probably don't need to know more about the word *sphere* to understand that part of the sentence. Your working definition of *sphere* is something like the following: *A sphere is something that can be living, and Earth is a sphere.*

At the end of paragraph 3, you can find the expression *Earth-dwellers*. In this case, the punctuation (the hyphen) helps you figure out the meaning.

Here is the expression in context:

> Then warm-blooded animals took to the air—the first birds. Fifty
> million years later, both birds and mammals were well established
> as *Earth-dwellers.*

From this context, you can understand that birds and mammals were living
on Earth. Do you need more information than that? It probably isn't
important to know more about Earth-dwellers than the fact that they were
on Earth, but paragraph 4 contains some more clues:

In comparison to fish, insects, and birds, <u>human beings have just arrived</u>.
In a geologic sense, people are newcomers. <u>Despite their short time on
Earth</u>, however, they have brought about enormous changes to the surface
of the planet—changes far out of proportion to <u>the length of time they have
occupied it</u>.

The meaning of *dweller* seems to be connected with living on Earth. The
hyphen connects the two words. And you are right: to *dwell* means "to
inhabit, to live in a place." A *dweller* is an inhabitant, a person who lives in
a place.

Here is one more example, the word *lifetime* in paragraph 2 of the reading:

> During one human *lifetime*, not many things change. Even trees live
> longer than people, and the Earth itself is very old.

The two sentences tell you the following information: that a lifetime is a
length of time, that it belongs to a human being, and that it is about living
and becoming old.

Strategy Focus: Figuring Out What Nouns Mean

Try to figure out the meanings of these important terms from the main reading.
The paragraph numbers in parentheses will help you locate these terms.

A. Look for clues and decide which of the definitions is best: *a, b, c,* or *d.*

1. (paragraph 3) dinosaur

   a. planet   c. continent

   b. period of time   d. animal

2. (paragraph 5) species

   a. special things   c. place

   b. groups like people   d. places

ٱ لمَقْرُو

3. (paragraph 6) poverty
  a. not richness   c. unhappiness like suffering
  b. change in the weather   d. crowded cities and small farms

4. (paragraph 7) a drain   خُفَّف
  a. an amount   c. an increase
  b. a loss   d. a kind of help

ٱلتَّلوُّث

5. (paragraph 7) contamination
  a. pollution   c. overpopulation
  b. suggestion   d. connection

ٱلنِّظام ٱلبيَّئِيّ

6. (paragraph 9) ecosystem
  a. a kind of forest   c. an environment
  b. a cycle of life   و ظيفة   d. a balance of all living things

7. (paragraph 11) a function
  a. a sign   c. an important part of the work
  b. a face or aspect   d. an odorless gas

8. (paragraph 4) newcomer
  a. a resource   c. a discovery
  b. an ancestor   d. a recent arrival

B. Write a definition for each word or term. Use words from the reading context for your definitions. The first one has been done for you.

1. (paragraph 5) manual dexterity = _the ability to make_
  and use tools

2. (paragraph 13) equilibrium = _____
  _____

3. (paragraph 14) indigenous peoples = _____
  _____

4. (paragraph 14) ancestors = _____
  _____

Strategy Focus: Figuring Out How to Identify Verbs

To pick out the verbs, you can use the same process that you used to identify nouns:

- Substitute the phrase *to do something* (to) or *to be in a special state* for the unknown word. Does the sentence still make sense?

- Check if the word is an action word or a be word (*is, are, was, were,* or *seem*).

- Look at what comes before the word. A verb needs a noun, a subject, before it—someone or something to *do* the action, someone or something to *make* something, or someone or something to *be*.

- Look for *-s* or *-es* at the end of the word; these endings show the present-tense, third-person singular form (as in *he, she,* or *it* does something).

- Look for *-ed* at the end of the word; it shows the past form of regular verbs.

- Look for a helping verb like *can, could, will, would,* or *have to* in front of the unknown word.

First identify the unknown word as a verb. Next you need to find clues to its meaning. Let's look at some examples. Here are two new words that seem to be verbs: *consume* (paragraph 6) and *strive* (paragraph 8). Look at these two words, one at a time, in their contexts:

> Yet people in rich nations use more of the available resources than people in poorer nations. As they *consume* these resources, they also waste large amounts of them.

You can substitute a verb phrase like *to do something to* (or *to be in a special state*) for the unknown words to determine whether they are verbs:

> People in rich nations use more of the available resources than people in poorer nations. As they *do something to* these resources, they also waste large amounts of them.

Note that the phrase *to be in a special state* doesn't fit into the sentence because of the word *resources,* a noun.

In the sentence from the reading, the verb *consume* is parallel to the verb *use*: People use more of the available resources, and they consume resources. It seems that part of the meaning of *consume* is *use*. (It is.) And perhaps, in this context, the meaning of *consume* relates to the meaning of *waste*. (It does.)

Read

Now look at *strive* in paragraph 8:

> As people *strive* to control the planet and make life comfortable, are
> they using up resources that are needed for their survival?

Again, substitute a verb phrase:

> As people *do something to* control the planet...

What is it that people do? To answer this question, look at the words near the verb for other clues to its meaning.

The heading of this section is "People try to control resources." Here is one clue: "strive to control" and "try to control." You can guess that the words *strive* and *try* have similar meanings. Therefore, *to strive* must mean "to make an effort; to try to get a result." And it does.

Strategy Focus: Figuring Out What Verbs Mean

Try to figure out the meanings of other important verbs from the main reading. Paragraph numbers in parentheses will help you locate these verbs.

A. Look for clues and choose the best definition: *a, b, c,* or *d.*   *interact ... class ... student.*

1. (paragraph 9) (to) interact   نتفاعل
   a. (to) act together with   c. (to) clean
   b. (to) be interesting   d. (to) be comfortable with
       نظم - ضبط - يحول

2. (paragraph 10) (to) regulate   *I regulate my school.*
   a. (to) destroy   c. (to) do (something) again
   b. (to) change   d. (to) make normal

3. (paragraph 13) (to) exceed   يتجاوز + يفوق   *exceed*
   a. (to) be more than   c. (to) make difficult   *exceed the limit.*
   b. (to) do something good   d. (to) make simple

4. (paragraph 16) (to) abuse   اساءة المعاملة
   a. (to) protect   c. (to) make (something) clean
   b. (to) hurt   d. (to) make an opportunity for

B. Write a working definition for each verb in bold type. The first one has been done for you.

1. (paragraph 6) to **waste** resources means to ___use carelessly___ .

2. (paragraph 7) to **renew** an amount of water means

   _____ .

3. (paragraph 10) to **pollinate** crops means _____ .

4. (Paragraph 10) to **dispose of** waste means _____ .

5. (paragraph 13) to **accelerate** permanent changes means

   _____ .

Strategy Focus: Figuring Out How to Identify Adjectives

Adjectives do different kinds of work in sentences. The most common task is adding meaning to nouns. Therefore, the definition of an adjective must tell what work the adjective does in the sentence.
An adjective can appear

- before a noun as a number word, an amount word, or a describer.
  Some people in rich nations use more of the available resources.

- after a *be* verb (*be, become, seem, appear*).
  Petroleum is *valuable*.

- after a noun as a complement.
  People strive to control the planet and make life *comfortable*...

Strategy Focus: Figuring Out What Adjectives Mean

Sometimes there are clues to the meaning inside the word. Look at *widespread*, in paragraph 3:

   Life was now *widespread*.

Do you see the two smaller words, *wide* and *spread*, inside the whole word? To spread means "to distribute evenly," as a person *spreads* butter on bread with a knife or *spreads* open a tablecloth over a table. *Wide* means "covering a large area." The word *widespread*, therefore, probably means "distributed evenly over a large area." A check of this meaning shows it fits the context. There were living things in many places; therefore, life was *widespread*.

Read

Sometimes you need to look for the same kinds of clues that you used to find the meanings of nouns and verbs. Read these sentences from paragraph 2:

> In human terms of years, the Earth was formed from a *swirling* cloud of gas and dust about five billion years ago. The turning slowed, and the planet cooled and became able to support life.

Look at the word *swirling* in the first sentence. Notice that

- it comes between *a* and *cloud*, so you know that it is a modifier, an adjective.

- it tells something about the quality of the cloud.

- the *-ing* ending tells you that this adjective comes from a verb (swirl), so you can look in the context for verbs or words that come from verbs. The most likely meaning lies in the word *turning*. According to the text, a swirling cloud is turning in a huge circle. Therefore, *swirling* tells us what kind of cloud it was.

Another example is the word *diverse* in paragraph 3. Check to see whether it does the work of an adjective. Does it come before a noun as a number word, amount word, or describer? Yes, it modifies the word *forms* (of life). The next seven sentences in paragraph 3 are a list of the *different* kinds of life on Earth. It seems reasonable to guess that *diverse* means *different*.

Here's another example. In paragraph 3, the word *marine* is used to describe a kind of animal. The rest of the sentence provides the meaning: "...and then *these sea* animals developed shells." Note that the word *these* tells you that the writer is discussing the same animals (*the marine animals*). This time, however, the word *sea* describes the animals. *Marine* animals must live in the sea. (They do.)

Here is another example of a modifier. See how the word *phenomenal* is used in paragraph 6:

> In fact, the increase in population is *phenomenal*. In 1900, there were 1.2 billion people on Earth. In 1950, there were 2.5 billion.

You can identify the word *phenomenal* as an adjective because it comes after a *be* verb. Now look around the word for clues to its meaning. You can see that the increase in population (more than double) in 50 years is *phenomenal*. Such an increase is not small. It is a great increase, so *phenomenal* must mean that the increase is not ordinary. It is a large increase.

Find these words and their meanings in the reading. Write definitions from the contexts.

1. (paragraph 9) *countless* = ___You can't count___

Hints: Do you know the word *count*? Do you know the word part *—less*? Like the word *careless* (*care* + *less*), countless has the combination of two parts.

2. (paragraph 11) *classic* = ___old,_____

Hints: You know the word *class*. A *class* of students is a group of people learning together. *Classic*, in the sentence in the reading, means "one that represents a *class* or a group of phenomena."

Strategy Focus: Figuring Out Words That Are Not Nouns, Verbs, or Adjectives

Sometimes a word does not fit into any of these categories. It is not the name of a person, place, thing, or idea. It isn't an action or state of being, and it does not modify anything. First try to figure out the use of the word. Where does it appear in the sentence? What is its function? Does its form give you useful information? Here's an example from paragraph 14:

> Rapid population increases and industrial growth *notwithstanding*, some groups of people have been able to live in harmony with the planet.

Where does *notwithstanding* come in this sentence? It comes:
- after a noun at the end of a phrase.
- before a comma.
- before a complete sentence.

How does *notwithstanding* function? It seems to connect the ideas *rapid population increases and industrial growth* with *live in harmony*. Consider some other ways to connect these ideas. There are five main ways that two sentences can be joined: using *and, but, or, so, because,* and *with* clauses. First try *and*: (There are) rapid population increases and industrial growth, and some groups of people have been able to live in harmony with the planet. (Answer: No, *and* will not work. The ideas do not follow logically with *and*.)

Will *but* work to connect the ideas? Again, try to rework the ideas of the sentence using *but*: (There are) rapid population increases and industrial growth, *but* some groups of people have been able to live in harmony with the planet. (Answer: Yes, the ideas seem to follow logically with *but*.)

However, the word *but* joins two sentences, and the group of words before *notwithstanding* is not a sentence. It seems that *notwithstanding* does the same function, but it comes in a different place in a sentence. You might ask yourself "What other ways are there to say *but*?"

Here is a list of connecting words that have the meaning of *but:*

however	yet	nevertheless
despite	in spite of	notwithstanding

All of these words will work to join the two ideas:

1. There are rapid population increases and industrial growth; however, some groups of people have been able to live in harmony with the planet.

2. There are rapid population increases and industrial growth, yet some groups of people have been able to live in harmony with the planet.

3. Despite rapid population increases and industrial growth, some groups of people have been able to live in harmony with the planet.

4. There are rapid population increases and industrial growth; nevertheless, some groups of people have been able to live in harmony with the planet.

5. In spite of rapid population increases and industrial growth, some groups of people have been able to live in harmony with the planet.

6. Rapid population increases and industrial growth notwithstanding, some groups of people have been able to live in harmony with the planet.

Strategy Focus: Practicing How Different Types of Words Relate to Each Other

Think about how these words are similar. Then write what you think the related word means.

1. **count, countless**

   I can **count** to ten in Polish.

   When I speak Polish, I make **countless** mistakes.

   Countless probably means *too many + you can't count*

2. **new, renew, renewable, nonrenewable**
Twenty years ago, we bought **new** furniture.
We **renewed** the furniture by washing it with a special soap.
Wooden furniture is **renewable**. You can paint it and clean it and make it seem new.
Plastic furniture is **nonrenewable**. There is nothing you can do to make it look new again.

Renew probably means *make new again* .

Nonrenewable probably means *can't make again new* .
can't fixed.

3. **opportunity, opportunism**
The new computer factory offered the worker an **opportunity** for a better job. Job **opportunism** means taking a better job when you find one.

Opportunism probably means *taking better job. chance* .
is the act of gaining

4. **vegetables, vegetation** *a chance. gaining*
Many small farmers grow **vegetables** like lettuce, carrots, and tomatoes. There is very little vegetation in a desert, but lots of it in a rain forest.

Vegetation probably means *place is able to grow plants.*
where plants are growing.

5. **nutrition, nutrient** *where plants are growing.*
Eating fresh foods and drinking lots of water are important for good **nutrition**.
Fruits and vegetables contain many important **nutrients** for a healthy body.

A **nutrient** is probably *organic, something healthy for* .
body

6. **equator, equatorial**
The **equator** is a line on a map or a globe. It divides the Earth into northern and southern halves. There are many tropical rain forests in **equatorial** areas. Most **equatorial** areas are hot.

Equatorial probably means *line between northern south*
something near to equatorial

7. **geology, geologists, geologic**
Geology is the study of the Earth's surface (its top layer of rock). Rocks take millions of years to form, so **geologists** search back in time. **Geologic** time is millions, not hundreds, of years.

Geologic probably refers to something that is *exactly very old.*

8. **protect, protectionism**

   Parents naturally **protect** their children. Parental **protectionism** is natural.

   Protectionism probably means _keeping Save_ .

9. **cure, curable, incurable**

   Doctors can **cure** many kinds of disease. Tuberculosis, for example, is **curable**. Some cancers, however, are **incurable**.

   Curable probably means _able to treat_ .

Strategy: Analyzing Cause and Effect

 Related Reading 1

Let's Clean Up the Mess

1   International conferences on global warming are in the headlines. The challenge of reducing carbon dioxide (CO_2) in the air causes great argument. Nearly everyone agrees that increases in world temperatures are caused by the greenhouse effect of carbon dioxide in the atmosphere. Nearly everyone agrees that the warming is affecting world climate patterns. More dangerous storms, for example, form because of the warming of the oceans. Floods destroy homes and crops because of the storms. And it happens because of our human impact on nature.

2   High above Earth a layer of carbon dioxide (together with water vapor and methane from rotting organic matter) acts like a blanket. It keeps heat from the sun close to our planet. Most of the problems with CO_2 come from burning fossil fuels (oil, coal, and natural gas) for energy. Fossil fuel burning increases this poison gas in the atmosphere. However, those fuels are the source of much of the world's energy. Moreover, few people believe that industrialization is going to decrease. In fact, as population increases, production of carbon dioxide is likely to increase from the eight billion tons of CO_2 that we are now producing every year.

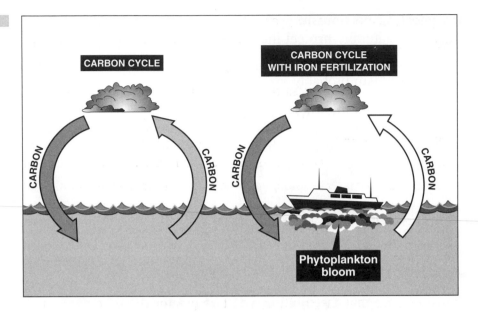

3   Just as tiny droplets of water vapor collect around specks of dust to form raindrops, solutions coalesce around these ideas:

1. reducing dependence on fossil fuels and industrialization
2. finding alternative energy sources (therefore reducing use of fossil fuels that increase CO_2)
3. increasing the number of plants like trees that take CO_2 out of the air
4. developing plants (through plant research) that will absorb more CO_2
5. finding ways of making the oceans absorb (use up) more CO_2

4   Analysis of these solutions shows some directions for science. Number 1 is unlikely to happen. Civilization is unlikely to return to simpler times. There are too many people to do so. Without science and technology, there would not be enough food, housing, or clothing for the world's population. Number 2 is on-going. Scientists and engineers are trying to find clean ("green") sources of energy. There is progress in finding alternative energy sources, but it is not happening fast enough. Number 3 is an effort that should involve everyone. Even

as people plant trees, however, other forests are being cut down because of the need for farmland. Solutions number 4 and 5 hold the greatest promise for reducing CO_2 in the air.

5   Earth's natural process of absorbing and releasing CO_2 is called the carbon cycle. The two main intake methods for CO_2 are through plants and the ocean. Plants use CO_2 and release oxygen as they make food through the process of photosynthesis. Solution number 4 concerns plants. The biologists' challenge is to create plants that have a great hunger for CO_2. It may be possible, through careful blending of plant characteristics, to create a super CO_2–absorbing plant that can be controlled. This way of cleaning up the mess is within the reach of botanists (plant scientists) today. However, they must be sure that the solution won't be greater than the problem.

6   Ocean waves absorb great amounts of CO_2. Waves "reach" up into the air, capture CO_2 and dissolve it into the water. Some of the CO_2 turns into carbonate (CO_3) and some is "eaten." Tiny marine plants, called *phytoplankton* or just *plankton*, use the CO_2 and grow (they "bloom" like flowers). Fish eat the plankton. It's part of the carbon cycle.

7   Scientists are trying to make the process happen faster. Years ago, oceanographer John Martin came up with an idea for a solution. He called it the "iron hypothesis." In his ocean studies, he noted that there are large areas in the ocean (especially around Antarctica and in equatorial Pacific waters) where water is rich in nitrogen compounds. However, this food for plankton is not being used, because these waters have very little iron. Plants, like people, need some iron. Martin believed that adding iron to the water would increase plankton growth and increase absorption of CO_2. Martin's experiments, carried out now by Kenneth Coale, have proved successful. Scientists believe that 20% of the CO_2 could be removed by "fertilizing" parts of the ocean with iron. It would be cheaper than large-scale tree planting.

8   Coale and his colleague Ken Johnson added iron to several patches of ocean. They found that plankton in these areas increased thirtyfold. That is, within a few days, there were thirty times as many plankton in that part of the ocean. The number of *zooplankton* (tiny marine animals) doubled. Many clumps of phytoplankton (plant plankton) grew large and sank to the ocean floor. The experiment was a success! Iron fertilizing offers hope of a way of reducing the carbon in the atmosphere. At the same time, there is concern about the effects of such increases of plankton on the ocean bottom. Studies continue.

9   Another plan for the reduction of CO_2 in the air comes from Monterey, California. Small amounts (a few gallons) of liquid CO_2 have been dropped to the ocean floor. Through video cameras, researcher Peter Brewer followed the liquid carbon dioxide. He noted that it dissolved quickly. It didn't affect marine life, and it spread out quickly. This process is called *carbon sequestration*. (To sequester means to separate, to remove.) The goal is to remove a billion tons of CO_2 a year by 2025. Adding CO_2 to the ocean makes the water more acid, so there is the potential of harming marine life. This possibility worries scientists. However, as oceanographers point out, the pH (a measure of acidity) of ocean water varies greatly around the world. Even so, concern about the effect of carbon sequestration means much more study before the program can begin.

10   The problem of removing CO_2 from factory smoke has been solved. Small chimney "scrubbers" (cleaners) pull the CO_2 out of the smoke. Now the challenge is how to take CO_2 out of the air. Scientists Klaus Lackner and Scott Elliot are working on the idea of a "scrubber" that could remove enough CO_2 from ordinary air to reduce the greenhouse effect. They say that it would have to be the size of a large city. In the past people have been successful in building many great projects with the purpose of controlling parts of nature. Centuries ago Chinese engineers built a wall along the north border of China. More recently China was successful in building Three Gorges Dam. The Canadians' James Bay Project is another example of success. Engineers have built canals through isthmuses like Suez and Panama. Huge road systems and incredible buildings around the world have made a modern way of life possible. Is it also possible to create a scrubber big enough to reduce the CO_2 in the air?

11   Another creative solution was proposed by physicist Edward Teller. Many scientists agree with Teller that the greenhouse effect could be reduced by shielding Earth from the sun. They suggest some artificial means, like a giant space umbrella and a cloud of sun-reflecting mirrors. Computer models show that blocking 1.8% of sunlight would reduce world temperatures to safe levels even if the CO_2 in the air doubled. The thinking and the studies continue. Where will the solutions come from? How will we clean up the mess?

Strategy Focus: Learning Vocabulary in Context

1. **methane, fossil fuels**
   High above Earth a layer of carbon dioxide (together with water vapor and **methane** from rotting organic matter) acts like a blanket. Farmers can collect animal and plant waste into an airtight container. The decomposition of the organic matter produces a gas (CH_4). This **methane** can be burned as fuel.

   Methane is a _____.

2. **coalesce**
   Just as tiny droplets of water vapor collect around specks of dust to form raindrops, solutions **coalesce** around these ideas.
   The two parts of the broken bone **coalesced** within a few weeks. Two months later, the condition of the bone was normal.

   For separate parts to **coalesce** means that they _____ .

3. **absorb, absorption, release**

We need to find ways of making the oceans **absorb** (use up) more CO_2.
Ocean waves **absorb** great amounts of CO_2.
Earth's natural process of **absorbing** and **releasing** CO_2 is called the carbon cycle.
Plants use CO_2 and **release** oxygen as they make food through the process of photosynthesis.
Martin believed that adding iron to the water would increase plankton growth and increase **absorption** of CO_2.

When something **absorbs** carbon dioxide, it _____ .

Absorption is the process of _____ .

If **absorbing** is taking something in, then releasing (the opposite) must be _____ .

4. **oceanographer, botanist**

Years ago, **oceanographer** John Martin…in his ocean studies…noted that there are large areas in the ocean (especially around Antarctica and in equatorial Pacific waters) where water is rich in nitrogen compounds.
This way of cleaning up the mess is within the reach of **botanists** (plant scientists) today.

It is clear that **oceanographers** study _____ and

botanists study _____ .

5. **hypothesis**

Scientists are trying to make the process happen faster. Years ago, oceanographer John Martin came up with an idea for a solution. He called it the "iron **hypothesis**."
A scientist watches (observes) and thinks about the problem, and then he comes up with an idea to test—his **hypothesis**.

A **hypothesis** is a scientist's _____ .

6. **increase thirtyfold**

They found that plankton in these areas **increased thirtyfold**. That is, within a few days, there were thirty times as many plankton in that part of the ocean.
Sales at the new store increased fivefold after the television advertising started.

An **increase** of **thirtyfold** or **fivefold** means _____ .

7. **potential**

   Adding CO_2 to the ocean makes the water more acid, so there is the **potential** of harming marine life. This possibility worries scientists. The **potential** for using the ocean to remove poison gases from the air is within possible science work.

   A **potential** for success is the _____ for success.

8. a **concern**

   Even so, **concern** about the effect of carbon sequestration means much more study before the program can begin.
   At international conferences on global warming, people's worries and **concerns** make headlines in newspapers.
   Many people have **concerns** about the greenhouse effect on global warming.

   A **concern** is the same as a _____ .

Strategy Focus: Making Inferences

From each of these facts, you can make some inferences. Write a check (✓) in front of each idea that you think is a good inference from the facts.

1. **Fact:** Plants use CO_2. The plants can be as small as microbes in the soil and plankton in ocean water or as large as redwood trees. They all use CO_2 to make food. The plants on Earth now remove nearly two billion tons of carbon from the air a year.

   a. _____ We should increase the amount of plant life on Earth to clean the air.

   b. _____ Small plants are more important than large ones in removing carbon dioxide from the air.

   c. _____ It should be against the law to cut down a tree.

   d. _____ It would be good to protect forests all around the world.

2. Fact: Areas with large forests clean more air than those without much plant life.

    a. _____ Forests should be protected.

    b. _____ We need to plant more forests to clean the air.

    c. _____ Deserts and grassy prairies have dirty air.

    d. _____ More people should live in the forests.

    e. _____ We should move factories to areas with lots of trees.

3. Fact: The oceans already absorb great amounts of carbon dioxide.

    a. _____ It is wrong to expect the oceans to absorb more CO_2.

    b. _____ The oceans are part of the carbon cycle.

    c. _____ Carbon sequestration and iron fertilization are similar to natural processes.

    d. _____ It is natural for CO_2 to go into ocean water.

4. Fact: Scientists have solutions to some of our global carbon dioxide problems, but they also have concerns about the impact of some of these solutions.

    a. _____ Some of these solutions might bring new problems that are even more difficult to solve.

    b. _____ On Earth everything affects everything else.

    c. _____ It takes time to study and experiment in finding solutions to problems.

    d. _____ Scientists and engineers have solved many problems before, and so they will find a solution to global warming, too.

5. Fact: Scientists are thinking about the challenge of building a huge scrubber to remove carbon dioxide from the atmosphere.

    a. _____ They should hurry up and build it.

    b. _____ Building such a huge scrubber would take many years.

    c. _____ They will build it when they want to.

    d. _____ There are many details to work out before they can build a huge scrubber.

Strategy: Anticipating the Topic

Before you read the next reading, look at the title; also look at the first sentence of each paragraph. They give you a good idea about the general topic in the reading. Knowing the general topic helps you read faster and better.

 ## Related Reading 2   9-24-02   Monday

Tropical Rain Forests

1   Areas in Africa, Central and South America, and Southeast Asia are dense with green growth, unusual insects, colorful birds, and exotic animals. Life is everywhere: beginning, thriving, dying, and beginning again. From these rain forests people harvest beautiful wood, delicious fruits and nuts, and powerful medicines. The lush vegetation of the tropical rain forest holds the greatest variety of species on Earth. A single hectare of Amazon rain forest in Brazil, for example, might support as many as three hundred different types of woody plants, a great range of biodiversity. In contrast, forested land in France normally supports only twelve different woody species—not much variety at all.

Rain forests are dense with hundreds of types of woody plants and unusual animal species. Although people have long thought that rain forests were indestructible, scientist are now realizing that the ecosystem of the rain forest is very fragile.

2   Rain forests have so much rich growth that people have long thought that they were indestructible: cut down one tree and two would grow in its place. The resources in these dense rain forests could surely be used freely. Governments, too, have assumed that the rain forests could be easily turned into profits. The growth seems so abundant; it seems to be easily renewable. To owners of large agricultural businesses, the rain forest is an enemy; it covers land that they need for fields. Surely, these businesspeople think, there are plenty of trees. It won't matter if we cut some down to make a large field. They may even believe that the rain forest will take over the land again when they stop farming. Such is not the case, however. Although the ecosystems of tropical rain forests include many plant and animal species, the ecosystems are fragile. The balance is easily upset.

3   All rain forests share certain characteristics. They grow in very wet, humid places where the annual rainfall exceeds 1,000 millimeters (40 inches). The tallest trees form an umbrellalike ceiling called a *closed canopy.* Such a top layer of vegetation forms when a large number of trees branch out horizontally at approximately the same height. Their branches hold vines; the leaves of the trees and the vines make a forest ceiling. Under a closed canopy, young plants grow in the shade. Only the plants with leaves at the top of the canopy get direct sunlight. In fact, the forest floor is quite dark. Because of the closed canopy in a rain forest, as little as one or two percent of the sunlight reaches the floor.

4   Another characteristic of most tropical rain forests is poor, thin soil. Only rain forests in volcanic areas might have somewhat better soil. People who wish to farm must move their fields frequently because of the nutrient-poor soil. Most rain forest land is exhausted after only two years of farming. That's why the farmers cut more trees and move to new land.

5   Many people want to understand: rain forests have so much biodiversity (many different kinds of plants). Yet, the soil is nutrient-poor. The answer is that the rain forest ecosystem depends on a long stringy fungus, *mycorrhiza* (MEE-ko-REEZ-uh). The strings of the fungus are the thickness of a spider's web. These strings connect fallen leaves with the roots of trees. Like tiny pipes, they carry nutrients from the rotting vegetation to the roots of the trees. The fungus makes it possible for plants to get food without taking it from the soil.

6   Rainwater washes nutrients from the leaves as it falls. This water goes straight to the trees. It is not surprising that a thick web of roots lies below the surface of the forest floor. The ecosystem of the rain forest does not depend on rich soil at all. When the trees are removed, the richness of the forest disappears. Rain forest ecosystems are really simple. Ignoring how the system works results in a wasteland.

Strategy Focus: Finding the Main Idea

Write a check (✓) in front of the statement that seems to be the best one-sentence summary of the reading.

1. ____ The canopy of a rain forest protects the vegetation from the sun.

2. ____ The way a tropical rain forest makes up for poor soil shows the fragile nature of the ecosystem.

3. ✓ The ecosystem of a tropical rain forest is dependent on large amounts of rain and a closed canopy.

4. ____ Large-scale agricultural operations on land that was once tropical rain forest are sure to fail.

How do the other ideas support the main idea?

Strategy Focus: Reading for Details

Decide whether each statement is true or false according to the reading. For each statement, circle *true* or *false*; then write the number of the paragraph that contains the answer.

1. Most of a tree's roots go deep into the soil of the rain forest.   true   (false) _____

2. A tropical rain forest is a fragile environment; the poor soil shows that nature is fragile.   (true)   false   4

3. The ecosystem of the rain forest depends on large amounts of rain and a closed canopy.   true   false   3

4. Large farming operations on tropical rain forest land are sure to fail.   (true)   false   4.

5. A rain forest canopy is like a roof of leaves and plants.   (true)   false   **3**

6. Farms on rain forest land have rich soil.   true   (false) _____

Strategy Focus: Understanding the Author's Perspective

Discuss the following questions with your classmates. Your instructor may ask you to explain your answers.

1. What does the author think about rain forests? Are they valuable? If so, how?

2. What is the author's opinion of farming in the rain forest?

3. What does the author think eventually happens to rain forest land that is cleared of all plant life? Do you agree? Explain your answer.

Strategy Focus: Scanning for Details

1. List three characteristics of tropical rain forests.

   a. They grow in wet, humid places.

   b. The tallest trees form an umbrella like ceiling

   c. Young plants grow in the shade.

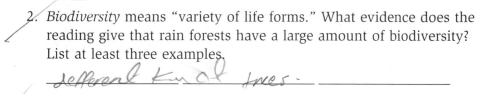

2. *Biodiversity* means "variety of life forms." What evidence does the reading give that rain forests have a large amount of biodiversity? List at least three examples.

   <u>different kinof trees.</u>

3. Why do small farmers in rain forests move their fields often?

   _____

4. What do *mycorrhizae* do for trees in the rain forest?

   <u>theSldings of the fungus -</u>

Strategy Focus: Applying Information About Key Ideas

Read this description carefully:

> Some plants grow in nutrient-rich water only, in special greenhouses. There is no real soil in these "hydroponic gardens" at all—only gravel or small stones.

Remember this key idea as you read the information and answer the questions that follow:

In Australia, the macadamia, an evergreen tree, produces a round nut. In the 1800s, the macadamia was brought to Hawaii, and the tree thrived there. Its nut was delicious, and the macadamia grew well in Hawaii's volcanic soil. However, land in Hawaii was expensive, and an orchard of macadamia trees needed a lot of land. Both pineapples and sugar cane also grow very well there. Farmers could make more money on these crops, so they usually grew them instead of macadamias. Then someone noticed that macadamia trees could grow where other crops couldn't on relatively new volcanic soil. Hawaii has a lot of rain,and that rain dissolves the necessary nutrients from the volcanic soil to feed the trees. The macadamia soon became profitable.

1. How is the macadamia tree orchard like a hydroponic garden?

   _____

   _____

2. In a rain forest, the rain dissolves the nutrients for the trees from the organic matter on the forest floor. How is the rain forest similar to a hydroponic garden?

_____

_____

3. How did the macadamia become profitable?

_____

_____

Strategy: Writing About the Ideas

1. With your classmates, identify some "messes" that need to be cleaned up. Then make a step-by-step plan for how you could do the project.

2. Go to the Internet and look up one of the biggest messes the world has ever seen. On March 24, 1989, shortly after midnight, the oil tanker Exxon Valdez struck a reef in Prince William Sound, Alaska. More than eleven million gallons for crude oil contaminated the ocean. The Valdez Oil spill threatened wildlife, a fishing industry, and a community.

   a. Make a list of what was done to clean up the mess.

   b. What new technologies have resulted from the Valdez oil spill?

   c. What is your opinion of the management of the disaster?

Strategy Focus: Keeping a Vocabulary Journal

Choose five words from the new words in this unit to be your target words.

Write the words here: _____ _____

_____ _____ _____

Now write them into your vocabulary journal. Remember to include the following parts:
  • your target word
  • the sentence from the unit in which your target word appears
  • a definition, including the part of speech.
  • some sentences of your own

Strategy: Increasing Reading Speed

Each unit of this book has a timed readings of 400 words each, with five questions at the end of each reading. Your goal is to finish reading in less than a minute and then to answer at least three of the five questions correctly. To meet this goal, follow the procedure outlined below.

The Procedure for ALL Timed Readings

1. SURVEY.
    First your teacher will give you a minute to prepare to read the article.
    *READ THE TITLE.
        What can you learn from it?
        What ideas do you expect?

    *NOTE THE NUMBER OF PARAGRAPHS.
        How is the reading organized?

    *READ THE FIRST PARAGRAPH.
        What are the key words?
        What is the main idea?

    *READ THE LAST PARAGRAPH.
        What do the first and last sentences of the last paragraph tell you?

    *LOOK FOR CLUES TO DEVELOPMENT.
        Is it a story?
        Is it a description?
        Are there many facts, names, and dates?

2. READ QUICKLY.
    Your teacher will give you a signal to get ready for the reading. When your teacher says, "Go!", read as fast as you can. Your teacher will write times (every ten seconds) on the board. When you have finished, look up at the board.

3. WRITE YOUR READING TIME AT THE END OF THE READING.
    There is a blank at the end of the reading for your time. Record your time in the blank and go quickly to the questions.

4. ANSWER THE QUESTIONS.
    Select *a, b,* or *c*—whichever best answers the question or completes the sentence.

5. CHECK YOUR ANSWERS.
   Write your time score and answer score on the record charts at the end of the book.

6. CORRECT YOUR ANSWERS.
   Work with your classmates. Do you understand your mistakes?

Strategy: Increasing Reading Speed

 Timed Reading

There Is No More "Away"

Everyone is talking about, practicing, and discovering new ways to be environmentally responsible. The word *recycle* tells the story: *re-* means "(to do something) again," and *cycle* is "a full circle, a return to the beginning." Therefore, *recycling* means recovering and reusing spent (used-up) products— finding ways to use products a second time. The motto of the recycling movement is "Reduce, Reuse, Recycle"; the term *recycling* covers the whole program.

The first step is to *reduce* garbage. Supermarkets sell products in expensive wrappings. A fast-food hamburger often comes wrapped in paper in a box in a bag. What a waste of resources! Every day, millions of plastic cups are used for coffee and tea. Each time someone buys a hamburger or uses one of those cups, energy and resources are wasted. To reduce garbage, the *throwaway* trend must stop.

The second step in the general recycling program is to *reuse*. If customers buy juices and soft drinks in returnable bottles, they can return them to the store. Manufacturers of drinks collect the bottles, wash them, and then fill them again.

The energy for making new bottles is saved. Where returning bottles for money is common, garbage dumps have relatively little glass and plastic throwaway bottles.

The third step in being environmentally sensitive is to *recycle*. Used motor oil can be cleaned and used again. Aluminum cans are easily recycled. When people collect and recycle aluminum (for new cans), they help save one of the world's precious resources. The problem of garbage has other aspects. People can't throw things away because there is no more space for dumps. Furthermore, liquids from garbage contaminate groundwater.

Recycling is a challenge because it requires a basic change in everyday life. For recycling to be successful, ordinary people must be aware of what they buy. They must also sort their trash and garbage into organic garbage, newspapers, steel cans, glass containers, and plastic. Waste materials of the same kind are *compacted* (crushed into blocks). A manufacturer buys the sorted, compacted blocks of material to make into something new. Once a customer buys and uses the product, the same materials follow the same cycle—being sorted, collected, and used again. Hence the word *recycled*. In the end, the real meaning of recycling is keeping planet Earth safe and clean for future generations. It is one way for everyone to contribute to a better world.

Time: _____

Now answer these questions as quickly as you can.

1. The waste in a fast-food restaurant comes from…

   a. the paper and plastic of packaging.

   b. the low quality food.

   c. the high cost of hamburgers.

   d. people throwing food away.

2. Which way is a good way to reduce waste?

   a. Refuse to buy foods that have lots of extra wrapping.

   b. Use a plastic cup for coffee.

   c. Get new appliances and throw away old ones.

3. To *compact* cans is to…

   a. to crush them and make a package of them.

   b. to melt them down to make new cans.

   c. to throw them away.

4. Some of the things we can recycle are…

   a. land and water.

   b. paper, glass, and metal cans.

   c. plastic cups.

5. What is the main idea of the reading?

   a. We should use things over and over.

   b. Aluminum is an important resource and should not be wasted.

   c. People can help the environment by making less waste.

BUSINESS: WATCHING THE BOTTOM LINE

 **Preparation**

Strategies for Anticipation

This unit is about business, world markets and local markets, where people buy and sell goods (materials and products), and the principles of business that make it work. Read the titles of all the readings in this unit.

What do these titles tell you about the topic of the unit?

Anticipate the ideas: Which of these pairs of ideas do you think is more likely to be in this unit?

1. a. advertising
   b. paying taxes

2. a. selling
   b. talking

3. a. finding a job
   b. setting up a business of your own

4. a. how to manage your time
   b. how to make a good meal

5. a. the way to make friends
   b. the way to succeed

Part of being a good businessperson is being able to prioritize. Priority means "most important." Prioritizing is putting things in order of importance. Write down six things that you want to do or need to do this week. These are your objectives for the week:

_____   _____

_____   _____

_____   _____

Which of your objectives is the most important? Which is the least important? Prioritize them. Put the most important item first, the next most important item second, and so on:

1. _____   4. _____

2. _____   5. _____

3. _____   6. _____

Now make a plan for accomplishing these objectives. When will you do each of them? Making a plan to accomplish your objectives is like a businessperson's schedule. You will know what to do when. You will be able to keep a focus. Moreover, you will know when you have accomplished a goal.

Strategy: Understanding Support of a Main Idea

The first reading has one main idea. There are several kinds of support in the reading too. There is a list of good business practices, for instance. There are also some principles for good relationships within a business. It is true that a business with happy employees puts a positive face to the community. These are the businesses that succeed.

As you read the reading, look for the main idea and write it here:

_____

What are the good business practices? How many are there? Write the list here:

_____

What is the writer's conclusion about good business?

_____

Main Reading

It's Good Business

1   The good businessperson has always followed a *code of ethics*, a way of behaving that allows everyone a fair chance to succeed. If a business practice shows good ethics, it's also good business. If it's good for the country and the world, it's also good business. The reverse is also true: If it's good business, then it's good ethics and good for the world. Good business gives everyone an equal opportunity. Many business practices are acceptable, such as trying to produce a better product for less money to sell more. Other business methods are considered *unethical,* somehow not quite honest or right. For instance, lying about the qualities of one's product in advertising is not ethical, nor is it moral to lie about the "other guy's" product.

Many critics of business believe that businesses have created many of the social and environmental problems of modern society; therefore, businesses should try to solve some of these problems. "If you aren't part of the solution, then you are part of the problem." In either case, the message is clear: Businesses today have a great opportunity to undo some of the damage that business has done in the world. Furthermore, good business practices make better citizens out of managers and employees, and being good citizens is "good for business."

2   What are good business practices? For many people, the answer lies in four concepts. These ideas separate good business from business that is damaging to society:

- clear purpose and goals
- balance
- order
- satisfaction for both customers and employees

3   These concepts can lead us into a discussion of successful business practices. Let us consider them one by one.

Clear Purpose and Goals

4   "If you don't know where you're going," reads the old saying, "any direction will get you there." Every business, large or small, needs to have a mission statement. This short statement (usually fewer than 50 words) summarizes the company's goals. This announcement tells the world (and the people within the company) what the purpose of the company is. It states the purpose of the organization in a clear way so that the people within the company can know whether or not they are accomplishing their mission.

5   For example, a company may have this goal: "Daly 4 Enterprises seeks to combine writing talent and editing skills for the purpose of supplying timely and interesting articles to magazines and newspapers and, at the same time, serving as a refining and distribution center for writers." Such a statement makes it clear that the company does not write advertising copy or provide typing services. The company's

editors might consider working with a promising writer to develop his or her writing skills, though. Its mission statement includes those kinds of activities.

Read

Balance

6   In business practice today, there must always be a balance between the need to be a worthy member of society and the desire for profit. To help maintain this balance, management (the people who make policy and direct employees) must keep good business practices always in mind. A good business makes money *and* enjoys a fine reputation. People like to buy from a company that makes good products and is thought to be good to its employees and good for the community.

7   Balance also means good planning. The *management* of a company will meet with the directors and sometimes with all employees to prioritize the goals of the company. Prioritizing means defining the important goal, the next most important, and so on—putting the goals in order. When a company has clear goals, the balance between desire for profit and responsibility to society is usually clear. For example, the Kimberly-Clark Corporation, a paper manufacturer, has long insisted on safety in its plants as its number-one priority. All employees are instructed in safe ways of doing their jobs and in keeping a safe environment for all others in the plant. Because Kimberly-Clark's workers feel safe in their work environment, the next goal, to produce high-quality paper, can be achieved more easily. Safety instruction is also considered essential at the many DuPont Chemical plants around the world. There are safety officers, for example, who study the work environment and make recommendations for improvements. Companies like Kimberly-Clark and DuPont Chemical reward workers for safe days and for good ideas that will make the work environment even safer. The companies, in turn, are rewarded with loyal employees, higher production rates, and low rates of *absenteeism* (happy people come to work; they aren't "absent"). An emphasis on safety before profit can actually mean higher profits, and that is good business.

Read

Order

8   Order grows out of *predictability*. In other words, there is an arrangement of parts that makes sense. In a business that has order, there are clear guidelines and *clear policies*. Employees know the decisions that the leaders have made on how to accomplish goals (ways of doing business). In other words, everyone knows how the company does business, and all know what to expect. Order makes a business run smoothly. In the grocery business, foods and other products are put on the shelves in a certain order. Older *stock* (items, things to sell) is always moved to the front of a shelf, for example. In that way, all the food that a customer buys is kept as fresh as possible. Without this simple policy, some food (at the back of the shelf) would be much older than the food that the customer selects and takes home. This policy (called *rotating* or turning around) is standard in most food stores. The food business runs better because of this common policy.

9   Order is also an aspect of each employee's life in the workplace. Workers need to plan their time well so that they can be efficient. For people who work in hospitals, schools, and offices, there is a strong need for *time management* skills. Time is always in short supply for busy people. Yet, people who plan how they will spend their workday almost always manage to accomplish more than those who go into work without a schedule to follow or a prioritized list of things that they need to achieve. For this reason, many companies offer time management classes for employees. In the end, the companies get the benefit.

Satisfied Customers and Employees

10   Satisfied customers buy from the company. A company will not sell its products if its customers don't like the company. Employees represent the company. So customers identify a company with its employees. That is the reason employees are so important. The most important aspect of an inside-the-company focus is the employees. Business consultant John Stewart-Cook calls it "'happy-fy-ing' the

Read

unhappy workplace." He continues, "When people work, they work for money. They work because they need the money for their own and their families' support. If the workplace is a happy place, then people work better, produce more, and please the customers. No business is worth more than the people it employs." It seems that a business owner, boss, or manager can create a happy work environment and improve the business at the same time. Here are some of the principles that Stewart-Cook recommends:

11   1. *Help employees feel a sense of ownership in the company.* Some companies combine employee stock ownership programs and participation in the day-to-day management of the company to foster this commitment to the company's success.

12   2. *Encourage employees to think of better ways to do things.* Give employees who have good ideas some of the profit (money made from the use of the idea). In a combined goal-completion and profit-sharing program, for example, the idea is to let people come up with ways to improve a situation within a specific amount of time and reward them for completing the improvement projects that follow. These programs can work because employees often work for long periods of time in one area of a company's business; therefore, they know best where the waste of resources is. A wise manager rewards employees for showing how and where there is waste. When waste of time or materials is obvious, something can usually be done about the situation to stop the waste and improve efficiency.

13   3. *Educate employees about the business and allow them to share its goals.* When employees know what is expected of them, they generally try to do it. By teaching people to be better observers, a company gets better watchers of the company's process. The employees learn what to look for. The change in performance can be dramatic when employees feel they are part of a team. In some companies, however, some workers have little self-respect. They think in terms of "them" and "us." "They" are the bosses, the management,

Read

the skilled and educated people. And "we" are just the workers. These class divisions cause some people to think, "The information doesn't pertain to me." By becoming better observers, employees can better evaluate what is going on. They feel more like partners in the business. These employees have invested themselves in the company; they want the company to do well. They can also begin to follow an important business rule: "Study mistakes and live up to ideals." Good business is an ongoing process.

14   4. *Promote egalitarianism (equal treatment) in the workplace.* "Level the playing field, and there is a reduction in energy wasted running uphill." In a place where there is a potential royalty class, like the doctors in a hospital, equality is especially important. Successful health care, for example, must be based on a team approach. The work of a hospital is to take care of patients, to heal the sick. Every member of the team must work with the other team members. Treating patients like kings and queens is better than treating doctors like royalty.

15   5. *Allow employees the right to complain and suggest.* One effective way to handle complaints is a multilevel grievance procedure. In this approach, if an employee feels that he or she has not been treated fairly, then a panel of peers listens to the details of the case and makes a decision. If the employee is not happy with that decision, he or she can go to the next level of management, and eventually all the way to the director of the company.

16   6. *Encourage employees to come up with new ideas for the company.* Employees often see ways to improve the productivity and efficiency of the company. Some companies actually give their workers time during working hours to be creative, to think about improvements.

17   7. *Help employees feel secure about their jobs.* If a company has to decrease the number of workers, efforts to find new jobs for the employees affected should be at the top of the priority list. In some situations, a company can temporarily lend employees to other

Read

companies instead of laying them off when they aren't needed. It helps employees (and their morale, or their feelings) to know that the company cares about them. The principle is, "What goes around, comes around." In other words, it pays a company owner or manager to "go the extra mile" (do a little more work) to protect employees' jobs. If a person is considerate of others, then others will be considerate of that person.

18   8. *Provide positive pay incentives for employees.* Pay for good performance, develop team spirit and peer pressure to excel, to do well and not make mistakes. It is also considered positive for a company to provide *state-of-the-art* (modern, up-to-date) support for working parents with on-site day care, help for parents with sick children, and flexible hours whenever possible. Companies are encouraged to allow and foster *job-sharing* as a preferred way of handling secretarial positions—sometimes two heads really are better than one. Cooperation between two working mothers, for example, means that one always has the job covered. Programs like these help employees feel at home while at work. The principle is part of an honor code: "It's not how many hours you put in. It's how much you get done in that time."

19   9. *Diversify hiring and promotion.* If you open up opportunities for people who have never had them, they can improve the whole company by excelling and raising standards across the board. One such practice is hiring *senior citizens* (people past retirement age) for part-time employment. As statistics show, older workers are better risks. They miss fewer days of work, and they have less need for expensive insurance plans. They don't usually have children at home to worry about, and they have good work habits and lots of good "people skills." Another kind of diversification is to hire people with disabilities. They can do many necessary jobs happily and effectively. For example, the person with a developmental disability can deal with simplicity and repetition. Jobs working in bulk mail, washing

dishes, putting price tags on merchandise are within their abilities. In some communities, there are job coaches who learn the job first. Then they teach the job to people with developmental disabilities.

20   10. *Do business in a way that promotes world citizenship.* Use your social conscience when purchasing supplies. Don't buy from a company that exploits children or one that violates environmental protection laws. Be socially aware in advertising: convey social improvement messages in advertisements. Prohibit socially exploitative advertising. Build a demonstration-quality social enterprise. Sponsor good programs. Be environmentally conscious in mass-market selling.

21   The four basic requirements for a business and the ten workplace principles tell how to be successful in business. The principles show that investment in the workforce and in building local and world community is the most important aspect of running a business. If you owned a farm, you would need to have balance and order, clear plans, and capable, motivated workers. If you also had two people, a married couple, working for you and with you on the farm, how would you treat them? Would you fire them if one got sick? What if something happened to their child? Should anything be different if you owned a factory and had a hundred people working for you and with you? No, because it wouldn't be good business!

Strategy Focus: Finding the Main Idea

Choose the answer that best expresses the meaning of the reading.

a. Good business practices are likely to make the business successful.

b. Every business needs to have a mission statement.

c. There are many ways of making a lot of money in a free enterprise system.

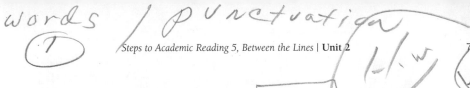

Strategy Focus: Learning Vocabulary in Context

Read each of the groups of sentences (contexts) from the reading. Note the words in **bold** type. In each context, there are some clues to the meanings of the words in bold type. Underline those clues. Then write or choose the correct meaning of the word.

1. If it's good **ethics**, it's also good business. If it's good for the country and the world, it's also good business. The reverse is also true: If it's good business, then it's good ethics and good for the world. The good businessperson always follows a **code of ethics**, a way of behaving that allows everyone a fair chance to succeed—an equal opportunity.

   a. Ethics and **a code of ethics** refer to ___ *a way of behaving that allows*

   b. If something is **fair**, it gives everyone ___ *equal opportunity*

2. [Lying] about the qualities of one's product in advertising is not ethical, nor is it **moral** to lie about the "other guy's" product. If a practice is **moral**, then it is…

   a. honest.

   b. ethical.

   c. both honest and ethical.

3. [Businesses] have created many of the social and environmental problems of modern society; therefore, businesses should try to **solve** some of these problems…"If you aren't part of the solution, then you are part of the problem."

   a. A question and a problem both have **solutions**. Another word for **solution**, therefore, must be ___ . *answer*

   b. To…a problem is to find the solution.

      1. create

      2. solve

      3. be part of

   c. The word **social** is related to the word **society**. Which of these problems are social problems?

      1. bad water, dirty air, sick animals

      2. sadness, lack of money, illness

      3. stealing, killing, dishonesty

4. [Businesses] today have a great opportunity to **undo** some of the damage that business has done in the world.

   Before one can **undo** a mistake, one has to make one! *Undo* is made up of two parts: *un-* and *do*. The words to *dress* (to put clothes on) and **to undress** (to take one's clothes off) show the opposite meanings.

   Therefore, **undo** must mean ___do back___ .

5. Every business, large and small, needs to have a **mission statement**. This short statement (usually fewer than 50 words) summarizes the company's goals and objectives.

   All the employees met in groups, and each group made a list of the company's goals. Then they compared their ideas and wrote a single **mission statement**.

   A **mission statement** tells ___goals of smith___ .

6. Companies like Kimberly-Clark and DuPont Chemical **reward** workers for safe days and for good ideas that will make the work environment even safer. The companies, in turn, are rewarded with **loyal** employees, higher production rates, and low rates of **absenteeism** (happy people come to work; they aren't "absent").

   a. To **reward** is to _____ .

      1. get something bad
      2. give something good
      3. avoid coming to work

   b. A **loyal** employee is one who _____ .

      1. doesn't come to work
      2. is happy to come to work
      3. is absent

   c. **Absenteeism** refers to _____ .

      1. not coming to work
      2. being a loyal employee
      3. company rewards

7. Order is based on **predictability**. In other words, there is an arrangement of parts that makes sense. In a business that has order, there are clear guidelines and clear **policies** (decisions on how to accomplish goals, ways of doing business).

   The weatherman's **predictability** of the weather is better now because of technology and satellite photographs.

   The company **policy** is to hire teenagers for summer jobs.

   Predictability refers to _____.

   A **policy** is a _____.

8. In the **grocery** business, foods and other products are put on the shelves in a certain order. Older **stock** (items, things to sell) is always moved to the front of a shelf, for example... This policy (called **rotating** or turning around) is standard in most food stores.

   a. What is sold in the **grocery** business? _____

   b. What is **stock**? _____

   c. Stock is **rotated** so that ...

      1. it stays around.

      2. no food gets old at the back of a shelf.

      3. there are always things to sell.

9. By teaching people to be better **observers**, a company gets better watchers of the company's process. The employees learn what to look for. The change in performance can be **dramatic** when employees feel they are part of a team.

   a. The job of an **observer** is to _____.

   b. A **dramatic** change is one that...

      1. no one will see.

      2. is small.

      3. is large and is easy to see.

10. Promote **egalitarianism** (equal treatment) in the workplace. "Level the playing field and there is a reduction in energy wasted running uphill." In a place where there is a potential royalty class, like the doctors in a hospital, equality is especially important. Successful health care, for example, must be based on a team approach.

A policy of **egalitarianism** means that all workers are treated ___equal___ .

Royal refers to kings and queens, the ruling class. In a hospital, doctors are the most likely group of people to be treated like **royalty** because ___ruling class___ .

11. Provide positive pay **incentives** for employees, pay for good performance, develop team spirit and **peer pressure to excel**, to do well, and to avoid mistakes.

  a. Pay is money that a person gets for working. Therefore, a pay **incentive** is likely to be ___pay for good performer___

  b. **Peer pressure** comes from…

    1. other team members.

    2. the boss.

    3. one's family.

  c. To **excel** is to ___do well___ and not to ___make Mistes___ .

12. It is also considered positive for a company to provide **state-of-the-art** (modern, up-to-date) support for working parents with **on-site** day care, help for parents with sick children, and flexible hours whenever possible. Companies are encouraged to allow and **foster job-sharing** as a preferred way of handling secretarial positions.

  a. If something is **state of the art**, then it is ___modern up to date___ .

  b. If a day-care center for children of factory workers is **on-site**, then it is…

    1. probably nearby.

    2. far away.

    3. at the factory.

c. To **foster** job-sharing means to...

   1. make it easy to do.

   2. make it difficult to do.

   3. define it.

d. **Job-sharing** means that two people have...

   1. one job between them.

   2. half a job each.

   3. Both 1 and 2 are correct.

13. **Diversify** hiring and promotion—if you open up opportunities for people who have never had them, they can improve the whole company by excelling and **raising standards** across the board. One such practice is hiring senior citizens (people past retirement age) for part-time employment... Another kind of **diversification** is to hire people with disabilities.

   a. In these sentences, **diversify** and **diversification** refer to ...

     1. people of different types.

     2. jobs of different types.

     3. part-time jobs.

   b. When someone **raises standards**, the quality...

     1. is different.

     2. is less.

     3. goes up.

Strategy Focus: Making Inferences

Do you know enough from the reading to make these statements? Check (✓) *enough* or *not enough*.

1. One of the unethical things that some companies do is to lie about their products.

   ☐ enough   ☐ not enough

2. A business or a company needs clear policies to run smoothly.

   ☐ enough   ☐ not enough

3. Most businesses in the world damage their communities.

   ☐ enough   ☐ not enough

4. Customers and employees tend not to like surprises from the business.

   ☐ enough   ☐ not enough

5. Happy people are better employees than sad people.

   ☐ enough   ☐ not enough

6. It is good business for a grocery store to make sure that customers get fresh food.

   ☐ enough   ☐ not enough

7. No employee should stay at one job longer than a few months; employees should rotate jobs.

   ☐ enough   ☐ not enough

8. Companies that share profits with employees have happy employees.

   ☐ enough   ☐ not enough

Strategy Focus: Thinking About Advertising and Marketing

Discuss these questions with a group of classmates.

1. How important is advertising? Every company wants to sell its products, so nearly every company spends some of its income on advertising. Look in a magazine at examples of advertising. What aspects of the ads are attractive? What makes an ad effective? How much are ethics and honesty involved in the advertising? What kind of advertising do you like?

   مجذب

2. Consider marketing as an aspect of business. One aspect of selling a product is making customers interested in it. What else is involved in selling a product? Here are some ideas. Decide if each idea is an important consideration for marketing:

   a. the package that the product is wrapped in

   b. the potential for selling the product in different areas

   c. a fair price for the product

   d. the best approach for advertising the product

   e. similar products that might be successful

Strategy: Scanning for Key Ideas

Look quickly through this reading for information on the following: *Linda Meadows, Hal Carpenter, disabled, coach, personnel manager*. Make notes of words or phrases that refer to these ideas. Then read carefully, adding to your notes as you go. Finally, compare your notes on these topics with those of a classmate.

 Related Reading 1

A Job Coach

1   Linda Meadows is thirty-eight years old. She attended a university and earned a degree in business management. For fifteen years, she worked in a busy company office. Then she had a car accident in which her head was hurt. Her brain swelled, and she lost some of her abilities. Linda is now considered disabled. However, Linda loves to be with people. She enjoys feeling as if she is contributing to a community. However, she can no longer do the management work that she used to do. She loses patience with people. She sometimes thinks that they are laughing at her. She cannot speak as clearly as she once did.

2   The personnel manager at her old company understood that Linda could not do the same work, but he recognized that she still had some of her organizing skills. The company policy is to keep employees, even if they are disabled. Perhaps Linda was now impatient with people, but the personnel manager also understood that much of her lack of patience came from her frustration. Linda wanted to do her old job, but she couldn't. Her inability made her feel angry inside herself, and she reacted negatively toward others. The personnel manager contacted Hal Carpenter.

3   Hal is a job coach. He works with disabled people to find them jobs and to help them learn to do them. The first step in Hal's process is

to talk with the clients. In this case, Linda and the personnel manager were his two clients. The personnel manager wanted to find a job that Linda could do. Linda wanted to do a useful job in the company. Hal went through the company plant, visiting every room, talking with people in various jobs, and taking notes. Then he tested Linda to see what her abilities were. He found three jobs that she might be able to do. None of them involved being with lots of people. Linda and the job coach went to the three work sites. Linda watched people in each of the situations and asked questions.

4   One of the jobs required a worker to use a computer to sort items into four different types. Linda sat down at the computer and wanted to work. Hal and the other employee showed her the system. It confused her, and she showed her frustration. However, the next job involved working with her hands, organizing reports. Linda immediately liked this job. Hal and the personnel manager discussed this job possibility. And Linda tried the job. Hal worked alongside her for two days. Together they figured out how Linda could manage all aspects of the job. They practiced what she should say when other employees needed one of the reports. Linda practiced filing them and retrieving them. She liked making order out of a box of reports. She was proud that she was contributing to the company's success. And Hal, the job coach, promised to come back the next week to see how Linda liked her new job.

Finding the Main Idea

Write a check (✓) in front of each title that you think is appropriate for this reading.

____   Losing One's Abilities

____   The Personnel Manager's Job

____   Hal and Linda Work Together

__✓   Linda Finds the Right Job

Strategy Focus: Learning Vocabulary in Context

Note that the meanings of these terms are in the context.

1. The **personnel manager** at her old company understood that Linda could not do the same work.

    A company needs to have someone to handle employee matters; that person is usually called the **personnel manager**.

    The **personnel manager** at asked a **job coach** for help with Linda. Hal is a **job coach**. He works with disabled people to find them jobs and to help them learn to do them.

    a. Which of these two people probably handles arrangements for child care and for insurance? _personnel manager._

    b. Which of these two people probably helps a person learn a new job? _personnel manager._

2. The company **policy** is to keep employees, even if they are disabled.

    The company has a job-sharing **policy** that allows two people to have half a job each.

    A **policy** is...

    a. a law.

    b. a decision about how to react to a situation.

    c. a method of achieving a goal.

3. Perhaps Linda was impatient with people, but the personnel manager also understood that much of her lack of patience came from her **frustration**.

    If a child tries many times to catch a ball and cannot do it, the child is likely to give up in **frustration**.

    A feeling of **frustration** comes from not...

    a. being fast.

    b. understanding.

    c. being successful.

Strategy Focus: Discussing the Topic

Hal Carpenter worked with Jim Marvin so that Jim could have a job. Jim has limited mental abilities, but a fast-food restaurant manager was willing to give Jim a job. Jim needed to learn how to do the job, so Hal came in to help. Jim's job was to pick up the trays that customers left in the dining area. He was supposed to empty the trays into the garbage container inside the restaurant and stack the trays. Then he carried the trays back to the dishwashing area and put them into a washing rack. These parts of the job he was able to do well. However, Jim also had to remove full black plastic garbage bags from the garbage containers, close and tie them up, and take them to the Dumpster in back of the restaurant. Jim didn't know how to tie a knot in the plastic bags. Hal taught him. First Hal tied up several bags, talking about the job and describing his motions. Then he went halfway through the tying, and let Jim finish. Next he and Jim practiced those motions until Jim felt comfortable with doing that part of the job. Then Hal showed Jim how to "snap" the bag to make two ends to tie together. Jim practiced that several times. Then Hall showed him how to begin the tying. Soon Jim could do that. Then the three steps were put together. Jim had learned not only how to tie the garbage bags, but now he could wear shoes with shoelaces because the jobs were the same.

1. What did Hal do to make the "big job" of learning to tie up a garbage bag easy?
2. Why do you think Hal started with the end of the job?
3. Why did Hal tell Jim exactly what he (Hal) was doing with the bag?

Strategy: Making Summary Notes

This reading contains principles for solving problems in groups. As you read, note each principle in a few words. As you find new principles, look back at your notes. Rewrite any notes that need changes. Try to write each principle clearly in the fewest possible words.

Related Reading 2

The Principles of Problem Solving

1   A principle of leadership is that a group of people might well have more information than a single person, even the leader. A wise leader, given this insight, will tell his followers where to go, but will not give them directions on how to get there. The solving of the problem by the group may show a better way than the leader imagined. If the group's solution isn't a better one, the leader can always help to refocus the group and change its direction. However, many leaders recognize the potential of letting people figure out their own solutions first.

2   What follows is a discussion of the major steps in problem solving. These steps should be taught to any group that is going to solve problems together.

1. *The first step is to state the problem and all the symptoms of the problem.* Describe the problem as clearly and completely as possible. The goal should be to state the problem objectively, without emotion or guilt. The problem should also be limited to one situation. Do not try to address all the problems in an organization at once. Too general a statement will not lead to a clear solution. In addition, every member of the problem-solving team needs to understand and describe the problem the same way.

2. *Next, make a goal statement.* What is the desired outcome? What results do you want? What do you want the situation to be when the problem is solved? This statement is extremely important because, like a mission statement, it provides a check to the question "Have the goals been achieved or not?" These goals should be written as a list of criteria for success. This list will be needed later in the problem- solving process. If the goal statement includes possible causes or solutions, then it needs to be revised (rewritten, changed).

The statement should be very short—fewer than twenty words. The shorter the statement, the more focused it is likely to be. A clear focus on goals will help in finding an answer to the question, a solution to the problem.

3. *The next step is to figure out how the problem got started.* What is the history of the problem? What caused the problem? The group should make a list of possible causes. If possible, the members might try to guess what the root of the problem is (how the problem got started). This step includes making two lists: the causes of the problem and the effects of the problem. Solving the problem will be easier if reasons and results are clearly stated for everyone. A pitfall (mistake, weakness) at this stage is to try to attach responsibility for the problem to one person. In an organization, responsibility for a problem situation hardly ever rests with one person; usually a number of causes interact to create the situation.

4. *The next procedure is brainstorming.* It is a technique for eliciting all of a group's ideas on a topic—both silly and serious. In brainstorming, people throw out ideas about possible solutions to the problem. No one is permitted to criticize any of the ideas, no matter how silly they might seem. The reason is that out of someone's silly idea, a serious and workable idea might form. After the list is written, participants choose the few that seem most usable.

5. *Next, the best solution is chosen from the list.* The remaining solutions are measured against the criteria for success that were developed in the second step of the procedure. The solution that fits the largest number of criteria is probably the best solution—and even this solution can probably be improved.

6. *Then, the participants have to decide on a plan of action.* Details are very important at this point. Who will do what and when? A timeline may have to be set up so that all the tasks in the project can be completed on time. A timeline is like a schedule of events. If the project is a large one, then planning and preparation are essential.

A plan of action must contain the job tasks, the people who will do them, the budget for each part of the job (the costs), and the amount of time and money that each part of the job will require. Attention to details clarifies the job.

7. *The action step—putting the schedule into action—is the "real" work.* The details of the plan of action are followed, and if everything is planned well, the project gets done, and the participants feel good about their work.

8. *The last step is evaluation or assessment.* After the project is completed, someone must determine its outcome. Was it done well? Was it done on time? Did the costs come within the budget? What does the end result look like? And, most importantly, what can be learned from the project so that the next problem-solving situation can be done even better, with greater efficiency?

By following this problem-solving sequence, any group of people can solve a problem. An additional positive aspect is that the people on the problem-solving team have an investment in the project. There is no such commitment to working through a problem if the orders on how to fix the situation come from management. Group problem solving really is a better way.

Strategy Focus: Distinguishing Fact from Non-Fact

Read each statement and decide whether it is a fact (*F*) or a non-fact (*NF*)—a judgment, inference, opinion. Write *F* or *NF* in the blank. Remember, your classmates might not agree with you. Explain why you think your answer is correct.

1. __*NF*__ A wise leader can always do a better job of making decisions than a group of people.

2. __*F*__ A budget is a statement of how much money can be spent on each part.

3. _____ A leader should use brainstorming for making all decisions.

4. _____ Another word for a *schedule* is a *timeline*.

5. _____ All leaders should agree on how to run a problem-solving session.

6. _____ A plan of action needs to have many details.

Strategy Focus: Learning Vocabulary in Context

Read each of the groups of sentences (contexts) from the reading. Note the words in **bold** print. In each context, there are clues to the meanings of those words. Underline those clues. Then write the meaning of the word or choose the best meaning of the word.

1. A **pitfall** (mistake, weakness) at this stage is to try to attach responsibility for the problem to one person. A **pitfall** is…

   a. where people are likely to make mistakes.

   b. a place of business.

   c. a dangerous area.

2. The goal should be to state the problem **objectively**, without emotion or guilt. If a job is done **objectively**, then there is neither _____ emotion or guilt. _____.

3. A **timeline** may have to be set up so that all the tasks in the project can be completed on time. A **timeline** is like a schedule of events. A **timeline** is _____ a schedule _____.

4. Next, make a goal statement. What is the desired **outcome**? What results do you want? What do you want the situation to be when the problem is solved? The **outcome** refers to the _____ results _____.

5. A plan of action must contain the job tasks, the people who will do them, the **budget** for each part of the job (the costs), and the amount of time and money that each part of the job will require. A **budget** must be…

   a. a new kind of job.

   b. a plan for spending money.

   c. like a timeline.

6. If the goal statement includes possible causes or solutions, then it
   needs to be **revised** (rewritten, changed). If a report is **revised** several
   times, the person who wrote it has _____ *rewritten, changed*

Strategy Focus: Discussing How to Start a New Business

Think about the problems that a new business faces. Here are some pitfalls
that a business can fall into. Why do you think these are weaknesses in a new
business plan?

  a. spending too much money on a place for the business

  b. expanding too fast

  c. charging too much for the product

  d. not doing market research to be sure there is a need for the product

Strategy: Scanning for Key Ideas

Look carefully at the title of the reading, and note down your ideas. Who is
the face of the company? What do customer service representatives do?
What personal qualities do they need for the job? Then look quickly through
the reading, making brief notes about the job duties and personality of a
customer service representative. Add to these notes as you read the reading
a second time.

 Related Reading 3

The Face of the Company

1   If the most important aspect of a business is its employees,
then the most important of the employees are the *customer service
representatives*. The customer service representative is the face of
the company to the public. He or she is often the first voice of the
company, the person who makes the first impression. A personality
survey of the ideal customer service representative shows a truly
"people-centered" person. The ideal customer service representative

likes to meet people, enjoys helping other people, and is good at remembering names and faces. He or she likes to see other people enjoy themselves, can communicate with children and adults alike, and takes pride in being a good communicator. He or she is *well-groomed* — clean, tidy, and well-dressed. In their training, customer service representatives learn that they get only one chance to make a first impression. That's why the ideal customer service representative also has a warm smile and uses it often.

Customer service representatives can be important to the success of a business. An ideal customer service representative has the skills to make customers want to return.

2   Learning to be an ideal customer service representative requires two things: first, understanding why customer service is important; second, learning how to be a good communicator for the company. *Trainees* (people who are learning how to do a job) get lessons in remaining positive even when the situation is quite negative. They learn how to set other people at ease, with a reassuring smile, a general pleasant remark, or a simple compliment.

3 Trainees also learn the importance of *body language*. A successful businessperson holds his or her head high and uses body movements (gestures) that are natural and appropriate. No movement should be hurried or too slow. The muscles of the face should be relaxed, in an easy natural smile. Also important is the trainee's ability to hold eye contact with the other person in a conversation.

4 The ideal customer service representative has a nice voice. Tone of voice can determine the difference between failure and success for a person in the public eye. When some people are upset or angry, their voices show these emotions by becoming louder or harsher. Neither of those qualities (loud or harsh) is good in business. The customer service representative should operate as though the customer is always right, but perhaps doesn't understand company policy. In such a case, the service representative must patiently and clearly explain the situation to the customer. A warm and understanding voice will be successful far more often than a loud, hard voice. Other positive voice qualities are clearness, directness, and naturalness.

5 The customer service representative may need to use the telephone frequently. Therefore, complete knowledge of how to use the telephone effectively is a must for a customer service representative. A positive attitude on the telephone is especially important because telephone contact is often the first contact. For example, it is unacceptable to keep a customer waiting a long time on the telephone, to fail to return telephone calls, or to give a rude response—even to a rude customer. Telephone service must be pleasant, positive, and smooth. Trainees are told to smile into the telephone—it will keep their voices pleasant, too. Telephone *etiquette* requires that the representative identify him- or herself by name and company. It is polite to give the reason for the call and to ask if it is a convenient time to call. Many people don't realize it, but it is good to talk a little more slowly than normal on the telephone, especially when dealing with numbers. It is also good policy to summarize the business of the telephone call before saying good-bye and hanging up. A rule of telephone communication that is often ignored is the "hang-up" rule: the person who called is usually the person who signals that the call is at an end.

6   The customer service representative must be aware of customers' basic human needs. Every person wants to feel welcome, to feel respected. A customer also expects timely service and possibly help or assistance. The customer does not want surprises, but comfort and orderly service in dealing with the company. In addition, every person wants to feel understood, recognized, and remembered. It is human nature to feel good when someone accepts you and appreciates you as a person.

7   The customer service representative also has to be aware of customers' business needs. Even before a customer knows what he or she needs or wants, a customer service person should have anticipated and planned for that need. It may sound like a difficult job, but a customer service person should know what the total number of possible needs are for a customer in a particular business. Therefore, the job is simple: prepare for each of the possible needs and then assess each situation. What might the customer need and want? The well-prepared service person is ready for rush periods when many customers appear, and can handle the stress of a number of people asking for help all at once.

8   Also important for the face of a company is the skill of listening well. Trainees for customer service are taught to follow these directions in learning to listen:

First, stop talking—because when you are talking, you cannot listen.

Next, concentrate on what the other person is saying— don't let little things distract you.

Then, try to find the "hidden" meaning: What does the customer really want?

Finally, repeat the message as you heard it; give information feedback.

In all communication, eye contact is recommended. There will be both content and feelings in any communication. A good customer service representative listens for the feelings first and the details of the content second. The real message is in the feelings.

9   The position of customer service representative is an important one in a company. Some companies have only one person through whom all customers make contact. In other companies, there may be many—as in grocery stores and department stores. In these businesses, every salesperson represents the company. A successful salesperson has all the skills to make customers want to return. That's the sign of success. That's also the bottom line. ∎

Strategy Focus: Filling in a Cloze Summary

Fill in the missing words that summarize the characteristics of a good customer service representative.

A good customer service representative is a people- _centred_ person who needs to have a lot of _communcation_ skills. The person can control his or her _emotion_ so that even when angry or upset, customers _cant_ not recognize the emotion. The person will remember _name_ and faces, be pleasant to everyone, even rude _customers_ The person will also be well-groomed and _dress_ neatly. The ideal customer service representative will also _deal_ good telephone etiquette and a pleasant voice. _ideal_ person will also understand the importance of making _____ feel comfortable, of anticipating the needs of customers, _____ of being prepared to answer all questions. The _____ customer service trainee also plans for the answers _____ questions so that the customers can be helped _quickly_ . Customers come back to a company if they _feel_ comfortable and respected at the place of business. It's proof of good business.

Make a list of the characteristics of a good customer service representative:

_____   _____

_____   _____

_____   _____

Strategy Focus: Discussing the Ideas

Discuss these questions with a group of classmates.

1. The principles of good customer service apply to many fields. Consider how a teacher compares to a customer service representative. What is a teacher selling? Consider how a doctor compares to a customer service representative. What is the doctor selling?

2. What is the "hang-up" rule of telephone etiquette? Why is it important in a business conversation?

3. Make a list of occupations. What "people skills" are important in each of those occupations? Which occupations require the most skill in working with people and getting good results from people?

Strategy Focus: Understanding Business Terms

In business, there are a number of two-sided relationships:

a. profit and loss
b. supply and demand
c. income and outflow
d. debit and credit
e. cost and profit
f. buyer and seller

Write the letter of the correct relationship in front of each question:

1. __a__ Which one refers to whether money is earned or spent?
2. __f__ Which one refers to people who are customers or merchants?
3. __b__ Which one refers to the need (or lack of need) for the product?
4. __d__ Which one refers to a bookkeeper's two sets of numbers?
5. __e__ Which one refers to money that is spent in doing business and money that is earned by the company?
6. __c__ Which one refers to money that is earned and the money that goes out?

Strategy Focus: Making Inferences About the Meanings of Business Sayings

There are a number of interesting axioms and sayings that are like general rules about making money, being successful, and doing business. For example, in the main reading, there were several sayings. The first one explains the importance of setting a goal: "If you don't know where you're going, any direction will get you there."

You will find other concepts from the reading in this list of twelve sayings.

a. *The customer is always right.*
b. *What goes around, comes around.*
c. *Buy and sell; sell and buy. The story ends with the bottom line.*
d. *A penny saved is a penny earned.*
e. *You have to spend money to make money.*
f. *Study mistakes and live up to ideals.*
g. *You cannot sell from an empty cart.*
h. *The early bird catches the worm.*
i. *Early to bed and early to rise makes a man healthy, wealthy, and wise.*
j. *If you aren't part of the solution, then you are part of the problem.*
k. *Waste not, want not.*
l. *Take care of the pennies and the dollars will take care of themselves.*

Try working with the sayings in the following exercise. Use these three steps:

The first step is to think about each of these statements and discuss them with classmates. What do these sayings tell us about beliefs about business? For example: *Penny wise; pound foolish.* First of all, *penny* and *pound* are terms from the money system in England. Some people are wise (careful, thoughtful) about how they spend pennies (small amounts of money), but they are not careful with large amounts of money (the money measured not in pennies but in pounds). They save little bits of money, but waste in general because they don't pay attention to the overall picture.

The second step is to match each of these twelve sayings with an explanation. Write the letter of the saying in front of the explanation.

1. __j__ It is not possible to avoid being involved in the business. You have to be working with the other people in the business—or else you are working against them.

2. __e__ In order to be a successful businessperson, you have to put money into resources (things to sell) because your customers will not want to buy only one thing from you. They'll want choices.

3. __a__   If you disagree with a customer, you will always lose the argument.

4. __k__   People who throw away useful things are foolish. They will need those resources later and not have them.

5. __d__   It is good to put money in a bank and not spend it. It's as if you had a job and earned the money.

6. __i__   The person who is well rested and gets up early in the morning to start work will be successful because he'll be there before his competitors.

7. __L__   A successful businessperson attends to details; if the small parts of the business are running well, the more important parts are, too.

8. __h__   The first one to see a business opportunity gets the chance to be successful in the business.

9. __c__   You can see the success of a business by subtracting the cost from the profit.

10. __g__   First you have to set up a shop, then you have to get things to put in it, and then you have to hire workers. After all that is done, then you can open for business.

11. __b__   You get back what you give out.

12. __f__   Try to figure out what went wrong—that's what a good businessperson does after a failure or a loss in business.

The last step is to think about (and discuss) the ideas for good business in the six sayings below. Do these principles also work in the management of a person's own life? How are these principles good in helping a person manage time and resources better?

a. *What goes around, comes around.*
b. *A penny saved is a penny earned.*
c. *Study mistakes and live up to ideals.*
d. *The early bird catches the worm.*
e. *Early to bed and early to rise makes a man healthy, wealthy, and wise.*
f. *Waste not, want not.*

Discuss the sayings that you have heard and liked. What sayings are important to you, in the way you live your life?

Strategy: Writing About the Ideas

1. Choose one of the sayings about business from the lists. Write a paragraph about it: why you think it is good, why it isn't very good, or how to explain it to a younger person.

2. Choose a large and colorful advertisement from a magazine. Write a paragraph in which you give your opinion of the ad. To what kind of person will the advertisement seem good? Why? How much real facts and information are given in the ad? How much is the reader supposed to infer?

3. Describe the job coach's task in working with a disabled person.

Strategy Focus: Keeping a Vocabulary Journal

Choose five words from the new words in this unit to be your target words.

Write the words here: _____ _____ _____

_____ _____ _____

Now write them into your vocabulary journal. Remember to include the following parts:

- your target word
- the sentence from the unit in which your target word appears
- a definition, including the part of speech.
- some sentences of your own

Strategy Focus: Exploring the Concept of Being Successful

Now consider these questions:

1. What makes a person successful in life? Make a list of characteristics of a successful person. How can a person imitate those characteristics?

2. How can time management skills help a person live a happier life in a modern business environment? How can time management help a student do better in school?

3. What are the most important relationships you have? How do you measure your success? How do you measure your own happiness?

4. Is saving money important to you? Why do some people think that it is important to save money? Who should save money?

Strategy: Increasing Reading Speed

 Timed Reading

Taking Care of Business

Business is about making money. Every business makes a product or sells services, collects money for that work, and subtracts the cost of doing business. The rest is profit. The profit is written on the bottom line of the record book. The bottom line is a measure of success in business. Every business needs to have a profit in order to continue to exist.

The person who keeps the records of a business is called a bookkeeper. This person—or a whole department in large companies—receives all the bills and all the payments for the company. At the end of every period (a week, a month, a fiscal year), the bookkeeper has to figure out whether the company is making money or not. For this purpose, bookkeepers keep two separate lists. Money that comes into the business as payment for goods or services goes into the computer as a credit. All income is recorded as credit.

Nowadays business records are kept on computers, but bookkeepers used to use black ink to write credits in record books. Therefore, if a company is "in the black," then it is making money. Money that goes out of the company is recorded as a debit. Debits include paying for supplies, paying rent on a business place, paying employees, paying for employees' benefits, insurance and taxes, and paying the cost of doing business—transportation, telephone bills, utility bills, and repairs. Money that goes out of the business was once recorded in red ink. So, if a company is "in the red," then it is losing money. When the bookkeeper adds up all the income and all the outflow (money paid out), the amount that is left is "the bottom line." For example, if all the bills that the company had to pay amounted to $5300 in a month, and if the company earned $7200, the bottom line would show a profit of $1900. In this case, the company is "in the black."

Because the business exists to make money, business leaders try to increase income by increasing sales—the amount of the product that is sold. They also try to run the company more efficiently. They try to lower their costs and advertise better than their competitors (businesses that sell the same products). The company that does best in all those areas will make the most money and the greatest profit.

Time: _____

Now answer these questions as quickly as you can.

1. The opposite of income is…
   a. come.
   b. outflow.
   c. expense.

2. Numbers written in red ink are…
   a. debits.
   b. profits.
   c. credits.

3. The measure of success in a business is…
   a. its bookkeeper.
   b. the amount of money that comes in.
   c. how much profit it makes.

4. Competitors are…

   a. customers, the people who buy from the company.

   b. other companies that make the same product or sell the same service.

   c. advertisers.

5. Choose the best title for this reading.

   a. The Red and the Black

   b. Bookkeeper's Problems

   c. Debits, Credits, and Profits

BIOTECHNOLOGY: FEEDING THE BILLIONS

Preparation

Strategies for Anticipation

The word *agriculture* literally means "to work a field." In Latin, *agri-* is part of the word *ager*, which means "field," and *cultura* (cultivation), refers to working the soil. Today we use the word *agriculture* to mean the art of farming, producing food.

Bio means life. *Techno-* means "skill," and *-logy* refers to the study of, or the thinking about, a field. *Biotechnology* is a new way of farming with the help of scientists.

Farmers who practice the art of farming will tend the soil carefully by enriching it and protecting it from too much wind and water. They plant seeds and care for the resulting plants in their fields, their *crops*. They *harvest* (gather, collect) their crops and prepare them for market or for eating. Some farmers raise animals for food or profit; these animals are called *livestock*. All farmers work hard to support themselves and their families through their efforts, but to succeed, they need something besides hard work. They need to have specific knowledge about soil, seeds, water, and weather. When hard work and knowledge meet, the result is agriculture.

Today's population is growing fast. There are more than six billion people on Earth, and one billion of them are hungry. The challenge of feeding the billions is here.

Stop and think about farming for a moment. Ask yourself these questions and prepare some answers.

1. What kind of experience do you have with growing things?
2. What is the most important crop that farmers cultivate in your area of the world?
3. How is land measured? (Hectares? Acres?) How large is an average farm?
4. Is the average size of farms staying the same? Getting larger? Or getting smaller?
5. What kinds of livestock are you most familiar with?
6. Do farmers make a lot of money? Are farmers highly respected?

Now discuss these questions and your answers. Make a list of ideas that you think will be part of this unit.

Strategy: Restating Main Ideas

Survey this reading. Note that it has three main parts. You can read each of the parts as a separate reading, but they all fit together into an argument. What are the two sides of the argument? Why are they organized in this way? As you read through this reading, think about ways to summarize the ideas.

 ## Main Reading

Feeding the Billions

1   For as long as people have been farmers, biotechnology has been a science. The first farmers noticed that some plants were stronger than others. They looked for the qualities that would yield a good crop, and they saved the seeds of those plants for the next year. Farming became more sophisticated because the need to produce large crops also grew. And science became more complex as well. Farmers needed seeds for plants that were not vulnerable to insects or funguses. They wanted plants that could tolerate sun and drought (not much rain). The farmers looked for the strongest plants. Again, they chose those plants for seeds. The tradition of seed-saving has a natural beginning.

2   Traditional ways of producing good seeds have been successful. Experiments to combine the strongest traits (qualities) of corn or soybeans, for example, give high yield. Also the use of fertilizers has made the soil richer. Pesticides (to kill insects) have also had a great effect on production. The increase in food production over the past forty years is a result of traditional biotechnology.

3   There is now a new kind of biotechnology, genetic engineering. This kind involves scientists in white coats in laboratories. Modern agronomists use genetic material and biologically active chemicals (like antibiotics or enzymes) to cause specific changes in seeds. In ordinary plant breeding, hundreds of genes are "crossed" or mixed, and the results are examined for desirable traits. Biotechnology is quite different. Plant biotechnology allows selection of one or two desirable traits and none of the undesirable ones. It seems possible to produce perfect crops. However, bioengineering of plants has caused great controversy. Is it good? Is it bad? Is it safe? Some people see great advantages in biotechnology. Critics of biotechnology have deep and serious concerns.

4   The opponents of biotechnology believe that we do not know enough about the science of genetics. These "unnatural" plants might not be safe for people or animals to eat. The new breeds of plants might be difficult to control, and they might affect other living things.

5   The proponents of biotechnology point out many advantages. They see these new plants as a way to save the world's vast population from starvation. There are pros and cons, advantages and disadvantages, benefits and risks. Who knows the truth of biotechnology? It is good for us as inhabitants of the earth and as consumers of farm products to know what we are eating. It is wise to question what seems like too much of a very good thing.

Pros: Advocating Biotechnology

6   Proponents of biotechnology believe it is the future. Billions of people can live well, and wildlife can be saved. Biotechnology can make it happen. Without biotech farming and biotech forest management, proponents believe those people will starve, and the wildlife will disappear. The key is high-yield agriculture. And high-yield farming is possible because of biotech work. Dennis Avery, the director of the Hudson Institute Center on Global Food Issues, believes in biotechnology. He gives six reasons why we need biotechnology.

7   First, he says, biotech will expand the gene pool for all crops. Therefore, genetic engineers will be able to breed strong crops. All plants will be better and produce more food.

8   Second, trees will become a crop. Biotech principles will create trees that grow faster, straighter, and closer together. High-yield forest farms will grow trees four times as fast as "regular" trees. Foresters will raise the wood products (for lumber and paper, for example) on small tracts of land.

9   Third, because of biotechnology the wild forests will be saved. The genetic diversity in the wildlands will be saved because forest products are grown on farms. With biotech, researchers can select genes from any plant or animal and insert those genes (and thus also the characteristics) into any other plant or animal. The world's great forests will be left untouched. Like a bank of valuable genes, the wildlands will hold the potential for developing new products. Because biotech forests will be managed like farms, there will be all the forest products society needs. There will be no profit in cutting down the natural forests.

10   A fourth advantage is that biotech can create a new diversity. Researchers are trying to develop bacteria that will eat oil and turn it into useful compounds. Such a bacterium would make oil spills on the ocean less damaging. Another example of new diversity involves two trees that were dying out: the American chestnut tree and the

American elm tree. Because of genetic engineering, these two trees have been saved. However, each of these tress is one gene different from the original species.

11   Fifth, biotechnology can reduce the amount of pesticide spraying on farms. Researchers have developed "B.t. crops" that resist insects. These crops include a gene from the *Bacillus thurigdiensis* (or B.t.), an organism that is found naturally in soil. B.t. produces a substance that kills many insects. That's why B.t. biotech crops can mean less water contamination. For example, there is now a potato plant that can fight off a Colorado potato beetle. This insect once destroyed a field of potato plants in a few days. A biotech company (Monsanto) has developed a potato (NewLeaf®) that protects itself against the beetle. There are many benefits from such a plant. It is not destroyed by the beetle. Farmers do not need to spray potentially harmful chemicals on their fields. That means farmers do not risk being hurt by the pesticide poisons, and the pesticides do not seep into groundwater. In addition, the work of the farmer in planting and harvesting is easier. Farmers know how large the crop will be, so they do not have to plant extra acres. This planning means less waste of water, too.

12   The sixth reason for supporting biotechnology is its potential for helping Third World countries. Here Avery suggests a cycle of social development that he thinks is related to food production. The poorer the country, the more children a family has. Children represent wealth and future security. The more children a family has, the greater the number of children who will die before adulthood. The reason is that large families mean greater competition for resources. If a country suddenly becomes richer because it has more food, in one generation family size will decrease. Parents won't have to have large families to be sure that some of the children grow up. In a food-rich country, children are expensive. In other words, zero-population growth is possible only when there is more than enough food. And there is more than enough food because there are not so many people.

13   Avery continues his argument with a discussion of pollution. Many blame the First World for causing pollution. In fact, he says, pollution is a far more serious problem in Third World countries. People in the Third World have reached the most polluted stage of their development. Their cities are dirty; they burn coal that dirties the air. They do not treat their sewage. First World countries are beyond that stage. They treat sewage, control industrial waste, protect wildlife, and try to correct environmental problems.

Cons: The Arguments Against Biotechnology

14   Seeds that are produced with genes from other sources are called transgenic plants. Crops of all kinds have come from this process—strawberries to corn, apples to potatoes. Many of these crops are called "B.t. crops" because they include a gene from an organism that is found in soil. The *Bacillus thurigdiensis* (or B.t.) produces a substance that kills many insects. Pesticide use can be reduced greatly. There are some worries, however. Will the insects change? Will they become tolerant of the B.t. plants? Agriculture could become vulnerable to stronger insect infestations.

15   Another danger is that the transgenic plant genes might spread from the plants in the fields to other nearby plants. Such spreading would mean that insects could develop resistance to the B.t. plants more quickly. Such foreign genes might affect the field crops and the wild varieties of similar plants. In another instance, a researcher at Cornell University noted that 50% of his Monarch butterflies (yellow with black patterns on them) died when they ate weeds with B.t. corn pollen on them. The concern is that transgenic plants may have something in them that could hurt human beings.

16   Yet another question comes from legal rights to seeds. If a biotech company puts millions of dollars into developing a special kind of plant, does the company "own" that plant? Does the company have the right to sell the seeds, and are the seeds from the crops also

the property of the company? Or do the seeds belong to the farmer? Can such plants be patented to protect the rights of the biotech company? Farmers, 1.4 billion of them, have always saved seeds from their harvest. They have always saved the best seeds. If a farmer saves biotech seeds, is he stealing from the biotech company? Obviously, these questions of ethics are not easy to answer. How will biotechnology be controlled?

17   Jules Pretty directs the Center for Environment and Society at the University of Essex. He believes that the world population will stabilize (reach its top point and then stay that point) at eight to ten billion people. He also figures that each person needs 350 kilograms of grain as food per year. He notes that much of that grain is wasted because it is fed to animals. The people eat the meat, milk, and cheese, not the grain. Pretty opposes most kinds of biotechnology because of the dangers it represents and the ethical questions it raises. He recommends sustainable agriculture, which uses farmers' skills and knowledge and not genetically engineered seeds. He prefers animal manure and composted soil to chemical fertilizers.

18   Norman Borlaug's Green Revolution, Pretty says, may have shown how to grow more food with fertilizers and pesticides. It has also contaminated the world with chemical fertilizers and pesticides. It would be better, Pretty says, to encourage natural enemies of the insects and to use natural products to fertilize the land. In his book, *The Living Land*, Pretty gives many examples of how education in sustainable farming has increased yield. Two hundred thousand Kenyan farmers doubled their production of corn. In southern and western India, 300,000 farmers are now using new water and soil management techniques. They have three times the crop yields of previous years. The solutions, Pretty says, must start with government policies. Taxes on pesticides and chemical fertilizers would make many farmers stop to consider sustainable farming as an alternative.

19   Pretty is obviously opposed to genetic engineering of crops. So is Ronnie Cummins, director of the Campaign for Food Safety. Cummins openly opposed biotech companies. One biotech development is bovine growth hormone. This chemical causes a cow to give 15 to 25% more milk. The milk also contains traces (small amounts) of the hormone. Also, because cows often respond to the hormone with infections, they are given antibiotic drugs. Traces of antibiotics also show up in the milk. Cummins also objects to genetically engineered farm products. He says these plants are making new toxins (poisons) and new allergens (things that people are allergic to). Furthermore, superweeds and superpests (plants and animals that can tolerate herbicides and pesticides) are developing. Like Pretty, Cummins recommends organic farming, sustainable farming.

Strategy Focus: Writing Your Opinion

Make a list of ideas that support biotechnology and a separate list of concepts that oppose biotechnology. Then make a statement about which side has stronger arguments.

Strategy Focus: Learning Vocabulary in Context

Choose the answer that fits the meaning of the words in bold type. (Some items have more than one answer; others require you to circle or write a check (✓) near the correct answer or to provide written answers.)

1. **High-yielding**: To **yield** means to give, to produce. The **yield** of a field is the amount of food that it produces. Therefore, wheat seed that is **high-yielding**…

    a. produces a lot of wheat.   b. produces little wheat.

2. **To double**: To increase by two times is **to double**. A farm in Japan produced 100 tons of rice last year. Therefore, this same farm would produce _____ this year if its yield of rice doubled.

3. **Critic**: A **critic** is a person who evaluates the good and bad things about a topic—but this person often focuses on the bad things. Which of these things might a critic do? Write a check (✔) in front of each possible answer.

   _✔_ a. Write for a newspaper

   _✔_ b. Attend theater productions and write reviews

   ____ c. Analyze results of a test or experiment

   _✔_ d. Read books for writers before they are published

   Can you think of other jobs for critics?

4. **To compete**: Whenever there is a "prize" to win, people will try hard to win it; they will **compete** with one another. The act of competing is called **competition**. Which of the following are examples of competition? Write a (✔) in front of each possible answer.

   _✔_ a. a football game

   ____ b. an examination in class

   _✔_ c. two farmers both wanting to sell their produce to the same person

   ____ d. two farmers working together to harvest their crops

   ____ e. an art contest

   ____ f. two plants growing next to each other

5. **Fertilizer**: To **fertilize** is to make richer. Chemical **fertilizers** add important chemicals to the soil, making it richer and thus able to grow better crops.
   Pesticide: A chemical that kills insects is a pesticide.
   Herbicide: A herbicide kills weeds. Most herbicides are chemicals that are sprayed on the soil.

   Use the three **bold** print words above in this short paragraph:

   A farmer's fields were not yielding much food, so he decided to buy _____ so that the richer soil would produce more. However, the weeds liked the enriched soil as much as the seeds for corn and beans that he planted, so he bought _Herbicide_. A few weeks later he noticed that some insects were destroying his young plants, so he bought _pesticide_

6. **Organic farming**: Natural farming, without the use of chemical fertilizers, herbicides, or pesticides, is called **organic farming**. **Agronomist**: An agronomist works with soil and plants to manage them better and to experiment with different processes and seeds. Every **organic** farmer is an **agronomist** of sorts because…

   a. in organic farming, chemical fertilizers, pesticides, and herbicides are used a lot.

   b. in organic farming, alternatives to the use of chemical fertilizers, pesticides, and herbicides are used.

7. **Trait**: (a) quality or aspect of a living thing (person, animal, or plant)

   Which of these adjectives describe good personality **traits**? Circle all the positive ones.

   cold   helpful   honest   blue   kind

   gentle   intelligent   angry   loud   giving

8. **Sophisticated**: complex, requiring much education and knowledge
   The opposite of **sophisticated** must be…

   a. simple.   c. funny.

   b. silly.   d. helpful.

9. What do a **virus**, a **pest**, and an **insect** have in common? Farmers hate them all because they destroy crops. The chemical poisons that kill them are called _____ .

   a. herbicides

   b. fertilizers

   c. pesticides

10. **Zero-population growth** is a goal of many countries because…

    a. they do not have enough resources to support a population that continues to grow.

    b. they do not have enough people, and people are a country's most important resource.

Strategy Focus: Finding the Main Idea

There are three main parts to this main reading. Write a check (✓) in front of the main idea for each of the three sections.

Part 1 – Feeding the Billions

✓ a. Genetic engineering is simply a new kind of biotechnology.

____ b. Farmers have always saved the seeds of their best crops for the next year.

____ c. Many people have deep concerns about the safety of using new biotechnology.

Part 2 – Pros: Advocating Biotechnology

____ a. Many people have deep concerns about the safety of using new biotechnology.

✓ b. Biotechnology could save the world from starvation.

____ c. Organic farming is the best way to raise food to feed the people of the world.

Part 3 – Cons: The Arguments Against Biotechnology

____ a. We don't know enough about the dangers of biotechnology to use it to produce the food we eat.

✓ b. Many people have deep concerns about the safety of using new biotechnology.

____ c. There are natural enemies that kill viruses and pests on plants.

Strategy Focus: Scanning for Details

1. Find the name of a biotech company: _monsanto_

2. Find the name of the bioengineered potato: _new leaf_

3. How many farmers are there in the world? _1.4 billions_

4. The names of two poisons used in farming are _herbicides_ and _pesticides_

5. Who is Dennis Avery? _director Hudson._

6. What does B.t. mean? _Bacillus thurigdnensis_

7. What color are Monarch butterflies? _yellow black_

8. Where is Jules Pretty from? _university of essex_

9. How many Kenyan farmers learned soil and water management techniques to improve crop yield? _2 hundred thousand_

10. Who wrote *The Living Land?* _, pretty_
   Jules

Strategy Focus: Discussing the Concepts   – diversity.

1. What advantages would come from biotech forests? 5

2. According to Dennis Avery, where in the world is pollution the worst? Why? _Third world countries_   17

3. How many kilograms of grain does it take to feed one person for a year? 350 kilogram
   hormone
4. How can cows be made to give more milk? Is it dangerous?

5. Where is the greatest biodiversity in the world?

Strategy: Understanding Definitions

Find definitions for these words and terms: *gene, organism, DNA, genetic engineering*

 # Related Reading 1

How Biotechnology Works

1   Genes are chemicals that contain information for making a plant or animal. Different genes can cause specific changes in the new plant or animal. Like a recipe, what goes into the soup determines what the soup will look and taste like. What goes into the DNA determines the traits the organism will have. A cook who is making soup might add potatoes, carrots, and cabbage to the broth. The soup would be very different if she used beets, spinach, and onions. In a similar way, genes can be changed in genetic engineering, depending on what the desired result is. Genetic engineers have taken genes from fish that make their own light in the dark waters of the ocean and added them to mouse genes. They made a mouse that shines in the dark.

2   All living organisms, both plants and animals, contain genetic material. The DNA of each plant or animal is unique, although all red roses have more in common than a rose and an African elephant do. In nature, a brown cow and a white cow may result in a cow of a different color, but traditional animal breeding is limited in the possible colors. For a genetic engineer, however, there are no such restrictions. To produce a purple cow, the genetic engineer needs only something that is purple color in nature, such as the purple gene from a purple iris (a flower).

3   Genetic engineering is radically different from traditional, natural methods of breeding. Gene transfer (adding genetic material from other sources) means unlimited combinations of genes and traits. Genetic engineers may be able to create completely artificial genes in a laboratory. There are many possible benefits from such new biotechnology. However, there are also new dangers.

4   DNA is basic genetic material. It is made up of four organic compounds (chemicals) with a sugar and a phosphate. It forms a pair of twisted spiral strings, a double helix. It contains the directions for

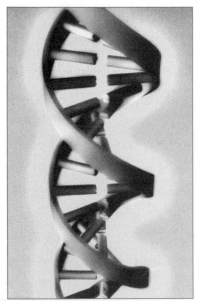

baby cells to grow into fully developed plants or animals. Human DNA has approximately three billion of these pairs of strings. In people, genes are arranged on 23 pairs of chromosomes, which are in the cell nucleus. Each chromosome has thousands of genes in it. And genes are made up of a series of DNA sections. When the DNA in genes gets mixed up, the person shows signs of disease. Bioengineering could change many aspects of life.

Double-helix structure of a DNA molecule

Medicines (biotech vaccines and antibody production) could improve our health. Biotechnology could be the source of cures for heart disease, cancer, and HIV/AIDS. The potentials are beyond our human understanding. Governments are making laws to control biotechnology. We simply don't know what all of the risks are. Nearly all scientists agree that genetic engineering could change the environment. Genetic engineers are changing how crops use water. They are showing that use of fertilizers may decrease greatly because biotech plants need less fertilizer, fewer chemical aids.

5   Biotechnology is playing with the building blocks of life. The dangers may be far larger than the promises. It is true that pollution could be gone and diseases could be cured. However, we need to examine other aspects of a biotech world. How would bioengineering of plants, animals, and people affect not only our environment but also our values and our ethics?

H-W

Strategy Focus: Writing the Definitions

1. A *gene* is ___chemicals that___ .

2. An *organism* is any ___plant or animal___ .

3. *DNA* is _____ .

4. *Genetic engineering* refers to the process of ___DNA of each gene plant or animal___ .

Related Reading 2

The History of Tea

1   Tea was the first brewed beverage. Preparing tea from boiling water and plant leaves is an ancient custom. Because people like variety and stimulation, they try to find ways to make the drinking of water more interesting.

2   The Chinese emperor Shen Nung in 2737 B.C. introduced the drink. (The word "tea" comes from the Chinese Amoy dialect.) Chinese writer Lu Yu wrote in A.D. 780 that there were "a thousand and ten thousand" teas. He said the tea leaf must be picked during certain moons in clear weather. He described how to process leaves for tea. First a leaf is rolled, then dried, then sealed. *close together*

3   Chinese tea was introduced to Japan in A.D. 800. Tea was introduced to Europe in the early 1600s, when trade began between Europe and the Far East. China was the main supplier of tea to the world at that time. In many languages, the word for tea showed the connection to China. In Turkish and in Polish, for example, the word for *tea* is *chai*. In 1834, tea cultivation began in India and spread to Sri Lanka (Ceylon), Thailand, Burma, and other areas of Southeast Asia. Today, Java, South Africa, South America, and areas of the Caucasus also produce tea.

4   There are three kinds of tea. They are black (fermented), green (unfermented), and oolong (semifermented). Green tea is produced primarily in Japan and China; most international tea trading is in black tea. Black tea preparation consists mainly of picking young leaves and leaf buds on a clear sunny day and letting the leaves dry for about an hour in the sun. Then, they are lightly rolled and left in a fermentation room to develop scent and a red color. Next, they are heated several more times. Finally, the leaves are dried in a basket over a charcoal fire. Green tea leaves are heated in steam, rolled, and dried. Oolong tea is prepared similarly to black tea, but with less fermentation time.

5   Three main varieties of tea—Chinese, Assamese, and Cambodian—have distinct characteristics. The Chinese variety, a strong plant that can grow to be 2.75 meters high, can live to be 100 years old and survives cold winters. The Assamese variety, the source of orange pekoe teas, can grow 18 meters high and can live about 40 years. The Cambodian tea tree grows almost five meters tall.

6   Tea is enjoyed worldwide as a refreshing and stimulating drink. It is also the oldest. Because so many people continue to drink the many varieties of tea, it will probably continue as the world's most popular drink.

▀

Choose the best answer.

1. The word *tea* comes from…
   a. India.   b. Assam.   c. a Chinese dialect.

2. Ceylon is the same place as…
   a. a part of China.
   b. the island of Sri Lanka.
   c. Assam.

3. Oolong tea is…
   a. a kind of green tea.
   b. the most popular kind of tea.
   c. a variety of tea.

4. Tea plants grow…
   a. over two meters high.
   b. in hot places.
   c. for two or three years.

5. The main idea of the reading is that people drink tea to…
   a. make drinking water more interesting.
   b. grow rich and healthy.
   c. survive cold winters.

Strategy Focus: Making Inferences

Is there enough or not enough information to make these inferences from the reading? Check (✓) *enough* or *not enough*.

1. Everyone in the world drinks and enjoys tea.

   ☐ enough   ☐ not enough

2. Black tea tastes best to most people.

   ☐ enough   ☐ not enough

3. Before 1600, there was not much trade between the Far East and Europe.

   ☐ enough   ☐ not enough

4. China is the main place that produces tea.

   ☐ enough   ☐ not enough

5. Centuries ago China had emperors.

   ☐ enough   ☐ not enough

Strategy: Understanding the Structure of a Reading

The first sentence of each paragraph in a reading alerts you to the information that is in that paragraph. Changing each of these sentences into a question will help you understand structure—the way a writer organizes ideas before beginning to write.

 Related Reading 3

Seed Banking Against Famine

1   In the 1840s, the island of Ireland suffered *famine*. Because Ireland could not produce enough food to feed its population, about a million people died of *starvation*; they simply didn't have enough to eat to stay alive. The famine caused another 1.25 million people to *emigrate*; many left their island home for the United States; the rest went to Canada, Australia, Chile, and other countries. Before the famine, the

population of Ireland was approximately 6 million. After the great food shortage, it was about 4 million.

2   Famine is no stranger in human history; it is documented in the earliest religious and historical writings. Usually, a famine has more than one cause. Disease, *drought* (long periods of time without rain), *flooding* (when fields are covered with water), violent storms like hurricanes, as well as war and other human activities, have all been causes of famine. In many ways, the famine in Ireland was not unusual.

3   One cause of the famine in Ireland was late *blight*, a *fungal* disease that destroyed the potato crop. The portion of the potato that people eat is an underground root called a *tuber*. Late blight fungus causes potato tubers either to rot in the ground before they can be harvested or to turn black and disintegrate after they are dug out of the ground. In 1845, when late blight hit the Irish potato crop, potatoes formed the basis of the Irish diet; they were the staple food, just as rice is the staple for most of Asia and wheat is the *staple food* of continental Europe. With their most important source of food destroyed, many Irish people had nothing to sell for *income*, and worse, nothing to eat.

4   Another cause of the Irish famine was the way potatoes were *propagated*. New potatoes can be produced from seed, but ordinarily they are not. Instead, when a farmer wants new potato plants, he or she normally cuts some of last year's tubers into pieces and plants them (potato farmers call these pieces *plugs*). New plants sprout from the plugs. This method of propagation results in *clones*—young plants with exactly the same genetic makeup as the tuber from which they were taken. When potatoes are propagated from seed, the young plants have genetic material from both a male and a female plant. This is sexual reproduction, and it results in new plants that are genetically different from either of their parents. Even if both the male and female reproductive materials are from one plant, the resulting seeds will produce plants that are different from the parent plant because the genetic material combines in new patterns.

5   In Ireland in the 1840s, only one variety of potato was cultivated; moreover, the crop was propagated almost entirely from existing tubers. As a result, there was little genetic diversity in the Irish potato crop. Because every potato plant had almost exactly the same genes, the potato crop reacted in the same way to the late blight fungus. Genes that might have provided some resistance to the fungus were either not present or not effective. Furthermore, there were no healthy tubers to serve as sources of plugs for next year's crop. An important cause of the famine in Ireland was this lack of genetic diversity.

6   Agricultural scientists point to critical food shortages such as the Irish famine to stress the importance of genetic diversity in food crops. Potatoes were brought to Ireland from South America in the 1500s. In South America there is a much larger *gene pool* with thousands of varieties of potatoes. In Ireland at the time of the famine, there was only one, and so late blight fungus destroyed the entire crop. After the late blight fungus infected the potato crop in the 1840s, agricultural scientists in Ireland and Europe improved the potato variety grown there. They used genetic material from varieties that grow in South America under similar conditions. The resulting *hybrid* could resist the late blight fungus, yet still had the taste that Europeans were used to.

7   A hybrid plant is produced by taking the yellow, powdery *pollen* (the male reproductive matter) from one variety of a plant and applying it to the *stigma* (the female plant part) of another variety of the same plant. The resulting seeds have genetic material from the two parent plants. The process can be repeated, so that some hybrids are a combination of many varieties of the same plant. (The hybrid potato that is now cultivated in Ireland is the result of mixing genes of potatoes that have special important qualities. The hybrid potato had to have appealing taste. It was also most important that the hybrid have the ability to resist late blight fungus.) Although hybrids are often developed to solve agricultural problems with diseases and

pests, they also create problems. For example, hybrids do not produce "true" seeds; that means the seeds they produce will not become plants with the same characteristics as their parents. Because they contain genes from at least two varieties of the same plant, their seeds may produce plants that are like any one of the parent varieties or unlike anything else. Sometimes hybrids' seeds are sterile—they cannot produce new plants at all. A field of potatoes from one hybrid is, therefore, a field with no genetic diversity; every plant has the same genetic makeup. Because no one hybrid can resist all diseases, the entire crop could be lost to disease, resulting in famine once again.

8   When agricultural scientists want to produce a hybrid with specific traits, they generally begin their work in a region where ancestral varieties of the plant grow wild. Scientists often find the land races. Land races are varieties of a food crop that have been cultivated for long periods of time and are especially well-suited to growing in a particular place. A land race, like its wild ancestors, has strong resistance to local common diseases and unique ways of keeping local insect pests away. It thrives under the particular local growing conditions—for example, climate, soil chemistry, and altitude. In the Peruvian Andes, for example, farmers grow at least three thousand land races of potatoes under an amazingly broad range of conditions— for example, potatoes are cultivated at sea level and at 14,000 ft. (4267M.) above sea level. Wild varieties of important food crops and their *domesticated* relatives, the land races, are extremely important to humanity's future food supply. They provide a necessary supply of genetic material, a gene pool that allows experts to solve agricultural problems. Unfortunately, both wild varieties and land races are disappearing at a very rapid rate.

9   Wild varieties are disappearing mostly because of *habitat* destruction. The places where they naturally grow, their habitats, are being changed so much that they can no longer live there. To make matters worse, farmers are replacing land races with hybrids. Hybrids

generally produce higher yields, so farmers can grow more potatoes to sell. Sometimes farmers plant hybrid seeds because they make an agreement with a bank or their government. The bank or the government agrees to lend farmers money only if they plant a hybrid seed. Many potato farmers in North and Central America grow a particular hybrid potato because they know that a big buyer in the food industry will buy only that one hybrid. For these and many more reasons, wild varieties and land races of important food crops such as rice, corn, wheat, and potatoes are disappearing.

10   Recognizing the importance of the wild varieties and land races of common food crops, and the very rapid rate at which they are disappearing, scientists have been collecting seeds and tubers in *seed banks*. The World Potato Collection in Peru is a collection of more than thirteen thousand strains of potatoes. It is an outstanding example of a seed bank. Similar banks exist for wheat, corn, rice, and other important food crops. These banks constitute a recognition that genetic diversity is necessary to ensure humanity's future food supply. Most seed bank experts, however, think their collections are incomplete—perhaps critically incomplete—and in urgent need of supplementing. Nevertheless, seed banks are a vital link to the past and a critical investment in the future. Seed banks are insurance against famine.

Strategy Focus: Writing Questions that Show the Structure

Write the questions for the paragraphs. The first one is done for you.

1. What happened in Ireland in the 1840s? _____

2. What is _____ ?

3. What caused _____ ?

4. What was _____ ?

5. What kind _____ ?

6. Why do _____ ?

7. What is _____ ?

8. Where _____ ?

9. Why _____ ?

10. Why _____ ?

Strategy Focus: Finding the Main Idea

Look at these five statements. Which one is the main idea of this reading? Are any of the statements *not true*? Which?

   a. The famine in Ireland shows why seed banks are necessary.

   b. There are agricultural solutions to famines like the one that occurred in Ireland.

   c. Wild varieties and land races of important food crops are disappearing.

   d. It will be impossible to feed the world's human population in the future.

   e. The potato is the most important food crop in the world today.

Strategy Focus: Practicing New Vocabulary

Use these new words to finish the sentences that follow. These words are *italicized* in the reading. Write them in the blanks.

blight	clones	emigrate
starvation	fungus	drought
famine	propagation	hybrid
income	gene pool	staple foods
habitat	floods	domesticated variety

1. In Ireland in the 1840s, the potato crop suffered from a _____ ,
   a plant disease. The rotting was caused by a _____ .
   The resulting lack of food caused a _____ . More than
   ten percent of the Irish population died of _____ .
   There was simply not enough food to keep them all alive.

2. To grow a potato plant, you can plant seeds or you can plant a plug, a piece of potato from last year's crop. The potatoes that grow from plugs are actually _____ , plants that are genetically the same as the plants from last year. Planting potato plugs is the most common method of potato plant

3. A great storm dropped large amounts of rain on India, and the rivers rose, causing serious, widespread _____ .

4. Three thousand varieties of potatoes grow in South America. Each type has adapted to a specific set of conditions, including available water, sunlight, soil type, and altitude. In other words, the plants adapted to their _____ . As a result, these three thousand potato plant types constitute a variety of genetic material for improving potatoes, a _____ for researchers to work with.

5. One _____ of potato became popular in Ireland.

6. Some parts of Africa have had little or no rainfall for years. Because of the _____ , there isn't enough water for gardens to thrive, so people have moved to other areas, and the desert has grown larger.

7. If a farmer produces more food than her family needs, then the extra food can be a source of _____ because she can sell the surplus.

8. The potato for the Irish; rice for the people in the Far East; squash, beans, and corn for the Iroquois—these are the _____ _____ of these people.

9. After a terrible famine, people are likely to leave their homes, to _____ to new country.

10. A _____ is "made" from the genetic material of two parent plants.

Stragegy Focus: Discussing the Ideas

Talk about the answers to these questions with a group of classmates.

1. What are the causes of famine? Can you think of a recent famine and its causes?

2. How did late blight fungus cause the famine in Ireland? (Talk about two ways.)

3. Why did the way the potato was propagated in Ireland make the entire crop react to late blight fungus in the same way?

4. What are the advantages of cultivating more than one variety of a food crop?

5. Why would a poor farmer, without enough money to buy seeds every year, probably choose not to plant hybrid seeds?

6. Why are wild varieties and land races of major food crops important to humanity's future food supply? How do seed banks help to ensure a future food supply?

Strategy: Understanding Sequence

Reading material is presented in a certain sequence. Sentences follow one another in an order that makes sense to the writer and that makes the writer's message easy to understand. The readings in this unit make use of two kinds of sequence: *logical sequence* and *time sequence.*

In logical sequence, a writer presents a topic, gives us information about it, and then draws a conclusion. The following sentences are an example of logical sequence:

> Car seat belts are belts that allow a person to strap himself or herself firmly into the seat. [Topic]

> In the past several years, seat belts have saved thousands of people from serious injury in car accidents. [Information about the topic]

> Therefore, people should "buckle up" and wear seat belts whenever they ride in cars. [Conclusion based on the information]

Notice the sequence of ideas: first the topic, then information about the topic, and finally, the conclusion. If the ideas do not follow the sequence, the reader can become confused.

Another type of sequence is time sequence. In time sequence, the writer tells a story, presenting a series of events in the order that they happened. Words and expressions like the following indicate time sequence:

> expressions like *first, next, finally*;
>
> prepositions with a "time" meaning, like *before, after,* and *during*;
>
> dates (1565; 1843); phrases indicating time such as *the summer of 1846* and *in 1845*.

The following paragraphs are all about the potato blight and the famine in Ireland. The paragraphs are not in the best order. Look for clues to logical sequence and time sequence that indicate the best order for the paragraphs. These clues include dates, expressions like *first* and *today*, and ideas that match or develop from one another. Then number the paragraphs. (Numbers 1 and 10 have been labeled for you.)

____ *Phytophthora infestans* lives on potato leaves. The fungus attacks a leaf and makes a tiny dark spot on it. Each of those spots sends out 300,000 *spores*, airborne seedlike carriers of the fungus. The wind takes the spores to new leaves, where new dark spots begin. Wet weather conditions are ideal for the spread of spores. In five days, each spore grows into a spot that sends out 300,000 more spores.

____ The summer of 1846 started off well in Ireland. The blight had had some effect in 1845, but there had still been enough food. The fungus, however, was still there. After a rainy July, it struck in August of 1846 and traveled cross Ireland at a rate of fifty miles a week, leaving black fields behind it.

_1_ *An Gorta Mor* is what the Irish call the great hunger of 1845-1852. That's when a late blight destroyed the potato crop and much of Irish society with it.

____ The first case of late blight was caused by a fungus that affected some potato-like plants in the highlands of Mexico. A collector of potato types in the northeastern part of the United States received a sample of the Mexican plant. In 1843, potatoes growing near the city of Philadelphia showed signs of the blight. In two years it spread all over the potato fields of the northeastern part of the United States and also appeared in Europe.

_10_ Today there are laws that control the importing and exporting of plants. Foods that are transported between continents are carefully checked for signs of plant disease. The agricultural disasters of the mid-1800s must never be allowed to happen again.

____ The potato was brought to Europe in 1565 from the South American Andes mountains. It reached Ireland in the late 1580s, where it quickly became important as a food crop. Because it grew well and was easy to store for the winter, it became a major source of food by the middle of the seventeenth century. By 1840, the average Irish person ate five pounds (over two kilograms) of potatoes every day. Potatoes were the most important food in the country and the staple food of poor farmers.

____ In the summer of 1845, the weather in Europe was sunny and beautiful until July, when fog and rain began. The blight began to spread and to affect crops. On the continent, potato plants turned black and died, but people had other foods to eat. The situation didn't seem so bad.

____ European *botanists* (plant specialists) were alarmed that America had a potato blight. No one knew what caused it. In an effort to prevent the spread of the blight, they imported different potato varieties to study them. They wanted to produce a blight-resistant kind of potato. Some of those imported varieties must have carried the *Phytophthora infestans* spores with them. Within weeks, the blight was reported in France, Germany, Belgium, the islands in the English Channel, England, and finally Ireland.

____ During this time, scientists were trying frantically to figure out what caused the blight. There were theories related to the weather and to the plants' ability to handle lots of water. Then it was noted that tomato plants were also affected by the blight. The fungus theory began to gain acceptance. However, it was not until 1861 that the fungus was identified as the cause of the blight. It took another twenty years before a copper sulfate solution that killed the fungus was discovered. By that time the fungus had indirectly killed millions of people.

____ Soon all of Ireland stank of dead vegetation and dead animals. Diseases like typhus killed thousands of people; typhus victims give off a terrible odor in the final stages of the disease. The smell of death was everywhere. Those who were not affected were too weak to bury the dead.

Strategy: Writing About the Ideas

1. "It was more than a decade ago, shortly before he died. I was sitting in the audience listening to Carl Sagan, the popular astronomer of 'Cosmos' fame. He spoke about the dangers to life on Planet Earth. One was the danger of collision with another heavenly body, like a meteor or a comet. Another was the danger of over-population and therefore widespread starvation. During the question and answer period after his lecture, someone asked him a difficult question. 'What can the world do to protect itself?' Sagan thought for a very short moment. Then he gave an answer that I will always remember. 'Educate the women,' he said." What do you think he meant?

2. In this unit, there are some ideas that are not simple. It is not easy to decide whether biotechnology is good or bad. What kind of evidence or facts do you want to know before you make up your mind?

3. Think about the potato famine in Ireland. How do natural disasters affect people in other places? Choose a place and write about the dangers the people face.

4. The major problems facing the world today are overpopulation, pollution, and starvation. The three blights are related. Populations in Third World countries are much higher than in more developed countries. Having children is the only way for parents to be sure someone will feed them when they are old. Infant mortality is high. How many children must a family have to be sure that some live to adulthood?

Strategy Focus: Keeping a Vocabulary Journal

Choose five words from the new words in this unit to be your target words.

Write the words here: _____ _____

_____ _____ _____

Now write them into your vocabulary journal. Remember to include the following parts:
- your target word
- the sentence from the unit in which your target word appears
- a definition, including the part of speech.
- some sentences of your own

Strategy: Increasing Reading Speed

 # Timed Reading

Health, Ethics, and Vegetarians

Claire has been a vegetarian for years. She stopped eating meat because of how she felt. As she told her doctor, she always felt tired. Her doctor found that her blood cholesterol was high. Therefore, her doctor suggested that she cut down on meat, especially red meat. Claire decided to "go all the way." She bought a vegetarian cookbook and stopped eating meat. She still eats eggs and cheese occasionally; now, however, most of her food consists of vegetables, fruits, and grains. Claire balances her diet to get all of the necessary vitamins, minerals, proteins, and carbohydrates. Claire became a vegetarian to improve her health.

Nancy is an animal lover. Nancy grew up on a farm where there were cows and chickens. As she grew older, she started to reduce the amount of meat that she ate. One day she realized that she had stopped eating meat altogether. It had never seemed right to her that animals were raised to be killed for food.

When Aaron was a student, he was on a strict budget. The little money that he had for food, he spent on rice, inexpensive vegetables, and spices. He learned to be a very good cook. Now Aaron is a successful engineer, but he still eats simple foods, and no meat. Aaron became a vegetarian from economic necessity; he is a vegetarian today by choice.

Twenty years ago, Kim's doctor told her that she had arthritis. Her bone joints (shoulders, knees, elbows, fingers) were red and sore. Her doctor told her that there was no cure, but that some people felt better if they stopped eating meat, potatoes, tomatoes, eggplant, and sugary foods. Kim tried these suggestions, and for twenty years she has avoided arthritis pain. Kim became a vegetarian to control the disease.

Simon is an environmentalist. He knows that the Earth can produce food for many people, but the amount of food is finite (limited). He knows that the population is increasing rapidly, but land for growing food is not increasing at all. He knows that it takes sixteen kilograms of grain to make one kilogram of meat; he thinks about the fifteen kilograms of grain that are wasted if he eats meat. "Somewhere," he says, "someone is starving, dying from lack of food. How can I enjoy a thick steak?" Simon's ethics—his ideas about what is right and wrong— make him a vegetarian.

Time: ___2,4٠___

Now answer these questions as quickly as you can.

1. A vegetarian never eats…
   a. fruits.
   b. grains.
   c. meat.

2. ____ is a disease that affects the bone joints.
   a. Arthritis   ردنيم
   b. Cholesterol
   c. A modern diet

3. Ethics is about...

   a. balancing one's diet.

   b. what is right and what is wrong.

   c. environmental issues.

4. A person on a strict budget...

   a. must be a vegetarian.

   b. has little money to spend on anything.

   c. is vegetarian because of ethical beliefs.

5. The main idea of this reading is that...

   a. people choose to be vegetarians for different reasons.

   b. meat is bad for one's health.

   c. people become vegetarians because they do not like to eat meat.

A CHANGING, LIVING PLANET

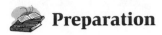 **Preparation**

Strategies for Anticipation

First check the titles of the readings in this unit. Then check the graphics (the pictures, drawings and photographs). What ideas do you think will be in this unit? The main ideas of a unit are called the key ideas. These key ideas open the topic by making us think about aspects of the general idea.

Which of the following key words or key phrases are likely to be part of this unit? Why do you think so? Write an *X* in the blank in front of the three or four most likely key words or phrases for this unit.

_____ art

_____ business

_____ health issues

_____ oceans

_____ the moon

_____ buying dishes

_____ differences between the
Earth and other planets

_____ earthquakes

_____ continents

_____ weather patterns

_____ agriculture

_____ emotions

_____ volcanoes

_____ making maps

Strategy: Using Context Clues

Read the following without using your dictionary. Remember that you want to strengthen your reading ability. You can learn to use the clues in the text to help you understand new words.

Main Reading

Part 1
Continental Drift

1   Thousands of times a person looking at a map of the world suddenly notices several things. The continents of South America and Africa look as if they fit together neatly, almost perfectly. The person notices that Europe and North America seem to fit together too, although not as closely as Africa and South America. In fact, as the person looks at the map, all continents seem to fit together like pieces of a giant jigsaw puzzle.

2   In the 1500s, mapmakers compiled all their information into the first reasonably accurate world maps. It was possible to see how the coastlines matched, even then. Is it a coincidence? Or do the maps show something about our planet's past? No one disputed the obvious way these land masses seemed to match to make one whole. No one offered a scientific explanation either—until 1912. In that year, Alfred Wegener, a German geophysicist and meteorologist, introduced a possible explanation. The theory of this earth scientist and weather observer came to be known as the *theory of continental drift*.

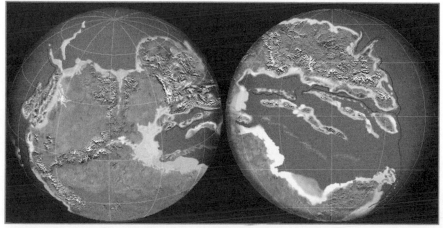

The theory of continental drift is Alfred Wegener's idea that all land was once a single mass, called *Pangaea*.

3   Wegener's idea was that all land was once a single mass. He theorized that about 300 million years ago, all present-day continents were joined in one supercontinent. Wegener called this supercontinent Pangaea [pan-GEE-ya], which means *all lands*. In Pangaea, the continent of South America fit under the "bulge" of Western Africa. North America fit around the "fat" part of that continent. Europe and Asia were far to the north, while Australia, Antarctica, and the Indian subcontinent were far south. Then, according to Wegener's theory, about 200 million years ago a mysterious force split the supercontinent into separate continents. He hypothesized that these land masses have always drifted on a fluid inner layer of the Earth. He thinks that they simply drifted apart. This inner fluid layer is known as the *mantle*. To Wegener the continents were drifting on the mantle like leaves drifting on a moving stream of water.

4   Wegener based the theory of continental drift on some strong evidence. And it explained why the continents seem to fit together. Nevertheless, most scientists of Wegener's time thought that his theory was ridiculous. Evidence like matching coastlines and similar rock formations in support of the theory was still insufficient. What force could could split Pangaea into separate continents and then move them about? In spite of its shortcomings, however, Wegener's theory was important; scientists today accept some of his basic ideas as fact. These ideas are part of a body of knowledge called *plate tectonics*. Knowing about plate tectonics is essential to understanding the way that modern scientists think about the Earth.

5   A very large body of evidence supports the idea of plate tectonics. Some of the most recent and most convincing evidence is actual measurement of plate movements. However, long before anyone developed the technology to make such measurements, scientists compared rock samples from layers of rock on the coastlines of widely separated continents. They found that some of these layers of rock were similar, thereby supporting the idea of continental movement.

Scientists compared and matched the types of rock, the sequence of layers of rock, and the magnetism in the rock.

6   Fossilized remains of plants and animals also support the idea that continents move. The fossil of one kind of very large reptile, for example, were found in both Africa and South America. This reptile would not have been able to swim across the Atlantic Ocean. The locations of the fossilized reptile and of the fossils of many other living things, therefore, gave valuable support to the basic concepts of plate tectonics. The discovery of coal in the Arctic, Antarctic, and other very cold zones helped to prove the ideas of plate tectonics, too. Coal deposits in such cold places as the North and South Pole regions indicated that these land masses had moved from one climate region to another. Coal comes from living matter, principally from plants. A lush forest—what coal developed from—could not thrive in the cold Arctic region today. Scientists have so much evidence in support of plate tectonics that the theory is now accepted as fact.

Part 2
What Makes a Living Planet

7   The Earth is an active ("alive") living planet, and it is sometimes a dangerous place to live. However, the planet must change to remain alive. Unlike some of the other planets in the sun's family of planets, our planet is renewing itself, from the inside out. Earth scientists agree that the Earth is made up of layers. The innermost layer, the *core*, is the hottest and densest. It is primarily composed of heavy metals like iron (Fe) and nickel (Ni). Some other heavy metals, like uranium (U), are also present. The radioactive decay of elements like uranium, which is slowly changing into lead (Pb), causes the high temperature of the Earth's core.

8   The next layer of the Earth is the mantle. Temperatures in the mantle are lower than temperatures in the core, but part of the mantle is so hot that it is molten. In other words, temperatures are so high

that some of the rock of the mantle melts; that is, it changes from solid to liquid. This molten rock is called *magma*. The mantle is covered by the hard outer layer of the Earth, the *crust*. Like the outside of freshly baked bread, this crust is very thin in comparison to the other layers. The Earth's crust has broken into huge pieces, which are called *plates*. The plates of the Earth's crust cover the entire surface of the planet; there is no exposed mantle. In some places the crust has cracked and buckled. That is, pressure on a piece of the crust makes a break in the crust. Part of the crust is pushed up (forming mountains.) These mountains are next to deep cracks. In the cracks, lakes and steep valleys have formed. The plates of the crust float on the magma. The movement of the plates is one reason why the crust is constantly changing.

9   No one is completely sure why plates move. Geophysicists' most common explanation at present is that giant convection currents in the magma of the mantle are the cause. A *convection current* is circular movement, like a loop. It carries hot material up and cool material down in continuous cycles. Convection currents of air are familiar: warm air rises and cold air falls. Convection currents carry hot magma up to and sometimes through the crust of the Earth. As the currents move under the Earth's crust, the magma and the plates floating on it also move. For example, the North American Plate is moving westward at a rate of 2.5 centimeters per year. That is as fast as a human toenail grows. A giant convection current is probably causing this steady, predictable movement.

10   Regardless of the cause, there is no doubt that the plates of the Earth's crust are moving. Sometimes two or more plates move toward one another from opposite directions and collide. On the western coast of the Americas, for example, there are places where the heavier Pacific Plate is slowly forced down under the lighter North and South American Plates. This process is called *subduction*. The edges of the

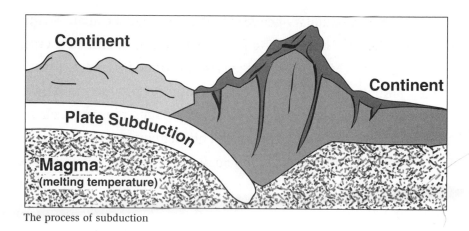

The process of subduction

Pacific Plate go down far enough to encounter very high temperatures. The edges melt in these high temperatures and become magma, part of the mantle again. The Pacific plate is being recycled. It is also getting smaller. Volcanoes are common in subduction zones because some of the magma from the mantle rises to the surface of the Earth. The many volcanoes along the western coast of the American continents are examples of volcanoes in a subduction zone.

11   Geophysicists know that plates under water act differently than land masses. When continental masses of plates strike one another, complete subduction is not likely to be the result. Because these plates are moving slowly, the pressure builds up slowly along the edges. So as the land on one plate pushes against the land on another, mountain ranges are formed. The process that resulted in the Himalaya Mountains began millions of years ago.

12   In places where magma is moving upward, it sometimes breaks through the crust. On the surface of the Earth, magma is called *lava*. This hot liquid rock is likely to come to the crust surface all along the 6,400-kilometer (4,000-mile) mountain range called the Mid-Ocean Ridge. Most of this mountain range is under the Atlantic Ocean, but geophysicists can observe the movement of lava and measure it with sophisticated underwater equipment. This ridge or *rift* (split) in the

Earth's crust is a boundary between plates. Plates move apart at rifts. Geophysicists have been able to measure that movement. New crust is forming at the Mid-Ocean Ridge (also known as the Mid-Atlantic Ridge or Rift). In other words, the Atlantic Plate is getting larger. Magma from the mantle emerges from the rift onto the crust as lava. It cools and hardens into new crust. This activity at the Mid-Ocean Ridge is called *seafloor spreading.* Seafloor spreading separated the Americas from Africa. These two continents have been moving apart for about 150 million years.

13   Some plates slide past one another. The place where this friction occurs is called a *transform fault.* Although two plates do not actually collide at transform faults, their motion past each other disturbs the crust on both plates. Earthquakes are common in transform fault zones. For example, Japan is in a transform fault zone where the Eurasian Plate and the Philippine Plate slide by each other. The movement of these two plates has caused countless devastating earthquakes in Japan.

14   Earth is a hot and sometimes dangerous place. However, the movement of plates renews the surface and recycles elements. If the plates didn't drift, Earth would not be renewing itself. This would be a dead planet.

Strategy Focus: Practicing New Vocabulary

Here are some contexts with the important words (in **bold**) from the readings. The words are presented in sentences to help you learn to pull the meaning out of the context. Underline *synonyms* (words or phrases that mean the same as the bold type word or phrase) or *antonyms* (words or phrases that mean the opposite of the bold type word or phrase) to show that you understand the meaning. Here is an example.

Example:
There are a <u>number of good reasons that support</u> the plate tectonics theory. The **body of evidence** includes matching fossils in South America and Africa, and matching coastlines.

1. The largest **continents** are Asia and Africa. The smallest land masses are probably Australia and Antarctica.

2. Water **is composed of** hydrogen (H) and oxygen (O). Sulfuric acid is made up of hydrogen, oxygen, and sulfur (S).

3. If you pick up a can of food to open it and you see a **bulge** at the top or bottom of the can, throw the can away. The swelling of the can—which makes it bigger—is caused by bacteria. These bacteria can be deadly.

4. When two automobiles **collide**, there is usually a lot of damage. Large bumpers on a car, however, can absorb much of the shock when one car hits another.

5. The **boundary** between Canada and the United States is an imaginary line. There is neither fence nor wall.

6. There are weaknesses in every person, but a person can overcome his or her **shortcomings**.

7. In a small airplane, you can feel the movement of warm air going up and cooler air falling as the airplane bumps up and down. These **convection currents** are a natural part of the winds on our planet.

8. The center of an apple is its **core**. That's where the seeds are.

9. French bread has a hard **crust**, but the inside is soft.

10. There are rich **deposits** of chromium (Cr) in Turkey. Mining these areas where the metal is found brings money to the country.

11. The children **disputed** the ownership of the new basketball that they found. They argued until the real owner arrived and stopped their argument with her thanks.

12. In geology, a **fault** is a large crack or **rift** in the Earth. Such a split shows places where two plates or land masses meet. At a **transform fault**, two **plates** meet and rub against each other. The rubbing or **sliding** can cause earthquakes. (Can you find five clues, one for each bold word?)

13. The remains of a plant or animal from millions of years ago might be found in rock. These **fossils** hold a great deal of information for scientists who study the **fossilized** forms of life in the stone.

14. Some very heavy metals break down into simpler metals because they are not "stable." The process is called **radioactive decay**. Uranium loses particles and energy as it changes into lead. In other words, the metal changes its form.

15. **Lava** is nothing but "super-hot" rock—so hot that it has melted like butter in the sun. It escapes from the **mantle**, the layer of the Earth that covers the core. Below the crust, this hot, molten rock is called **magma**. Both lava and magma are liquid, **fluid**—though lava cools and becomes solid rock again. (Can you find four clues, one for each bold word?)

16. A **theory** is a set of ideas that someone is trying to prove to be true. Solid evidence is necessary to change the theory into accepted fact, but it is sometimes almost impossible to find information and facts that prove a theory. Such work, however, is important for scientists— what one person can imagine or **theorize**, another person can prove.

Strategy Focus: Finding the Main Idea

The purpose of a title is to give the main idea of a reading. Here are two lists of possible titles for each of the two parts of the main reading. Note that they are labeled Part 1 and Part 2. Some of the titles are appropriate, some do not fit the reading at all, some titles are too narrow (too small for the topic), and some are too general (too large for the reading). With your classmates, discuss these titles and judge them. Select the best title in each group of four titles and decide what is wrong with the other suggested titles.

Part 1

   a. Wegener's Theory   c. The Life of Alfred Wegener

   b. The Planet Earth   d. Making Maps

Part 1

   a. The Breaking of Pangaea   c. A Giant Jigsaw Puzzle

   b. The West African Bulge   d. The Indian Subcontinent

Part 2

   a. Pacific Islands of Lava

   b. The Principle of Radioactive Decay

   c. The Living, Changing Earth

   d. What Happened 300 Million Years Ago

Part 2

   a. Great Mountains and How They Were Formed

   b. Magma, Lava, and Rifts: A Theory of Planet Earth

   c. The Birth of the Himalayas

   d. Australia, the Long-Forgotten Continent

Can you think of yet another title for each of these parts of the Main Reading? Write your ideas here:

_____

_____

Strategy Focus: Understanding the Author's Perspective

Read this list of paired sentences. Which sentence of each pair seems to show the author's feelings about the topic?

   1. a. Plate tectonics is a weak theory.

      b. Plate tectonics is probably true.

   2. a. Earth is constantly changing.

      b. Earth is rapidly changing.

   3. a. Alfred Wegener was a brilliant observer and scientist.

      b. Alfred Wegener had a ridiculous theory.

   4. a. It would be better if we didn't have earthquakes and volcanoes because they serve no purpose.

      b. Earthquakes and volcanoes are necessary parts of the Earth renewing itself.

   5. a. The force that broke apart Pangaea is easy to understand.

      b. The break-up of Pangaea is not easy to understand.

Strategy Focus: Analyzing Problems

Read about these situations. What do they prove? What questions do they make you think of ? Discuss your conclusions with your classmates.

1. In Africa, running north and south along the eastern side, there is a great split in the Earth. On one side of the rift there are layers of rock that match layers of rock on the other side of the crack that are a hundred feet higher. In one part of this split in the Earth, there is an enormous body of water, Lake Victoria. At one end of the crack, there is a low area where natural hot water and sulfurous gases come out of the Earth.

2. Iceland is a green island far to the north where hot springs can heat people's homes. One day there was a lot of shaking and trembling of the Earth, and a new island (Surtsey) appeared off the coast.

3. In the deserts of Arizona, you can find layers of rock with seashells and fossils of fish.

4. In California, there is a mountain that has a "plume"—a cloud of steam. Mount Shasta (the mountain) is not considered an active volcano, but it has a hot spring near its top.

Strategy Focus: Understanding Cause and Effect

Reread the main reading if you need to, to fill in the missing causes and effects. If you can, add examples:

Cause	Effect	Example
two continental plates collide	mountains are pushed up	*India Asia, the Himalayas*
magma rises to the surface		
friction at a transform fault		
	coal deposits in Antarctica	
lava cools off	subduction	
pressure builds up under a volcano		
	a deep valley is formed next to a high mountain	

Strategy: Prereading

Look quickly over the next related reading, scanning for names of places, unusual words, or any other items that catch your interest. Stop at three or four places in the reading as you read the sentences that contain these items. Think about what you may already know about the items.

 ## Related Reading 1

Earthquake Mentality

Evidence of earthquake damage is visible throughout the world.

1   Under ideal conditions, people would know when an earthquake is going to happen and how bad it will be. Both Japan and China are vulnerable to earthquakes. The people have an earthquake mentality. For example, they believe that earthquakes can be forecast. They simply have not found out how, yet. In Japan, scientists have wired the Earth and sea to detect movements. The Chinese have traditionally watched animals and plants for warning signs of earthquakes. For example, the Chinese have noted that before an earthquake, chickens' behavior changes: they keep their feet on the ground rather than roosting on a pole or branch—which they normally do at night. They have also noticed that snakes come out of the ground and that dogs

bark a lot, even normally quiet dogs. Before the Hanshin earthquake in Japan, there were reports of large schools of fish swimming near the surface of the water. Crows and pigeons seemed to be especially noisy, too. They were reported to be flying in unusual patterns before the quake. Perhaps most interesting, and most easily measured, is a chemical change in groundwater before a quake. Data seem to indicate that the amount of *radon* (Rn) in the water under the surface of the Earth increases before an earthquake.

2   People would also like to be able to prevent great property damage from earthquakes. After all, most of the people who die in earthquakes are killed by falling buildings. Therefore, building structures that can withstand the power of earthquakes is a major concern. Steel seems to be the best material, but not if it is welded to form a rigid structure. Many new structures are built with a new type of steel joint, an I-joint. It appears to be the most flexible, most resilient type of joint. These joints of steel can move without breaking. Also, to prevent property damage, buildings are now constructed with columns and horizontal beams of equal strength. Support columns (also called pilings) are placed deep in solid soil. In addition, many new houses have relatively light roofs and strong walls. Concrete expressway pillars for bridges and overpasses are now encircled with steel.

3   Besides working to improve building structures, people in areas prone to earthquakes need to prepare for the possibility of a devastating earthquake. As part of their earthquake mentality, they regularly check and reinforce their homes, place heavy objects in low positions, attach bookcases and cabinets to walls, and fasten doors so that they will not open accidentally during an earthquake.

4   In addition to preparing their houses, people in these regions prepare themselves. They have supplies of water and food at home and at work. They store several gallons of water per person. They keep something, a disinfectant, to clean or purify water with—such as a bottle of chlorine bleach or iodine tablets. Just a few drops of bleach

or an iodine tablet can purify a gallon of water, making it safe to drink. They try to store one week's food for each person. A well-prepared family has a radio, a flashlight, extra batteries, a first-aid kit, a shovel, a tent, and warm clothing.

5   Government experts also give advice to the people in earthquake areas. If you live in an earthquake region, their advice is valuable:

- Keep a fire extinguisher handy. You should have one at home, at work, and in your car (if you have one). The fire extinguisher should be able to put out any type of fire.
- Have a wrench or other tool to turn off gas and water lines if necessary.
- Arrange an alternate cooking and heating source. For this purpose, store a barbecue grill (for example, a hibachi), charcoal, charcoal starter, and matches. Another alternative is a camping stove with small gas canisters.
- Keep a pair of heavy, comfortable shoes in your home, at work, and in your vehicle. If there is an earthquake, there will be lots of broken glass. Light shoes will not protect your feet as well as heavy shoes will.

6   It is also important for a family to have earthquake emergency plans. How will family members leave the area? Everyone should agree on a meeting point outside of the area—perhaps in a town several miles away. Also important is an arrangement for family members to communicate if there is an earthquake. Cellular phones offer good communication. However, if an earthquake happens in a large city, many of the regular telephone lines within the city are likely to be down. The remaining working lines will be busy with the calls that naturally occur after a disaster. It will be difficult to call from one part of the city to another. It might, however, be possible to call outside the city. A sensible arrangement is to have all the members of the family call to check in with someone who lives more than a hundred miles away. That friend or relative can serve as a news center.

7   Although scientists still cannot predict earthquakes, they are learning a great deal about plate tectonics, the stresses between plates, how faults work, and general earthquake potential. Someday soon it may actually become possible to predict earthquakes with accuracy. However, even if prediction becomes possible, people who live in earthquake-prone areas will still have to do their best to prevent disaster. These precautions can make a great difference in saving lives and preventing loss of homes and supplies.

■

Strategy Focus: Discussing the Reading

1. What have the Chinese and the Japanese noticed about earthquakes and animal behavior?

2. What does radon have to do with earthquake prediction?

3. What do you need to have available if you live in an earthquake-prone zone?

4. Check (✓) all the things necessary for an earthquake survival kit:

☐ car	☐ gasoline	☐ newspapers
☐ tent	☐ blankets	☐ television set
☐ knife	☐ batteries	☐ books to read
☐ radio	☐ swimsuit	☐ warm clothes
☐ maps	☐ flashlight	☐ camping stove
☐ shovel	☐ first-aid kit	☐ gallons of water
☐ wrench	☐ can opener	☐ fire extinguisher
☐ raincoat	☐ canned food	☐ telephone numbers

5. What other things would you want to have after an earthquake?

6. Why is it good to have plans for calling a person in a different city after an earthquake?

7. Why are escape plans a good idea?

8. What makes a building stronger and more likely to withstand an earthquake?

9. What happens to a rigid building in an earthquake?

10. What is an I-joint? Why are I-joints important in earthquake-prone areas?

Strategy Focus: Practicing with the Meanings of New Words

Part A. In the left column there is a word that means nearly the same as a word or phrase in the right column. Draw lines to match the words or phrases with similar meanings.

precautions	region
construct	handy
pilings	preparations
detect	forecast
data	disinfectant
zone	build
available	support columns
predict	information
chlorine bleach	see warning signs

Part B. Now complete these contexts by writing a second sentence with the word or phrase that matches the word in **bold** type from the left column. Here is an example:

> Example: The best **precautions** for safety in an earthquake are about building safety. *The best preparations include making sure that your house is strong and flexible.*

1. If you add a few drops of **chlorine bleach** to a gallon of water, you can be sure it is clean. _____

_____

2. Cascadia is in an earthquake **zone**. _____

_____

3. The scientist collected **data** on animal behavior. _____

_____

4. Frank Lloyd Wright once **constructed** an earthquake-proof building on a floating base of concrete. _____

_____

5. Scientists have not been able to **predict** earthquakes. _____

_____

6. How much money do you have **available**? _____

_____

7. It's easy to **detect** radon in groundwater. _____

_____

8. The bridge has enormous **pilings** of concrete. _____

_____

Strategy Focus: Scanning for Details

1. the names of three kinds of birds: _____

_____ _____

2. the names of two hand tools: _____

_____ _____

3. the names of three chemical elements: _____

_____ _____

4. the names of two pieces of communication equipment:

_____ _____

Strategy: Looking for Meaning in Context

As you read, look for the meanings of words in context. The next related reading contains many new terms, some of which you need only for this reading. Being able to find the meanings in the context is an important skill, one you want to practice.

 Related Reading 2

The Wandering Continent, Antarctica

1   Antarctica today is a frozen wasteland. It is at the southernmost (the farthest south) part of the planet, at the South Pole. Today *glaciers* cover much of the surface of Antarctica, like huge rivers of ice. Strong winds, extremely low temperatures, and heavy snowstorms make Antarctica the most dangerous place on the planet for human life.

2   Once, however, that land mass was part of a great single land mass. And it was not a frozen wasteland. Geologists have theorized that the continents of today were once joined with Africa in the center. Above Africa was the great Europe-Asia mass, Eurasia. Going clockwise around Africa, on the eastern side, there was ocean. To the southeast lay what is now India. Antarctica and Australia were like two great plates at the southern end of the supercontinent. South America and North America were along the whole western side, with South America fitting under the bulge and North America between South America and Eurasia at the top. Geologists date this land mass, Pangaea, at 250 million to 300 million years ago.

3   Geologists are still studying and trying to understand how the great continents were formed. There are a lot of unanswered questions. For example, there are *coal* deposits on Antarctica. That means that thick forests once covered Antarctica—coal is ancient plant life in a carbon fossil form. Those thick forests did not exist when Antarctica was so far south. Another unanswered question is where Washington,

Oregon, California, and Arizona came from. There is evidence that a continental mass ripped away from the North American Plate along a North-South line. (And that mass is not today's American Far West.) Furthermore, this line appears to be where the Rocky Mountains are today. What is now Washington, Oregon, California, and Arizona was under water at that time—although some islands may have collided with the land mass and become part of the American Southwest. It has always puzzled geologists that some of the oldest rocks in the world are at the bottom of Arizona's Grand Canyon. Furthermore, there is clear evidence that large regions of the American Far West (much of which is *desert*, a waterless wasteland, today) were once seafloor. Fossils and ocean sediment indicate that it was once under water. So the geological research continues.

4   Two geologists, Eldridge M. Moores and Ian W. D. Dalziel, think they have an answer to part of the puzzle. Earth's surface is not only a giant jigsaw puzzle, but it is also a constantly changing one. Moores and Dalziel have found evidence that perhaps Antarctica was once attached to the western side of North America. They theorize that Antarctica was in this location 550 million years ago.

5   Moores and Dalziel note that the capitol building of Texas is built of *granite*. This billion-year-old stone came from a North American quarry (a mine for stone). The Texas granite comes from a rock layer called the Grenville orogeny. An *orogeny* [o-RAH-ge-nee] is a rock layer that forms mountains. The Grenville orogeny has some *unique* and easily identifiable characteristics; therefore, if there is granite like it in another part of the world, it can be identified. In Antarctica there are some mountain tops that stick up out of the snow. These mountain tops, called *nunatuk*, are composed of the same granite, with the same characteristics, as the granite in the Texas building. It seems, then, that both the North American and Antarctic Grenville granites were once part of the same mountain range.

6   If Antarctica was joined to North America, then where were the other land masses? Using the Grenville granite, Moores and Dalziel have theorized a continuous chain of mountains. It ran through North America, around East Antarctica, into Australia and the island of Madagascar. At this time, North America was a *wedge*, a pie-shaped piece, between South America and Antarctica.

7   More than 300 million years ago, Africa, South America, Antarctica, and Australia were joined as a supercontinent. Geologists' name for this supercontinent is Gondwanaland [gon-DWA-nuh-land). Many millions of years later, North America, Eurasia, and North Africa joined Gondwanaland to form Pangaea. Then the continents separated. Plates, it seems, floated off to other places.

8   For years, however, geologists have wondered where Antarctica came from and also what happened to North America. Only recently, by studying phenomena using magnetism in rocks, types of rock, locations of mineral deposits, and the like, they have concluded that the answers to the two questions are related. They now believe that Antarctica used to be part of the North American Plate. It simply broke off and floated away.

Strategy Focus: Figuring Out What the Words Mean

The reading contains a number of words that have been defined within the reading itself. Read quickly to find definitions of the words that follow. Remember that new words are sometimes presented in *italic* type. Also remember to look for commas, which sometimes show where there are definitions. Write the paragraph number in which each word is defined:

New word	Definition	Paragraph
1. nunatuk	_____	_____
2. granite	_____	_____
3. orogeny	_____	_____

New word	Definition	Paragraph
4. wedge	_____	____
5. glacier	_____	____
6. coal	_____	____
7. unique	_____	____
8. desert	_____	____

Strategy Focus: Finding the Main Idea

Here is a list of ideas from the reading. Which of these ideas is the main idea? Write *M* in the blank after the main idea. Then choose the sentences that state the main ideas of individual paragraphs. Write *P* in the blank after each of those sentences and also the number of the paragraph. Some of the sentences are support ideas and not main ideas at all. Write *S* in the blank after each of those sentences. Find one main idea, seven paragraph main ideas, and six supporting sentences.

1. _____ The Texas capitol building is built of granite.

2. _____ Geologists have theorized that a single land mass existed 250 million to 300 million years ago.

3. _____ Another name for land mass is continent.

4. _____ Antarctica hasn't always been where it is today.

5. _____ Eldridge Moores is a geologist.

6. _____ Scientists are trying to figure out where Antarctica came from.

7. _____ Gondwanaland is the name of a supercontinent.

8. _____ North America might have been connected to Antarctica.

9. _____ Pangaea was a supercontinent.

10. _____ Antarctica is a frozen wasteland.

11. _____ Much of Arizona is a desert.

12. _____ The Grenville rocks were probably part of a chain of mountains.

13. _____ The continents have joined and separated.

14. _____ Some granites of both North America and Antarctica are Grenville in type.

Strategy Focus: Understanding Cause and Effect

In this section, you will see how one or more actions cause a reaction. In other words, there is an effect (something we can see or hear or feel) and there is something else that caused that effect. Another way of describing this phenomenon is that first one thing (action) happens and then another thing (result) can be observed. There is a reason for the result.

First think about and, if possible, answer these questions:

1. What causes ice to form? What conditions and what materials are necessary for ice to form?
2. Why does it rain? Why doesn't it rain?
3. If you have two plants and one grows and the other doesn't, what reasons could there be for these results?
4. Why would a desert have fossils of marine animals like fish?
5. Why would an icy continent like Antarctica have coal deposits?

Each of these questions has a result or an effect that is in focus. In the first one, for example, the result is "ice," but what is necessary for ice to form? In the second question, the result is "rain." Our question is "What causes rain?" The third example is about plant growth, the effect or result. What causes it to happen or not to happen? Put the causes and the effects in the correct boxes in this table:

Cause	Effect
1.	
2.	
3.	
4.	
5.	

Strategy: Identifying Causes

In the short related reading that follows, you will learn about many different effects. As you read, look for the causes of these effects. Put the causes in this table:

Cause	Effect
1.	Ocean plates dive under the continental plates.
2.	People breathe in oxygen and breathe out carbon dioxide.
3.	There are convection currents inside the Earth.
4.	The rocks at the bottom of the ocean are carbonates.
5.	The amount of carbon dioxide in the Earth's atmosphere from volcanoes is not significantly increasing.
6.	Rocks form at the bottom of the ocean, layer by layer.
7.	The Earth's mantle is warmer than its crust.
8.	The seafloor is spreading.
9.	Radioactive materials in the Earth's mantle create heat.
10.	The crust of the world today shows the most recent 5% of its history.

Related Reading 3

A Rocking, Rolling, Living Planet

1   If life were to choose a planet to exist on, why would it choose a planet that has the great destructive upheaval of earthquakes? There are other planets in the universe. Why is a violent place like Earth the planet with people? Scientists now believe that the earthquakes that shake this planet may be part of a process that maintains life on Earth. Earthquakes, they think, may be one aspect of a planet-wide recycling system.

2   Earth is a living planet with a system of life that is based on carbon, oxygen, and hydrogen. Living things—plants and animals—are made up of many elements, but mostly carbon, oxygen, and hydrogen. All living things, furthermore, either use or release oxygen or carbon dioxide. Tracking or following the course of carbon, oxygen, and hydrogen, therefore, may give scientists some important clues about how a planet stays alive.

3   This is how the Earth works: a *thermal* (heat-producing) "engine" in the Earth's core creates a great amount of energy. The energy or heat from this hot, liquid center rises through the Earth's molten mantle, where radioactive decay adds more heat. The heat flowing upward and the cooler material flowing down create huge convection currents— which, because they are moving through thick liquids (molten rock) or nearly solid material (rock) in the mantle, seem to move very slowly— just a few centimeters a year. If we could speed up time, however, so that a million years were a hundred years, it would seem that this Earth matter is gently boiling, like water in a pot.

4   To put these numbers in perspective, we need to know the age of the planet and how old the planet's crust is. Geologists can tell us: the Earth itself is about 4,500,000,000 years old (4.5 billion years).

The Earth's current ocean crust is about 200,000,000 years old (that's 200 million years). In other words, what we can see of the present crust is the result of the most recent 5% of the whole active life of the planet. That means that 95% of the Earth's history is not evident in the Earth's present form.

5   The Earth is changing constantly and steadily. Most of the change is happening under its oceans. The newest surface crust is forming where plates are moving apart—for example, at the Mid-Atlantic Ridge. The seafloor is spreading because magma wells to the surface and cools to become rock. The new rock is pushed to the side by more magma, which makes the ocean plates larger. Where the growing ocean plates meet land plates, earthquakes are likely to occur. Ocean plates dive under the lighter continental plates (subduction), returning surface material to the mantle. Descending plates also make deep valleys (ocean trenches) and push up volcanic mountains on the land.

6   What is important to life on Earth is that surface material on descending plates returns to the mantle. As scientists track the surface carbon, oxygen, and hydrogen, they see how the system works. The atmosphere is made up of many gases; one of these gases, oxygen (which is necessary for life), combines with carbon to become carbon dioxide whenever burning of any kind happens. Technically, by breathing, people "burn" food by using oxygen for energy, just as wood or oil or gasoline that burns also turns oxygen into the oxide part of carbon dioxide. Volcanoes also release huge amounts of carbon dioxide (CO_2)—a colorless, odorless gas. Plants remove some of the CO_2 from the atmosphere in the process of making chlorophyll. However, much more of the carbon dioxide is removed by chemical processes in the sea. The wind whips the waves up; they seem to reach up and dissolve the carbon dioxide gas (and all other parts of air) into the water. Some of the dissolved carbon dioxide combines with parts of the water to form carbonates (CO_3). Carbonates combine with other elements to form rocks like chalk, marble, and limestone.

These substances precipitate (become solid flakes and fall to the bottom) and form carbonate precipitate seafloor rocks. Some of the carbon dioxide is used by tiny marine plants and sea. These plants and animals live out their lives in the sea water, then die and fall to the ocean floor. Layers of carbonate compounds lie under the weight of the ocean water and form rocks. As the sea plates descend, the carbonate reenters the mantle, removing carbon dioxide from the crust and returning it to the mantle.

7   If there were no earthquakes (and therefore no descending plates—no subduction—to cause earthquakes), the concentration of carbon dioxide on the Earth would soon make the climate too hot for plants and animals to live here. Subduction, a process that also causes earthquakes, reduces surface CO_2. For these reasons, geophysicists think of the earthquake-generating aspect of plate tectonics as an important part of the planet's life cycle. In other words, earthquakes are part of the planet's way of staying alive.

--- ■

Strategy Focus: Understanding Cause and Effect

Part A. Read each incomplete sentence. Try to determine the cause or the effect to complete it.

1. The Earth's mantle is warmer than its crust because _____
   _____ .

2. When the ocean plates dive under the continental plates, they can
   cause _____ .

3. Because radioactive materials _____ ,
   they create heat in the mantle.

4. _____ , so the seafloor is spreading.

5. Convection currents inside the Earth cause _____
   _____ .

6. When people breathe in oxygen and breathe out carbon dioxide,
   they are actually _____ .

7. Because _____ , the rocks at the bottom
   of the ocean are carbonates.

8. The rocks that form, layer by layer, at the bottom of the ocean are
   caused by _____ .

9. Carbonates precipitate out of sea water because _____
   _____ .

10. Marine plants and animals add carbonate to the ocean floor because
    _____ .

Part B. What causes each of these things?
   1. Deep ocean trenches are caused by _____ .
   2. Volcanoes are caused by _____ .
   3. The Mid-Atlantic Ridge is caused by _____ .
   4. Carbonate layers on the seafloor are caused by _____ .
   5. Convection currents are caused by _____ .
   6. Carbonate precipitate rocks on the seafloor are caused by

      _____ .

Part C. Here are some other questions about the reading:
   1. Where does all the CO_2 in the Earth's atmosphere go?

2. Why is carbon dioxide dangerous? Circle all the appropriate answers:

    a. People die if they breathe too much of it and not enough oxygen.

    b. It is poisonous to all animals.

    c. It is colorless and invisible.

    d. It has no smell, so it cannot be detected easily.

    e. It causes too much heat from the sun to reach the surface of the planet.

    f. Plants use it in the process of photosynthesis.

3. How much of the Earth's geological history is obvious? Why?

Part D. Try an experiment: If you have a glass of hot water and start adding salt, what will happen? If you keep on adding salt, what happens? What happens when the water cools?

Strategy: Scanning

Here are some questions to look for in the next related reading. Find the answers before you read it. Look for clues like numbers, capital letters, and punctuation marks.

1. Who is Kenji Satake? _____

2. At what time did the great quake occur? _____

3. On what date did it occur? _____

4. Where did the earthquake happen? _____

5. How long does it take for a shock wave to travel between British Columbia and Japan? _____

6. Who is Glennda Chui? _____

7. Who works for the Geological Survey of Japan? _____

8. What are the Wiyot, the Yurok, the Polowa, and the Chetco?

    _____

9. What happened in Miyako on January 28 in 1700?

    _____

10. What is Knight-Ridder? _____

Related Reading 4

The Big One

1   What do Japan and the Pacific Northwest have in common? Well, there are lots of things, like seacoast and fishing industries. According to a group of Japanese earthquake researchers, they also share the great earthquake of January 26, 1700, and the tremendous damage it caused. Furthermore, these researchers think the quake happened at 9 P.M. on that day, and that it was a magnitude 9 quake, by far the worst earthquake in the area's recorded history. The only problem, of course, is that in 1700 events in the Pacific Northwest were not recorded in history books. In the 1700s the population of the area was sparse; the indigenous people numbered in the thousands, not millions. They lived in small villages along rivers rich in fish and in forests filled with wildlife. Nonetheless, these people experienced a terrible earthquake.

2   Recently a story of the 1700 quake came from records and research done in Japan. The story of Japanese geologist Kenji Satake, his colleagues, and their work on a 300-year-old earthquake was reported by Glennda Chui, a Knight-Ridder Newspapers correspondent. How Satake and his coworkers came to their conclusions about the big earthquake is rather interesting.

3   Satake is a geophysicist from the Geological Survey of Japan. He knew that there were historical accounts of a tidal wave (*tsunami*) that hit Japan two days after the great earthquake. He also knew that it would take two days for a shock wave to travel the distance from the Pacific Northwest to Japan. Satake began sifting through public records. He concluded that the tsunami could only have originated in the Pacific Northwest (Northern California, Oregon, Washington, and the southern part of British Columbia)—an area that geologists call Cascadia. Furthermore, the quake had to have been an extraordinarily large one.

4   Actually there are lots of pieces of evidence, but not all this evidence was easy to study. Four Native American tribes—the Yurok, the Wiyot, the Chetco, and the Polowa—all have stories of a huge earthquake and tidal wave that struck long ago. Scientists Deborah and Gary Carver have collected stories from the oral history of these native people about the disaster. According to the Carvers, half of the dozen individual stories about the earthquake mention that it happened at night. No other time of day is mentioned in any of the other stories. Gary Carver, who is a paleoseismologist at Humboldt State University, has gone to the places where the native people say the earthquake struck and the tidal wave hit. Paleoseismologists like Carver study ancient earthquakes. He knows that earthquakes cause tidal waves; the larger the magnitude of the earthquake, the greater the tsunami is likely to be. He also knows that tidal waves carry sea plants, trees, even houses which they pick up as they rush to the shore and beyond. Where a tsunami has hit, there are deposits of these kinds of things. In the places that the indigenous people talked about, Carver found evidence of a great tsunami. He found the deposits of a giant tidal wave, one that was 60 feet (or almost 20 meters) high. Most important, these deposits were exactly where the native people said the tidal wave had hit. What he found was scientific evidence of the truth of the oral history reports.

5   On the other side of the Pacific, Satake and his colleagues were studying the remains of other trees—trees buried in the sand of the tsunami deposit. Using tree rings, they were able to date these trees to a time near 1700. They studied civil records, too. In the public records of several coastal regions they found reports that a three-meter (9-foot) tidal wave had washed away houses in Miyako, rice fields in Otsuchi, and a storehouse in Tanabe. The records show that the tsunami hit the Japanese coast on January 28, 1700.

6   Japanese geophysicists used this information to set up a computer model of the tidal wave. Such a model would show that amount of damage in those places. The geophysicists worked backward. They found the path of the shock wave that caused the tidal wave. They found that it must have come from the Pacific Northwest. They determined that the earthquake must have happened at 9 o'clock at night on the twenty-sixth of January.

7   Every detail fit: the tribal stories, the evidence, the historical records of the damage on the other side of the ocean. There is no question about it: the region of Cascadia (the Pacific Northwest) is seismically active. The magnitude 9 earthquake that hit was sixty times more powerful than the magnitude 7.2 earthquake that devastated Kobe, Japan, almost 300 years later. In 1700, there were few people living in the Pacific Northwest. Today, from Victoria, British Columbia, down the coast to northern California, 9 million people live near the ocean—within the danger zone of the fault and a 60-foot tidal wave. If an earthquake like the earthquake of 1700 hits, people on both sides of the ocean will be in mortal danger. It is impossible to imagine the loss of life and the property damage that such an earthquake would cause today.

8   What fear do the Japanese and the people of the Pacific Northwest have in common today? The answer is obvious: another earthquake like the earthquake of 1700. Paleoseismologists know that earthquakes of that magnitude happen in subduction zones about once every 500 years, but earthquakes are not predictable. Every day there are small earthquakes, ones that people don't even feel. But the next "Big One" could happen at any time. The historical account that Satake and his colleagues have pieced together, however, gives people a great deal of information to work with. They can plan to strengthen buildings below a certain level. They will build buildings on higher ground, far from the fault, and limit building along the coast. But if the "Big One" comes, there may be nothing anyone can do to prevent loss of life and property.

Strategy Focus: Analyzing Evidence

1. Write a check (✓) in front of each kind of evidence that scientists investigated to come up with the story of the "Big One" of 1700.

   a. _____ deposits from past tsunamis

   b. _____ records of damage to property in Cascadia

   c. _____ public records of damage to property in Japan

   d. _____ the oral history of the Wiyot people

   e. _____ computer-generated models of tidal waves

   f. _____ the history books of the Chetco

   g. _____ the records of Gary Carver at Humboldt State University

2. What kinds of things can you find in civil records? Write a check (✓) in front of each kind of information that might be part of public records.

   a. _____ the date of a person's birth

   b. _____ population count information

   c. _____ weather reports

   d. _____ information about accidents

   e. _____ records of when people died

   f. _____ the dates of floods, fires, earthquakes, hurricanes, and other disasters

   g. _____ marriage and divorce records

3. Now make a list of three more kinds of information that might be found in public records:

   _____

   _____

   _____

4. Think about the following ideas and discuss them with your classmates.

   a. the limitations of oral history

   b. why witnesses at a trial don't all tell the same story

   c. how a story "improves" with age

5. Why was the Kobe earthquake so much more damaging than the "Big One" of 1700 in the Pacific Northwest? Write a check (✓) in front of each correct answer.

   a. _____ The Kobe area has a large population today.

   b. _____ Cascadia was sparsely populated three hundred years ago.

   c. _____ Cascadia's buildings were not high three hundred years ago.

   d. _____ In large Japanese cities nowadays, there are many tall buildings.

   e. _____ Today's architecture is far superior to the architecture of 1700.

   f. _____ People no longer fear earthquakes.

6. What is a paleoseismologist? Underline each phrase that applies to the definition.

   a geologist   an earthquake expert

   a human being   a musician

   a scientist   a person interested in ancient earthquakes

   a historian   an investigator of tsunami evidence

   someone who digs   a storyteller

7. What is a geophysicist? Underline each phrase that applies to the definition.

   a geologist   a seismologist

   a scientist   a computer user

   an earthquake   an expert on tidal waves

   a physicist

Strategy: Writing About the Ideas

1. Some parts of the world are more likely to have natural disasters than others. For instance, there are hurricanes in Bangladesh and the Caribbean; earthquakes in Turkey, China, Japan, and the western coast of North America; sandstorms on deserts; dangerous floods along the river; and snowstorms (blizzards) in the far north and on mountains. How do people who live in those vulnerable places prepare for the natural dangers that are sure to come? Make a list of preparation plans for one kind of natural disaster. Then write a paragraph about those preparations.

2. Geography is earth science. Write about a part of the world that you would like to visit. Include your reasons that this part of the world interests you.

3. Go to the Internet and search for < world + map + Peters > on your favorite search engine or
go to http://www.webcom.com/ ~ bright/petermap.html.

   "The Peters Projection World Map is one of the most stimulating, and controversial, images of the world. When this map was first introduced by… Dr. Arno Peters at a Press Conference in Germany in 1974, it generated a firestorm of debate.…The earth is round. The challenge of any world map is to represent a round earth on a flat surface. There are literally thousands of map projections.…The Peters Projection is an 'area accurate map.' "

   In other words, this map shows the relative sizes of land masses. Examine the map and make a list of things that surprise you. For example, you might not have realized how much larger Australia is compared to all of Europe.

Strategy Focus: Keeping a Vocabulary Journal

Choose five words from the new words in this unit to be your target words.

Write the words here: _____ _____

_____ _____ _____

Now write them into your vocabulary journal. Remember to include the following parts:

- your target word
- the sentence from the unit in which your target word appears
- a definition, including the part of speech.
- some sentences of your own

Strategy: Increasing Reading Speed

 Timed Reading

More Sensitive than Machines, More Aware than People

After every major earthquake there are reports of strange animal behavior. Birds of many kinds have acted strangely before the earthquake. Chickens do not fly up to roost on a pole or branch; they stay on the ground. Pigeons and crows fly in unusual patterns. Canaries and parakeets stop singing in their cages. Normally quiet dogs start to bark; noisy dogs fall silent. Fish that normally stay deep in the water swim near the surface of the water in large schools. Snakes come out of their holes. Is this behavior related to earthquakes? Can scientists use animal behavior to predict earthquakes?

Scientists are not likely to start focusing on animal behavior as a way of predicting earthquakes. There are too many animals and too many ways that they behave. Instead, scientists will look for the causes of these changes in animal behavior. Perhaps people can sense what the birds, the fish, the dogs, and the snakes are sensing (feeling).

The Kobe earthquake in Japan happened on January 17, 1995. A lot of water in that area is bottled for sale. Therefore, there were supplies of dated water in bottles. Scientists studied this water. Between October and January 10, the water showed a sharp increase in chlorine and sulfates. Another study focused on radon in the water. Between October and the end of December, the amount of radon increased fourfold. There was another dramatic increase of radon on January 7. On January 8, the radon level was ten times higher than the October level. Then the radon began to decrease. A week later, disaster struck. Perhaps some animals are sensitive to the changes in these gases.

Just before the Loma Prieta earthquake, a seismologist at Stanford University, noted a burst of magnetic noise. Some physicists began experiments with squeezing dry rocks. They found that the rocks generated electricity just as they crumbled. Because earthquakes squeeze rocks, the researchers set up equipment to monitor earthquake-prone zones. Their results seem to support the conclusion that animals sense electric current.

In California, researchers have "heard" the groans and rumbles of faults for several years. Now they are beginning to understand that a sound from one fault gets "answers" from other nearby faults. These noises are evidence of changes in the Earth's crust, and geologists may learn to understand their messages. Perhaps animals are able to detect these sounds and know that something is going to happen.

Time: _____

Now answer these questions as quickly as you can.

1. Scientists today cannot understand animal behavior as a sign of a coming earthquake because...

   a. there are too many animals.

   b. there are too many scientists.

   c. animals have so many different ways of behaving.

2. The Kobe water study was possible because of...

   a. rain.

   b. bottled water.

   c. an accident.

3. If you squeeze a dry rock hard enough, it will...

   a. give you water.

   b. send out an electrical signal.

   c. cause an earthquake.

4. One fault moves and causes...

   a. noises in nearby faults.

   b. strange animal behavior.

   c. changes in the mountains.

5. The main idea of this reading is that...

   a. birds have a number of interesting behavior patterns.

   b. scientists are trying to find out what animals are sensing before an earthquake.

   c. earthquakes may be predicted by checking different kinds of signals in the Earth.

LIVING TOGETHER IN A WORLD OF PEACE

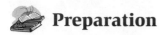 **Preparation**

Strategies for Anticipation

Between any two groups of people, there can be either **understanding** or **misunderstanding**. There can be **harmony** or **discord**. There can be **peace** or **war**. The difference between **agreement** and **disagreement** can affect every person who lives in the world.

Special schools in most countries train young people to be good soldiers and leaders in times of international trouble. These military schools teach, among other things, war education. In these schools, the young people learn to fight, so that they can protect the people of their countries from young people of other countries. However, there is something missing: education for peace.

Military school students lean to handle weapons, tools like knives, guns, and bombs, used to hurt other people. What would students learn in a peace school? What are the tools of peace? Do you have any ideas? Look at the list and check (✓) each box in front of each idea that is or could be part of teaching peace:

☐ work   ☐ teaching
☐ competition   ☐ good business
☐ using weapons   ☐ free trade
☐ city life   ☐ making money
☐ cooperation   ☐ mediation
☐ conflict   ☐ finding solutions to problems
☐ science   ☐ art lessons
☐ conferences   ☐ rain forests
☐ listening   ☐ making mistakes
☐ sharing ideas   ☐ negotiation
☐ lawyers   ☐ good communication
☐ making peace   ☐ agreements between governments
☐ helpfulness   ☐ understanding cultural differences

Now look quickly through this unit. Which of the ideas in the list are discussed in the unit? You might want to underline each of those ideas.

In general, **conflicts** begin because people do not understand a situation or because someone feels a strong emotion (like anger, not being needed or wanted, fear, or jealousy—wanting what someone else has). Even age-old conflicts probably began with/from such basic human responses.

Conflicts take many forms:
- arguments (heated words between two people or two groups)
- fights (physical violence between two people or two small groups)
- battles (fights between two groups of soldiers, each with the goal of killing the soldiers on the other side; actions that are part of a war)
- wars (organized fighting between two armies or groups of armies)
- attacks (surprise violence of one person or group against a second with the purpose of hurting or destroying the second person or group; the actions of terrorists)

What causes disagreements or conflicts between people? Here are some reasons people fight:
- money (how to spend it, not having enough of it)
- time (how to spend it, not having enough of it)
- decisions (who will make them)
- values (ideas of what is right and what is wrong).

Can you think of an example when people's values or beliefs made a difference and caused a conflict? What personal skills can help a person understand and resolve conflicts? Why do people believe different things?

 Main Reading   *important*

Understanding Cultures

1   Cultures are not right or wrong. Cultures are merely different, and those differences result in interest and in conflict. We human beings live within a culture, and the culture gives us guidelines as to how to live. The culture that we grow up with tells us how to act among other people. It defines who we are and what we are.

2   Anthropologists and sociologists are social scientists who study cultures and societies. They divide cultures into groups using different criteria. One dividing point, for example, is whether a culture is rural or urban. Of course, no society is all one or the other; however, the difference is clear under some circumstances. If we put the extreme urban culture on one end of a line, and the extreme rural culture on the other, we have a continuum. A continuum is a line, like a mathematical graph, that connects two extremes. All cultures fit somewhere between the two extremes. Some cultures are more rural or more urban in their values than others.

3   In general, rural cultures are called *Gemeinschaft* societies. This German word is used to describe societies that tend to have strong extended-family ties (grandparents, aunts, uncles, and cousins). People in *Gemeinschaft* societies think about themselves as part of a unit, such as a family or a village. People cooperate with one another. They live in harmony, and they live collectively. They tend to live in small villages, and their livelihood is usually farming and animal raising. If everyone does his or her work, there are few disagreements. The members of the society support one another psychologically, and they depend on others in their group for financial and emotional support. The emphasis in this kind of society is in being or becoming a certain kind of person. A student as a member of the group might receive help from the other members so that the student can go to a university to learn more about farming. In this way, when the student returns, he or she can help the whole community. In the *Gemeinschaft* society people tend to hold similar beliefs, and they tend to act in carefully defined ways.

4   Urban dwellers tend to be on the other end of the continuum in a *Gesellschaft* society. They usually work in industry or business. The emphasis is not on being or on becoming, but on *doing*. Their families are small (mother, father, and two children). They tend to live far

from other members of their extended families, so they must be more independent than rural dwellers. Members of a *Gesellschaft* society do not expect support from anyone other than a family member. A student must get a scholarship from an organization, take out a loan from the bank, or work to save money to go to a university. The city would never think of supporting a student to go to school. Therefore, the value of strong individualism becomes part of members of this kind of society. People do not dress like others, for example. Their beliefs are likely to be different as well. The emphasis on individualism can cause discord in society, disagreements, and lack of harmony.

5   Rural communities tend to be *high-context*. Urban communities tend to be *low context*. This definition reflects how much influence or control over the behavior of the individual person the society has. A person from a high-context society knows exactly what the others in the society expect of him or her. There is no need to ask or to discuss one's responsibilities. Furthermore, there is relatively little opportunity for misunderstandings. The person from a low-context society, on the other hand, has fewer rules to limit his vision. He or she can explore more freely. The low-context person is likely to make a lot of mistakes in the process of figuring out the best (new) way to accomplish a goal. The person in a low-context situation needs to ask questions and negotiate responses (talk over possibilities) to the situations that he or she faces.

6   Religion and politics are part of every culture. A high-context society is likely to have a single religion and one main specific brand of politics. The people will tend to agree with one another on both spiritual and political matters. The same is not true for a low-context society. There will probably be many religious groups, religious freedom is likely, and politics will include many different groups with greatly varying ideas. There may be conflict between groups within the society. This conflict will be part of the cultural expectations of

people in the society. They will know how to live comfortably with disagreements and discord around them. They will feel uncomfortable if everyone agrees.

7   People from different cultures deal with time, the relationship between nature and people, and interpersonal relationships differently. They are likely to have different attitudes toward work and the amount of influence one person can have on others. Differences like these mean that people will respond to outside forces in different ways. To a person from one culture, warning that a storm is coming is reason to cover windows and protect belongings. To a person in another culture, a storm warning is a reason to turn to belief and faith in an all-powerful being for protection.

8   In a similar way, masculinity and femininity (the qualities of being manly and womanly) are defined by culture. Which jobs are women's work? Which jobs are done by men? People in every culture face the same problems: how to define the self, the family, society, human nature, nature, and the supernatural. Each culture is likely to define these parts of life in unique ways. Furthermore, the people in that culture will find a set of ways to solve these problems that not only fit together but also are unique to that culture.

9   Culture is not as easy to learn as language. Therefore, even if people "speak the same language," they might not mean the same things by the words. It is the difference in culture and the lack of understanding that leads to all kinds of conflicts—from small misunderstandings in business deals to major wars. The difference in cultures is why we all need education for peace.

Strategy Focus: Analyzing the Reading

Read carefully for the answers to these questions.

1. (Paragraph 1) What is the role of culture in daily life?

2. (Paragraph 2)
   a. What is a social science?
   b. What is a continuum?

3. (Paragraph 3)
   a. What is an extended family?
   b. Where is one likely to find a *Gemeinschaft* community?
   c. What is the most common work in a *Gemeinschaft* society?

4. (Paragraph 4)
   a. Where is one most likely to find a *Gesellschaft* society?
   b. What kind of work do most people do in a *Gesellschaft* society?

5. (Paragraph 5)
   a. What is the difference between a high-context and a low-context society?
   b. Why does a person from a low-context society have to negotiate (discuss with others) before making a decision?

6. (Paragraph 6) Which kind of society will most likely have one major religion?

7. (Paragraph 7) In what attitudes are cultures most likely to differ?

8. (Paragraph 8) Why do people from all cultures have to face the same kinds of problems?

9. (Paragraph 9) Why are there likely to be conflicts between people of different cultures?

Importent

Strategy Focus: Discussing the Ideas

1. Reread the last sentence of the reading: "The difference in cultures is why we all need education for peace." What evidence is there that we need education for peace?

2. Why are people in a rural environment more likely to have a large number of rules to live by than people in an urban and industrial environment?

3. Which kind of society is more likely to have disagreements and conflicts within it? Why?

Strategy Focus: Learning Vocabulary in Context

Here are some of the most important words from this unit. For each one, there are several sentence contexts to help you learn about the word. Read each of the contexts and try to figure out the meaning of the words from the contexts. Try to determine whether each word is a noun, a verb, an adjective, or an adverb. Complete the sentences.

1. **criterion, criteria**

   The main **criterion** for a good book is a good plot. Other aspects that are important to me are the characters and the overall message. I use these **criteria** in selecting a book to read.

   Anyone who meets the entrance **criteria** can enter the contest. The first **criterion** is that a person must be over eighteen years of age.

   A **criterion** is _____ .

   Criteria are _____ .

2. **continuum** (plural, **continua**)

   Black is at one end, the dark end, of the range of an artist's paint colors. White is at the other end of the **continuum**.

   On the **continuum** between rich and poor, most people are closer to poor on the line.

   A **continuum** is a _____ .

3. harmony, harmonious

Good music contains notes that are **harmonious**. The harmony of the music makes it pleasant to listen to.

As children, brothers and sisters often argue, so there isn't much peace in a family with children. However, when the children grow up, they usually learn to live in **harmony** with one another.

Some of the colors in this painting break up the **harmony**. This orange color, for example, looks bad with the other soft colors.

When things are in **harmony**, _____.

4. a conflict [KAN-flict], to conflict [kan-FLICT]

Your secretary said that you have a time **conflict** today. The schedule shows one appointment at 10 A.M. and another at 10:15. And, your secretary says, you have an all-morning meeting starting at 9 o'clock. The meeting **conflicts** with everything else in the schedule.

Just before an election, there seem to be many issues or topics for politicians to argue about. However, many of these **conflicts** seem to disappear right after the election.

Teenagers seem to have many **conflicts** within themselves. They want the feeling of safety and security of being children, but they also want the rights of being adults. They want to drive cars, but they don't want to work to pay for insurance or gasoline. They need their parents' guidance, but they want to be independent.

The people in the neighborhood were having **conflicts** over parking places, so they all met to set up parking rules for everyone. The meeting stopped all the bad feelings.

A **conflict** is _____.

When two things **conflict** with each other, they _____.

5. discord

Most people, if given a choice between harmony and **discord**, will choose harmony.

Even the happiest family will experience some **discord** because disagreements will arise. Not everyone is going to agree on how the family resources should be spent. Not everyone is going to agree on places to go and things to do. The secret, however, is to keep talking about how one feels about a situation. If everyone talks about the situation, then each person can understand the other's perspective. By talking about other points of view, everyone has the opportunity to change his or her mind. Then the effects of the **discord** can be managed, and harmony can return to the family.

In a business, at the first signs of discord among employees, a person should come in to mediate. This person in the middle listens to all sides, tries to understand where the conflicts come from, and attempts to end the **discord** through good communication.

Discord exists when people do not _____ .

6. **to cooperate, cooperation**

Working together in groups makes work go fast. That's why farmers have always liked to **cooperate**. **Cooperation** is also good business. Today, farmers own some of the huge machines they need — together with their neighbors. They all work to harvest the crops, and they send their crops to market in trucks that a group of farmers owns together.

The school was built with the **cooperation** of the parents and the local government. The government provided the money for the equipment and supplies. The parents did the construction work, and together they finished the school on time.

The kindergarten teacher asked her tiny pupils to **cooperate** with her in cleaning the classroom. They all helped, but it was clear that they thought **cooperate** meant "obey" and not "work together."

To **cooperate with** someone means to _____ .

Cooperation means _____ .

7. **dweller**

She lives in a small town, but he is a city **dweller**. In cities, many people live in apartments. Apartment **dwellers** seldom know their neighbors, but some town folks almost always do.

A **dweller** is a _____ .

Strategy: Discussing Ideas About Culture

1. How can a difference in culture cause conflict?
2. Most people believe that their culture is the right culture, and therefore other cultures should follow their ideas. How can such an attitude cause international conflicts?
3. What is the difference between learning a language and learning a culture? Which is harder, and why?
4. How can the media (TV, radio, and newspapers) influence culture? How are people's ideas influenced by the media? Can the media cause wars? Can the media cause peace?

Strategy Focus: Turning Concrete Statements into Abstract Concepts

Below is a story about a young man who goes on a quest, a search, for some important values in his life. As you read, look for the general conclusions he draws from concrete experiences. Can you interpret story events by changing them into general or abstract statements?

 Related Reading 1

An Allegory of Values

1. A young man was sitting on a rock near his home one day. A group of wise people from his village walked by. "What are you doing, young man?" one of the wise ones asked.

2. "Nothing," the young man said. "There is nothing to do here in this simple little village." He picked up a stone and threw it at a bird that was singing in a tree. "There's nothing in this place worth doing, and there is nothing worth even thinking about."

3. "And yet you sit here and do nothing about it?" said a white-haired woman. "Go and find what is important in life." The young man looked up at her, thinking how old she looked. She continued, "Find what is important, or your life, as you are living it now, isn't worth living. Go!"

4   The young man sat for a few moments longer. The old ones were telling him what to do—again. But then, because he really didn't have anything else to do, he started out on the road. He thought that he was starting on a journey to find nothing; certainly he wouldn't find the meaning of life. But he would escape the village.

5   One of the wise ones in his village said that the secrets of life could be found on the road from the seashore to the mountaintop. "Well, maybe…" he thought as he walked away. "Anything is better than staying in this place." He would go from the seashore to the mountaintop.

6   Soon he was at the shore. He walked along the seashore for miles. He watched the waves as the tide moved in on the sand of the shore. He listened as he watched the birds flying through the air. All was quiet, and then he heard a whisper, words in the wind. He stopped and tried hard to understand the words.

7   The wind said, "I am the world, and I am open to you. I am open to the birds in the air and the starfish in the waves. I am here for you and for all the animals. There are opportunities for all, and none are special in my mind. All are subject to the same laws. Everyone must follow the laws of the Earth. Rights are earned by hard work, by taking responsibility for what one does."

8   The young man thought how foolish the wind was. People were obviously more important than other creatures. People are more powerful than the birds or the fish or the animals of the field and the forest. As the young man listened, he noticed that a wave had left a live starfish to die on the beach. He bent to pick up the stranded starfish from the sandy beach and threw it back into the life-giving water; he nodded, and he walked on. "There are rights only for those who take responsibility," the wind whispered after him. The young man nodded to himself; he felt good about saving the starfish. He had earned the right to feel good about his actions.

9   The young man walked into a long and narrow valley. He saw a bear and a deer at a spring. They were drinking water from a pool, and the young man was thirsty. He picked up a long, heavy stick and walked toward the water. He was just about to shout at the bear and the deer and swing the heavy stick when something stopped him. It was strange—a bear and a deer drinking together. He put down the stick and spoke.

10   "May I take a drink?" he asked. The bear and the deer looked up and said, "There is plenty of water. There is no scarcity. The water belongs to us all." And the young man bent low to the water and drank his fill. And he heard the message, repeated in the breeze, "There are no scarcities; there is plenty for all to share."

11   The tired young man sat down to rest, and the bear and the deer came to rest with him. The man asked if the two were friends. The bear said, "No, we are not friends, but we have learned from each other." The deer continued, "One day Bear and I came to the spring at the same time. Bear wanted the water, and so did I. I kicked Bear with my sharp hooves."

12   Bear continued, "And I scratched Deer with my claws. We fought until we were both hurting and bloody."

13   Deer continued. "Neither of us was happy about the fighting; we were both still thirsty, and we were both hurting. It seemed better to agree not to fight, and to share the water of the spring." And the wind whispered into the young man's ears again, "It is wrong to fight when both want the same thing and there is enough for both." The young man rested a while and then left the deer and the bear sleeping in the warm sunlight.

14   The young man walked until he grew weary again. He found a place to rest near a bush that was heavy with flowers. On the bush, a butterfly was struggling to escape from the tight cocoon that held it. Fascinated, the young man sat down on a nearby rock and watched

as slowly the butterfly emerged, unfolded its wings, and moved softly as the wings dried. Then the butterfly flew off. The young man heard a crackle among the flowers on another branch and turned his head. Another butterfly was fighting to emerge. Eager to help, he broke the cocoon. The new butterfly inside the cocoon fell free, struggled to open its wings, and then became quiet, silent in death. The young man watched, unable to move. This butterfly would have slowly crawled out of the cocoon, opened its wings, dried itself in the sun, and then flown away—if he had not tried to help it. The young man felt bad. Again he heard whispered words in the wind: "Let others do their own work. Do not try to do it for them. It is the Iron Rule."

15   Then he noticed rain clouds on the mountaintop. A harsh, cold wind began to blow. Then lightning lit the hillside with its brightness, and the thunder roared. As rain came screaming down from the sky, the young man found shelter in a small cave. He watched as the storm whipped the leaves from a great, solid oak tree and saw the great tree split in two. He watched a willow tree bend and sway, bowing low to the ground. He heard the fallen oak say, "I am strong, rigid, solid, and now broken." Said the willow, "I am flexible. I am a toy to the wind. I bend." As the storm became quiet, the young man heard a whisper, "Bend, and move like the willow in the current; for then you can watch great things and learn from them without breaking."

16   Soon the rain stopped, the sun came out, and the young man got up and walked on. He was getting tired. He started talking to himself, saying that it didn't matter if he went to the top of the mountain. He sat down in the shadow of a cliff, and the earth shook beneath him. The wind whipped around the rocks in warning, "No giving up!" it shrieked at him. "Get up, and fulfill your promise. Get up!"

17   So onward and upward he struggled. Suddenly the young man was looking into a lovely meadow. The smell of flowers and sweet music seemed to fill the air, and the young man was drawn in. There were

people laughing and dancing, and eating good food. And the young man wanted to join in their fun. He bent to pick some of the flowers to make a necklace of blossoms, and a large sunflower spoke gently to him. "Don't let your head be turned by the beauty of this moment. Do not let the laughter of the party change your vision. Do not allow this temptation to change your path." The young man listened to the flower. He looked longingly at the people who were playing, and he turned to follow the path to the top of the mountain.

18   He was sweating and tired when he saw the top of the mountain. A horse came along, fresh and spirited. The young man reached to catch the horse to ride it to the top. But the wind blowing through the horse's mane said to him, "Be strong; you can do it on your own. You do not need a rescue."

19   At the top of the mountain, the young man saw an eagle with a long ribbon of paper in its mouth. The young man thought, "At last, the words of wisdom!" He reached to pull the ribbon of paper from the beak of the eagle. But the eagle spread its huge wings and took to the air. In the screech of the great bird, the young man heard these words, "Don't try to take it from me. Keep no secrets! Ask for what you want."

20   The young man fell to the ground and wept in frustration. "I've come so far, walked many miles, and now I need the wisdom of the mountain," he cried. Again and again he begged the eagle to give him the wisdom that he had sought. Exhausted, the young man was soon asleep.

21   He woke to find the sun up, the birds singing, the flowers and trees swaying in a gentle breeze. The ribbon of paper from the eagle lay at his feet. He picked it up to read it. To his surprise, he found nothing on it. He rolled up the paper and put it in his pocket. Slowly the disappointed young man began the long walk to his village. He had climbed the mountain, he told himself, and he had learned nothing.

It was just as he had thought. There was nothing to learn on such a journey.

22　　However, as he walked, the young man thought about what he had seen and heard. He had learned something. Whenever he rested, he wrote what he had learned on the paper.

23　　The path back down from the mountain was easier to travel than the road up the mountain, but as the young man walked, he noticed many things for the first time. The trip toward the seashore and home seemed much longer.

24　　Weeks later, the young man arrived back at home. The village seemed brighter, cleaner, nicer than it had been. He sat on the rock to look around. A group of the wise ones of the village stopped to ask him what he had learned. He took out the ribbon of paper and he read:

25　　"From the wind on the seashore I learned that human beings have rights if they earn them by being responsible for themselves and for others. I saw that the waves had left a starfish to die on the sand. I was able to save it. I picked it up and threw it back into the water. I earned the right to feel good about what I did. I learned to use my abilities, my power, for something good.

26　　"From the deer and the bear and the pool of water, I learned that competition makes scarcities, but there are enough resources for all— if we choose to use them well. The bear and the deer are not friends; in fact, they are very different. But they understand that all creatures need some things, and that if they fight over those things, both of them lose.

27　　"The bear and the deer also taught me that it is wrong to fight if two want the same thing; by talking about the problem, they can solve it. Fighting wastes resources and energy.

28　　"From the oak and the willow, I learned the danger of being rigid and the wisdom of being flexible. An oak tree is perhaps the strongest of all trees. It can stand strong against many storms.

However, if there is a storm more powerful than the oak, the storm can destroy the whole tree. The willow tree is thin and its branches are like pieces of string. The storm blows the willow tree's branches, but the branches do not break. The whole tree bends and sways in the wind. The willow tree, therefore, is really stronger than the oak tree.

29   "From the butterflies I learned to let others do their work by themselves, that I cannot rescue them. The wind called it the Iron Rule: No one should do for another what that person can do alone. I tried to help a butterfly that needed no help, and my attempt to help it destroyed it.

30   "From the earthquake I learned that it is wrong to give up when I still have the resources to continue. I wanted to stop, to rest, to quit, but the earth shook beneath me. My values and my beliefs were clear to me because I was in danger. The danger helped me to realize what work I must do. To make my life a life worth living, I must be strong. I must avoid giving up.

31   "From the sunflower I learned not to give in to temptation, for there are those who would sabotage a noble effort. I learned to recognize the things that would tempt me from the purpose of my work. There are many distractions, and although there are times for fun, one must complete one's work first. There will always be people who will try to stop a person from doing a job. They are wrong to sabotage someone else's work.

32   "From the horse I learned to use my own energy first and not to seek a rescue. I learned to trust myself, to rely on my abilities, and to see that my work was done myself.

33   "From the eagle I learned to ask for what I want, not to keep it secret within myself because others cannot read my mind. They do not know what I think unless I tell them. And I learned that it is wrong to use force to get my way."

34   A wise one of the village said, "Yes, you have learned the way of peace and the wisdom of a life well lived. A young man who understands these rules knows how to live in peace within himself, and he has learned how to live in peace with others. Now come and live in our village."

35   The young man looked at the wise ones, who no longer looked old to him. He got down from his rock and walked with them back through the village.

Strategy Focus: Exploring the Meaning

A. Write the lessons that the young man learned.

1. What did he learn from saving the starfish?

   _____

2. What did he learn from the deer and the bear?

   _____

3. What did he learn from the butterfly?

   _____

4. What did he learn from the earthquake?

   that it is wrong to give up when I still have the resources

5. What did he learn from the oak tree and the willow?

   learaed the danger if being right

6. What did he learn from the sunflower?

   _____

7. What did he learn from the horse?

   _____

8. What did he learn from the eagle?

   _____

H.W

B. Determine the meaning of the word **allegory**.

From this reading, it is clear that an *allegory* is most like...

a. a story   c. a rule

b. an animal   d. a lesson   *Important*

Strategy Focus: Learning Vocabulary in Context

1. **rigid, flexible**

Every government needs rules; however, in some societies the rules are **rigid**, and in other cultures they are **flexible**. Where the rules are strict and no exceptions are made, the police are quite powerful. However, in areas where laws are considered **flexible** guidelines and are not so strictly enforced, the police do not have as much power.

The thick steel rods of the bridge broke in two under the stress of the earthquake because the rods were too **rigid**. More **flexible** rods would have been able to bend.

A house is a permanent and **rigid** structure. A tent is temporary and **flexible**.

Rigid refers to the quality of ___*stiffness, unchanging*___.

If something is **flexible**, then it ___*easily*___.

2. **to sabotage, a sabotage**

During the war, an enemy soldier broke through the line of defense and **sabotaged** [SAB-a-tajd] a bridge. After the bridge blew up, there was no way for big trucks to cross the river. **Sabotage** accounted for the destruction of a tunnel and an airport, as well.

We had planned to go to the movies, but my friend's mother **sabotaged** those plans by insisting that her daughter stay home tonight.

An automobile blew up in the capital city. The police investigation showed that the car had been **sabotaged**. The newspaper account reported that such cases of **sabotage** were quite rare.

Sabotage means ___*destroying*___.

To **sabotage** something means ___*luck*___.

important

3. <u>scarcity</u>, <u>scarce</u>

There hasn't been any rain in months, so there's a **scarcity** of water.

California has a lot of Japanese restaurants, but there is a **scarcity** of Polish restaurants there. In Chicago, however, a tourist can find a lot of Polish restaurants but Japanese restaurants are relatively **scarce**.

Two-dollar bills are rare, but there is no **scarcity** of five-dollar bills.

A **scarcity** of something means that there is not enough Something .

If something is **scarce**, it means that there _____ lack _____.

It is _____ to find something that is **scarce**.

4. **rights, privilege** قصة و استاذ

Adults have the right to do some things that teenagers cannot. An adult can do what a teenager is criticized for. One of these special **privileges** is to be able to stay up late at night.

People who live in the Hidden Valley neighborhood have the **right** to use the swimming pool at the Hidden Valley Club. They can also use the Hidden Valley golf course, tennis courts, and gymnasium. Rich people have many more opportunities for education, travel, and good housing. That's why people say that the wealthy have many extra **privileges**.

A **privilege** is a right for d Something that is reserved for som .

A **right** is permission to do the realbility .

5. **artificial** . كاذب

This ring may look valuable, but the stone is **artificial**, and the gold isn't real either.

The states of Wisconsin, Minnesota, and Michigan each have thousands of natural lakes, but in the western states, most lakes are **artificial**. They are made by building dams to stop the flow of streams and rivers.

Some football stadiums may seem to have lots of thick, natural green grass, but the fields are actually covered by **artificial** grass.

If something is **artificial**, then it is to some body or .

Somethig .

اكتشف – كي ٨

Important

6. **to rescue, a rescue**

A child was playing in the sand on the beach when a big wave pulled him into the water. A man who was running by **rescued** the child even before the child's father could get into the water to pull him out to safety.

Some of the best mountain climbers, strongest hikers, and most skilled skiers on the mountain are part of the mountain **rescue** team. When people get lost on the mountain, a group of team members goes looking for them.

A little kitten climbed up a telephone pole and got frightened. The little cat cried until a firefighter climbed the pole to **rescue** it. Last year, the same firefighter was in the newspaper twice: once for the **rescue** of a dog that fell through the ice on the river, and another time for freeing a young eagle that got caught in an old fishing net. The firefighter's friends now call him Doctor Zoo.

To **rescue** someone is to _____ .

A person who performs a **rescue** _____ .

Strategy Focus: Discussing the Ideas

1. "Experience is what we call our mistakes." What do you think of this quote?

2. What role does the wind play in the allegory?

3. Why was the eagle's ribbon of paper blank?

4. What changed in the story? Explain your answer.

Strategy Focus: Ideas for Writing

1. Which of the young man's lessons is the most important lesson for you? Which lesson do you need to learn?

2. Why did the trip back to the village from the mountaintop take much longer than the trip to the mountaintop? (What was the young man doing as he returned?)

Strategy: Understanding the Negative and Positive Sides of Words

Some of the new words in the introduction and in the allegory are positive words—they relate to ideas about peace. Others relate to war and unhappiness in the world.

1. Divide this list into positive words about peace and negative words about the troubles of conflict.

war   harmony   disagreement
anger   agreement   understanding
fighting   negotiation   communication
discord   cooperation   misunderstanding

<u>Peace Words</u>   <u>Conflict Words</u>

_____   _____

_____   _____

_____   _____

_____   _____

_____   _____

_____   _____

2. What is the best title for the story?

    a. A Long Walk

    b. The Wisdom of the Wind

    c. Peace Education

    d. Walk to the Mountain

    Why did you choose the title you did? Discuss your conclusions with a classmate.

MEDIATION
MEDITATION

Strategy Focus: Thinking About the Title of the Next Reading

Think about the meaning of the words in the title of the next related reading. Look them up in a dictionary if you need to. Then list the topics and ideas you expect to find in this reading.

_____   _____

_____   _____

_____   _____

_____   _____

Related Reading 2

Choose Mediation

1   An elderly woman lived in a small house next to a young couple. She complained to the Community Dispute Settlement Center (CDSC) that these two young people came and went at all hours of the day and night in a noisy sports car, that they played the car radio much too loudly, and that they had no consideration for her. She was so afraid of the two young people that she asked for police protection at the CDSC. It seems that they wore their hair in what seemed to her to be strange hairstyles. Furthermore, they were of a different race than the elderly woman.

2   When she went to the CDSC, she met a mediator (the person who would help to solve their problem) and the two young people. At the mediation, she found out that the young man and woman both worked at the hospital. They were residents (doctors-in-training) and were often called in to the hospital at a moment's notice. The young man admitted that he often turned the car radio up very loud. "It helps me wake up fast!" he explained. "Sometimes I've only been asleep for an hour or two when I'm called in to work."

3   When the young couple realized that they had frightened the elderly woman, they felt very bad. "I could use earphones," the young man suggested. "And," his wife added, "we could get that broken muffler fixed. Then the car wouldn't make so much noise and wouldn't be so disturbing to our neighbors."

4   The elderly woman felt bad that she had been afraid because of the racial difference and the unusual hairstyles. When she found out that her neighbors were really nice people, and doctors too, she felt much better. After the mediation, she said that it was a miracle how the mediation changed her life. "I had lived in fear, but now I live next to two wonderful people."

5   In many cases two people (or two companies, or two countries) who have troubles with each other often look to the law to decide who is right and who is wrong. Laws exist so that there are guidelines for behavior—what is the right thing to do and what is not right.

6   Everything in a mediation is confidential. There is no public record (no one can walk in off the street and listen to a mediation), and there is no publicity in the newspapers. Furthermore, public mediation centers provide high-quality service for very little money. In fact, many of them are absolutely free. For a mediation, no lawyers are necessary.

A mediator can help the people on two sides of a dispute find a peaceful solution to their problems.

In addition, the solution to a dispute (a fight, an argument, or any kind of misunderstanding) is fair because the solution comes from the people who asked for the mediation. The mediator helps them understand what each side feels it needs from the situation. Together they work out the details with the mediator and between each other. When you add to these points the fact that more than 80% of all mediations are successful, mediation appears to be far more reasonable than going to court. People and their feelings seem less important in a court of law than in a mediation center. In mediation centers, however, people who emerge from a successful mediation often like one another better. The people might never have really listened to the other side before.

7   Mediation exists in some cultural traditions as the first way of handling interpersonal or even business problems. In Japan and in China, for example, most disputes are taken to mediators first. Mediators are trained people. They do not make decisions, and they do not suggest compromises (halfway solutions in which each party "gives in" on some points). All bargaining happens between the two parties in the dispute. —> خيرمناهم

8   Of course, not all cases are appropriate for mediation. Serious crimes like murder and burglary need to be decided by a judge. Threats to people's lives and property need to be taken to court, and so do attempts to ruin a person's reputation (defamation of character). For many cases, however, the best first step is mediation. The two sides come to understand each other's perspectives on the problem, and a small amount of understanding can go a long way toward finding a solution. Like the woman with the noisy and "inconsiderate" neighbors, some people find peace of mind at a mediation center.

Strategy Focus: Thinking About the Reading

1. What advantages does mediation have over going to court?
2. What kinds of problems are best handled in court? What kinds of problems are best handled in a mediation?
3. What serious crimes are mentioned in the reading?
4. How does mediation work?

Strategy Focus: Discussing the Ideas

1. How does your culture deal with problems like the problems between people?
2. Why is a mediator, a person in the middle, necessary at all?

Strategy: Looking at Mediation Case Studies

 ## Related Reading 3

A Classic Case: King Solomon's Decision

1   One famous case of a mediation happened in the days of King Solomon, who was known as a wise mediator. One day, two women were fighting over a baby, each claiming that the baby was hers. They brought their dispute to King Solomon to solve. King Solomon asked what they were fighting about. The first woman said, "The baby is mine, and this other woman is trying to take the child from me."

2   The second woman said, "That's a lie! This child is mine." The first woman said, "How can you say that? The baby is mine! Look at the child. The baby even looks like me!"

3   As King Solomon listened, his eyes went from one woman to the other. He couldn't tell which woman was truly the mother of the child.

4   King Solomon's Solution: The king said, "Stop! You shall share the child. Guard, cut the baby in half with your sword, and give each woman half of the baby." As the guard stepped forward with his sword raised, the king watched the two women. One nodded her head and looked pleased. The other woman cried out, "No, no! Give the child to her. She can have my child. Please don't hurt my baby."

5   King Solomon turned and pointed to the woman who had cried out; he said to the guard, "Stop! Give the whole baby to that woman. She is truly the mother." He turned to the other woman and, pointing at her, said to two other guards, "And throw her in prison—a prison for liars. She is not the mother of the child."

Strategy Focus: Mediating Case Studies

Today kings are seldom mediators. Instead there are people who are trained in mediation. Here are some other problems that were solved by mediation. The problem is given to you first from two different perspectives. Read the two views of the problem and try to decide the key points for mediation. Then make suggestions for a mediator. How do you think a solution can be found? Compare your observations with a classmate's.

1. **The Case of the Brown Streaks on the Driveway**

   Tony Adamson: I had a new driveway put in. After a couple of months, I noticed several large, long streaks of brown color on my new cement driveway. I called John Franklin, the owner of the company that made the driveway, and complained. Mr. Franklin and I had once had a good relationship because we had done business before. But now...

   John Franklin: I put in a new driveway for the Adamsons. On the day I came to put the sealing liquid on the driveway, it had started to rain. Rainwater makes the sealant less effective. I explained to Mrs. Adamson that it would be better to spray the protective sealing compound on the driveway on another day, a sunny day. Mrs. Adamson, however, wanted the job to be finished, and she insisted that I finish the job. Mrs. Adamson is responsible for the streaks, and Mr. Adamson has lost his temper. His neighbors have told him to sue me.

Mr. Adamson wants faster action than the courts could provide, so he called a mediation center. Mr. Franklin agreed to come. With the mediator present, the two men explained their sides of the story.

What solution do you see for the two people? Remember, the mediator cannot make suggestions.

2. The Case of the Garbage Can

Angela Clark: I like living in a tidy neighborhood. Every day I take a walk around the block, and I usually carry a plastic bag into which I put all of the bits of paper that I see on the sidewalk, along the side of the road, or on the ground. When my plastic bag is full of trash, I put it into one of the garbage cans in the alley, the little road behind the houses in her neighborhood.

Robert Billison: I saw a woman from my neighborhood put a bag of garbage into the garbage can behind my house. I complained to the city sanitation service that this woman who lives down the street is using my garbage can. One day I got in my car and followed her home, noting the address of the house she entered, so I know who she is. I am very angry that this Mrs. Clark is putting her garbage in my garbage can, and sometimes I don't have room for my own garbage! I called the supervisor at the city sanitation service. He suggested that I contact the mediation center, so Mrs. Clark was called and invited to mediation.

Insight into the situation: Mrs. Clark had no idea why she was being called to the mediation center, but she was told that one of her neighbors wanted to discuss an important matter with her. She and her husband came to the mediation center, full of worries and stress. Robert Billison was there, too, and they recognized one another in the waiting room. While they were waiting, Mr. Billison said, "So you're the lady who fills up my garbage can." Mrs. Clark was quite surprised. She said, "Well, I thought the garbage cans belonged to the city and we're all supposed to use them for garbage." Mr. Billison said, "I often run out of space in my garbage can, and I saw you putting a bag of garbage in my garbage can."

At that point the mediator came out of the office and invited both people into a mediation room. How do you think this case of the garbage can could be solved in mediation?

Strategy Focus: Reading the First Sentence to Get the Main Ideas

Read the first sentence of the following paragraph in the following related reading. Then stop to discuss what you think the reading is about.

Related Reading 4

Man in the Middle: The Process of Mediation

1   The first principle in setting up a mediation is to bring together the disputants, the people on the two sides of the argument. Mediators are people who put themselves between two people in an argument. Their purpose is to make sure that the two people or the two sides hear the other side's explanations. Mediators see a danger, for example, in speaking to the disputants separately, mostly because the mediator must speak to one disputant first and the second disputant after the first. Such separate interviews can cause serious problems—whichever person speaks to the mediator first gets a chance to "bend the mediator's ear" in his or her direction. Even a trained mediator can "take sides," that is, believe that one of the two parties in the dispute has a better case or is "right." One person's complaint can become part of what a mediator says to the other disputant. Therefore, it is best to have the first interview with both sides present. Then everyone knows what everyone else knows—there are no secrets.

2   Trust is the basis of the process of mediation. Both disputants must believe that they can trust the mediator. Therefore, discussions must be "out in the open," and not belong to or come exclusively from one side or the other. However, when two people or two groups of people are in disagreement with each other and a mediator brings them together, what is likely to happen? They are likely to show their feelings.

3   At this point, the second principle comes into play; the mediator must be in control. The disputants both want to gain the favor of the mediator—to feel that the mediator is "on my side." The mediator, however, must stay in control and stay neutral. The effective mediator stops all kinds of fighting, simply by not allowing it. The rules are these: no insults, no angry words, and no negative body language, and no attacks on the other disputants. And furthermore, only one person speaks at a time. The mediator indicates whose turn it is to talk and tolerates no interruptions from the other side. Some mediators use a timer to give both sides equal time. While one side is talking, the other may not interrupt. The job of the side that is silent is simply to listen and take notes during the other side's time to talk.

4   It is equally important for a mediator to choose the place of the meeting—it must be "neutral territory," a place that belongs to the mediator and not to either of the disputants. The place shows who is in charge.

5   The meeting must also be formal: the disputants should have a clear arrangement to show up at a specific time for the meeting. They should both meet in a waiting room or reception area and wait in the same room for the meeting, so that it is clear that there is no chance that either has had an opportunity to speak with the mediator before the scheduled meeting. At the time of the meeting, the telephones should be turned off so there will be no interruptions. The disputants and the mediator should sit at a round table or on chairs in a triangle. With this chair arrangement, there is less opportunity for the two disputants to argue with, to glare at, or to hit each other. The mediator can stay between them at all times, and thus remain in control.

6   The mediator even tells the disputants where to sit. Chair choice is an important part of mediating as well. The rule of thumb (general guideline) is to put the angriest person in the softest and deepest chair. The mediator, on the other hand, must be in a straight chair—one that allows for quickly rising out of the chair if it is necessary to keep the disputants from fighting physically. The mediator always sits on the edge of the chair as well—thus holding control by "body language." The person whose body is the highest in the room usually has the most control, at least psychologically, so the disputants should be in low, comfortable chairs. All participants (mediator and disputants) should be close enough to allow for eye contact—but the two disputants should be somewhat farther apart from each other and equally distant from the mediator.

7   Another rule of thumb is for the mediator to keep the disputants from talking to each other. The disputants should direct all commentary to the mediator and just listen when another person is talking. In many cases, while one person tells the mediator what happened, the other hears the story for the first time from the other person's perspective. The mediator keeps pointing to himself or herself, saying, "Talk to me; tell me." Trained mediators do not allow the disputants to talk directly to each other. If the two sides do start talking to (or at) each other, the mediator should stand up and put out his or her hands toward the disputants and say something like, "Stop immediately. I will talk to each of you, one at a time, and only one person at a time will talk to me."

8   The mediator's control of the situation is a measure of how well he or she can use body language. It is also important to be firm, to stop any breaking of the rules, and to match the level of force that either of the disputants uses. The mediator wants the two people to feel "listened to" and understood, so establishing rapport is necessary at this point in the mediation. The mediator can make a person feel understood (that's what rapport means) by echoing what that person says with "active listening" techniques.

9   Active listening is telling a person what you understand of what he or she is saying. The principle is simple, but nothing is more important to the two sides of a dispute than feeling that the mediator understands and is truly listening to what they are saying.

10   The next important point is that the mediator must not agree with either side and must not show sympathy with either side. Both sides are likely to try to sway the opinion of the mediator—to win the mediator "to my side." An effective way is to ask the mediator a question. However, a good mediator recognizes the trap and asks another question that will keep the conversation going. A good mediator is careful not to talk too much (not to try to solve the problem until the disputants are "all talked out"). Instead, the mediator tries to talk about twenty percent of the time. Each disputant talks about forty percent of the time. The mediator does not allow the disputants to ask questions—and certainly doesn't answer any questions that either of the disputants asks. The mediator also avoids "leading questions" (questions that put ideas in the heads of the disputants) and "closed questions" (those that can be answered with a "yes" or "no," because they are almost always leading questions).

11   A good mediator requires disputants to speak only for themselves. A disputant should not try to interpret what another person—either the mediator or another disputant—is thinking.

12   Because mediation is not easy, good mediators use principles to guide their actions. Here are some other important principles of mediation:

- Deal with one problem at a time.
- Keep everyone focused.
- Remain neutral.
- Pay attention to the body language of the disputants, always looking for signs of nervousness, worry, or fear.
- Accept at surface value what either or both of the disputants say and avoid making judgments.
- Avoid making suggestions.
- Remember that inside an angry person is a hurt person.

13   The mediator, the person in the middle, uses many principles for one purpose—to see that the two disputants listen long enough to each other to ensure that they understand each other. That's how, and why, mediation works.

Understanding the Principles: True or False?

Are these statements true or not, according to the reading? Circle *true* or *false* after each statement.

1. A mediator needs to take one person's side against the other side.

   true   false

2. Talking to one side first and then the other could change a mediator's point of view and affect the mediator's neutrality.

   true   false

3. One of the disputants always chooses the place for the mediation.

   true   false

4. A mediator is a person in the middle.

   true   false

5. The mediator's job is to help both sides in a dispute understand the other's point of view.

   true   false

6. Body language is a mediator's tool.

   true   false

7. A mediator should try to solve the problem for the disputants.

   true   false

8. Making suggestions is an important part of being a good mediator.

   true   false

Strategy Focus: Telling the Difference Between Fact and Non-Fact

Read each of these statements carefully. Is the information a fact, or is it a non-fact—a judgment, opinion, or inference? Circle *fact* or *non-fact*.

1. Mediation is a problem-solving method.

   ~~fact~~   non-fact

2. A mediator's job is to keep two disputants physically apart.

   fact   ~~non-fact~~

3. The mediator must be in control of a mediation session.

   fact   ~~non-fact~~

4. A mediator's office is always neutral territory.

   ~~fact~~   non-fact

5. If two disputants start hitting each other, it is the mediator's fault.

   fact   ~~non-fact~~

6. Sitting in a low, soft, and comfortable chair makes a person feel less angry.

   ~~fact~~   non-fact

7. You can establish rapport with another person by smiling at that person.

   ~~fact~~   non-fact

8. To prevent the two disputants from talking to each other, a mediator says, "Tell me; talk to me."

   ~~fact~~   non-fact

9. A "leading question" is one that can put ideas in the head of another person.

   ~~fact~~   non-fact

10. It is best to deal with one problem at a time.

    ~~fact~~   non-fact

Strategy Focus: Recognizing Fighting Words

Some words and expressions are inflammatory. They make the people who hear them feel angry or upset. As you read through the following conversations, circle the words or expressions that you think will make the other person or people in the conversation feel bad, angry, or resentful.

1. At the dry-cleaning establishment:

   Ann: I've come to pick up my clean laundry. Here's the slip.

   Clerk: I'm sorry, sir. This slip is for Tuesday pickup. It's only Saturday.

   Ann: You mean my laundry isn't ready yet?

   Clerk: I'm afraid not, sir.

   Ann: Things are never done right here. You must have a bunch of lazy workers running this place.

2. On the telephone:

   Adamson: You listen, John Franklin; it's about these ugly brown streaks on the new driveway I paid you to put in just a couple of months ago.

   Franklin: Listen, Tony, I told your wife that would happen.

   Adamson: Are you saying that those streaks are her fault? When you're the one who made the mess?

   Franklin: That's right. She was too stupid to listen to what I was saying and too pigheaded to try to understand the problem. She was the ignorant one who got on a high horse and overruled my decision.

   Adamson: Who are you saying is stubborn?

3. Robert Billison calls Angela Clark:

   Billison: Mrs. Clark?

   Clark: Yes?

   Billison: Are you the one who is always stuffing your stinking garbage into my garbage can?

   Clark: I beg your pardon?

   Billison: I saw you this morning—secretly dumping your trash into my bin. Were you or were you not in the alley this morning?

   Clark: Yes, I walked through the alley this morning, picking up the trash that careless people like you drop on the ground.

Billison: And did you or did you not put your garbage in my bin?

Clark: Really! I have no idea where I put the filthy mess I picked up—whether it was in your garbage can or someone else's.

Billison: Aha! So you admit it! You are the thief who is stealing the space in my garbage can!

4. In the parking lot:

Man 1:   Just look at the way you parked! Couldn't you park straight? Now whoever parks there is going to hit the side of my car when he opens the door of his car. Don't you care about parking straight?

Man 2:   I had to park this way; there were no other places, and the cars on both sides of me were parked crooked.

Man 1:   Sure, nice guy! Go ahead, blame someone else. Don't you ever take responsibility for your own actions?

Man 2:   And why don't you take responsibility for your mouth?

Strategy: Writing About the Ideas

1. How do you know when a person is angry? Words? Actions? The look on the person's face? Write about how you know what a person's feelings are. First make a list of feelings, and then write about how you know that another person has those feelings.

2. Some words in every language are considered "bad language." Think about this idea, that words can be "bad." How do they become "bad" words? Think about absolute language. Words like *always* and *never* are absolutes. If something never happens, then it can't *sometimes* happen or even happen once in a while. What do you think of using bad words or absolute words?

3. Other words are inflammatory; they cause anger as a response. In English, expressions like *big*, *fat*, and *stupid* cause fights. Expressions that compare people's actions to animal actions are also inflammatory: *Don't hog the food*, *Don't pig out*, *Don't monkey with that*, and *Stop horsing around*. What other words or expressions make people angry? Write a list of reasons that some language has so much power over people's emotions.

Strategy Focus: Keeping a Vocabulary Journal

Choose five words from the new words in this unit to be your target words.

Write the words here: _____ _____

_____ _____ _____

Now write them into your vocabulary journal. Remember to include the
following parts:
- your target word
- the sentence from the unit in which your target word appears
- a definition, including the part of speech.
- some sentences of your own

Strategy: Increasing Reading Speed

 Timed Reading

Excuses, Excuses

To err is human. To blame the other person
is even more human.

Common sense is not all that common.

Why tell the truth when you can come up
with a good excuse?

These three popular misquotes are meant to be jokes, and
yet they give us a great deal of information about human
nature. To err, or to make mistakes, is indeed a part of being
human, but it seems that most people don't want to accept
the responsibility for having made a mistake. They naturally
look for someone else who could be responsible for the problem.
Perhaps it is the natural thing to do. The original version of
the misquote was a quote about human nature. When it was
first said, it went like this: "To err is human, to forgive, divine."

In this saying we have an ideal: people should be forgiving of others' mistakes. Instead, it seems, we are likely to do the opposite—find someone else to shift the blame to. However, taking responsibility for something that went wrong is a mark of great maturity.

Common sense is what we call clear thought: "That's not brilliant. It's just common sense." Having common sense means having a good general plan that will make things work well, and it also means staying with the plan. Common sense means that you buy the food you need for a dinner party with enough time to cook it, but not so early that you need to store the food. Common sense tells you that you take an umbrella out into a rainstorm, but you leave the umbrella home when you hear a weather forecast for sunshine. Common sense does not seem to be common for large organizations (like governments, for example) because there are so many things going on that one person cannot be in charge of everything. People say that in government, "the right hand does not know what the left hand is doing."

And what is wrong with a society that thinks that making up a good excuse is like creating a work of art? One of the common problems with making excuses is that people, especially young people, get the idea that it's okay not to be totally honest all the time. There is a corollary to that: if a good excuse is "good," even if it isn't honest, then where is the place of the truth?

Time: _____

Now answer these questions as quickly as you can.

1. Common sense is something that…
   a. most people should have.
   b. one learns in school.
   c. governments use well.
   d. contains the answers to many questions.

2. The meaning of the word err is…
   a. a mistake.
   b. to solve a problem.
   c. to make a mistake.
   d. to go away.

3. According to the reading, which is the most human?
   a. to forgive
   b. to blame others
   c. to search for truth
   d. to find a way

4. According to the ideal, it is good to…
   a. shift the responsibility to others.
   b. blame others for things that go wrong.
   c. misquote popular sayings for fun.
   d. forgive other people's mistakes.

5. A better title for this reading is…
   a. Getting Food for a Dinner Party.
   b. It's Human Nature.
   c. Listen to Your Weather Forecaster.
   d. Using Quotes in Your Writing.

A SLICE OF LIFE

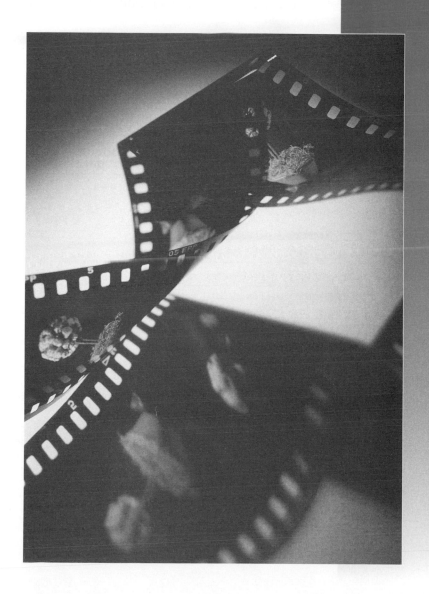

 **Preparation**

Strategies for Anticipation

Think about the title and the word *slice*. Think of a slice of bread, a slice of cake, a slice of meatloaf, a slice of cheese. What could a *slice of life* mean?

Look at a loaf of bread. You see the outside. It is brown, the color of baked flour. When you cut it, however, the inside may be white or brown—depending on the flour. Is a slice of life the same way? Is what you find inside also a surprise?

How is a short story or a novel like a slice of life?
When you read a story, do you look into people's lives?
How much do you see?

How is a movie like a short story or a novel?
How important is the *setting* (the place where the story takes place)?
How important is the *plot* (the series or sequence of events in the story)?
How important are the *characters* (the personalities of the people in the story)?

Survey this unit.

What are the titles of the readings? List them here:

_____

_____

_____

_____

_____

As you look into these pages, what do you understand about this unit?
What are the main ideas?
Which of these ideas is likely to be in the unit? Write a check (✓) in front of each likely idea for this unit.

_____ Information about actors and the difficulties of being famous

_____ How a movie is made

_____ Geographical information about Hollywood

_____ The responsibility of a moviemaker

_____ The kinds of movies that people enjoy most

_____ Information about poetry and people who write poetry

Main Reading

A Slice of Life

1 It always starts with a story. Here is Laurie's story. Laurie was born almost forty years ago. When she was still quite young, Laurie's mother became m*entally ill* and was taken to a hospital for *treatment*. For a while Laurie lived with her grandmother, Thelma, and the rest of her aunts and uncles on a poor *ranch* in Utah. Thelma had to move to a community in northern Mexico because she couldn't *support* her children. There, among *relatives*, she and her large family were able to survive. When Laurie was about eight years old, she was taken by one of her uncles to live with his family in the *jungle* in Nicaragua. For seven years, she lived in the hot, wet, tropical forest with her aunt and uncle. She worked hard, doing the housework and taking care of her baby *cousins*, living under harsh conditions.

2 When she was about sixteen years old, she escaped. With the help of some kind people, she made her way to California. She got a job doing what she had always done—taking care of children. This time, however, she lived with a family. The parents were busy professionals, a professor and a medical doctor. Shirley and Ted had two children to take care of and needed help. Shirley (the doctor) hired Laurie.

She gave Laurie a job, a home, and a family. She also helped Laurie find her mother and visit her in the hospital where she was living. When Shirley and Ted's children grew up and no longer needed a *nanny*, Laurie left the best home she had ever had and got several other jobs. Eventually she took the GED exam (a exam that shows whether a person knows as much as a high school graduate), and went to college. She wanted to be a writer.

3   Laurie wrote a book of stories about her life. These stories were like slices of her life. They were about a child who was *observant*, clever, and sensitive. They were about her life with her mother and grandmother. Laurie tried to sell her book of stories to publishers, and she collected *rejection* letters. No one wanted to publish her book. Then, she decided to try to turn her story into a *screenplay*. For this purpose, she read screenplay after screenplay and books about how to turn a story into a *script* for a movie. She had written her stories about the things that were familiar to her, about life on a community farm in northern Mexico, and about living in the jungle of Nicaragua.

4   Now she was going to write a play for a movie, so she had to change the stories. She had to create a single plot or story line out of her own life. Toward this goal, she introduced some new characters and *reduced* the number of members of Thelma's family. They were not necessary for the story that she wanted to tell. It was necessary to *fictionalize* her story; that is, she had to change details to make an interesting story. Just any story won't make a good movie. She had to describe the setting: the mango trees, the river, the jungle storms. And she had to put it all into 125 pages of screenplay.

5   Laurie's screenplay is in Hollywood now. She has to convince someone in a movie *agency* to read the screenplay because no one will buy it if no one ever reads it. She has to find an *agent* for it because movie producers only deal with agents. When Laurie finds an agency to represent her, she hopes the agency will find a producer to make her story into a movie.

6   Laurie's story is about a child and her warm and loving mother who is also mentally *unstable*. It is the story of a child who grew up speaking two languages, both Spanish and English. The screenplay is for a family movie. Of course, there are many different types, or *genres* (ZHAN-raz) of movies such as cowboy movies, detective or police stories, spy movies, historical movies, and comedies. A family movie contains nothing that children should not see. Laurie's screenplay is about a family, although it is an unusual one. And it is a story that children will enjoy.

7   Every movie, like every good story, must have a conflict of some kind. The conflict is the problem that must be solved. For Laurie the conflict was how to escape from her uncle because she was only a servant to the family. She wanted a life of her own. In addition, she wanted to know where her mother was. Although her mother was *mentally ill*, she was also a kind and loving mother. Laurie loved her mother and worried about her when she was so far away. She knew in her heart that she wanted to be able to take care of her mother. That's why she wanted to escape.

8   Laurie thinks her story will make a good movie. Meanwhile, the screenplay is sitting on a desk somewhere in Hollywood. Perhaps someone will pick it up and start reading it. Perhaps that person will like the story, and maybe you'll be able to see the story of Laurie's mother, May Blossom, on the screen one day.

Strategy Focus: Analyzing the Sequence of a Story

The story of Laurie in "A Slice of Life" is mainly written in chronological order, or time order. Notice the words that indicate time and underline them as you complete the following exercise.

In each set of sentences below, number each sentence according to the time order in the story. Write *1* or the first event that happened, *2* for the second, *3* for the third, and so on. The first one is completed in each set.

1. Laurie…

   ____ found her mother and visited her in the hospital.

   ____ moved with her grandmother to northern Mexico.

   ____ lived on a poor ranch in Utah.

   _1_ lived with her grandmother because her mother became mentally ill.

   ____ lived with Shirley and Ted.

   ____ made her way to California.

   ____ was taken to live in the jungle in Nicaragua.

2. Laurie…

   ____ went to college.

   _1_ took the GED exam.

   ____ wrote a book of stories about her life.

   ____ read many screenplays.

   ____ wrote a screenplay.

3. She…

   ____ needs to find an agent.

   ____ introduced some new characters.

   ____ described the setting.

   _1_ changed the book of stories.

   ____ created a single story line about her life.

Strategy Focus: Discussing the Ideas

1. Why did Laurie move so many times? (to a ranch, to Mexico, to Nicaragua, to California)

2. Where did she truly have a home? What made that place a home for her?

3. Laurie feels a great deal of love for her mother. She also wants to take care of her. Why do you think she feels this way?

4. What is the difference between a book of stories and a screenplay? Why is the difference important?

5. What is the job of a nanny? What are a nanny's responsibilities? Why was Laurie a good nanny?

6. What conflict did Laurie feel when she was in Nicaragua?

7. Why does a movie have to have a conflict at the center of the story?

8. Do you think you would like Laurie? Why or why not?

9. Why does a beginning writer have to have another job?

10. What plot do you see in Laurie's life? Is it exciting enough to make a movie? Why or why not?

Strategy Focus: Finding the Main Idea

A. Which of these titles could work for Laurie's story? Note that more than one might be appropriate. Check (✓) all that are suitable, and tell why the others are not.

____ A Doctor Named Shirley

____ May Blossom's Daughter

____ On a Ranch in Utah

____ My Grandmother Thelma

____ Laurie's Story

____ Making a Screenplay for a Movie Out of a Book of Short Stories

B. Make up another title for the story: _____

Strategy Focus: Learning Vocabulary in Context

1. **agency**, **agent**

   Laurie has to convince someone in a movie **agency** to read the screenplay because no one will buy it if no one ever reads it.

   She has to find an **agent** for it because movie producers only deal with **agents**.

   A real estate **agent** can help a family sell a house or buy a house. Agents know all the laws, and they know how to get the best price, arrange for insurance, and set up payments. Usually there are several **agents** in one **agency**. They share office space and expertise.

   An **agent** is a _____ .

   An **agency** is a _____ .

2. **relative**, **cousin**

   Thelma had to move to a community in northern Mexico because she couldn't support her children. There, among **relatives**, she and her large family were able to survive.

   For seven years, she lived there with her aunt and uncle. She worked hard, doing the housework and taking care of her baby **cousins**, living under harsh conditions.

   Parents, grandparents, aunts, uncles and **cousins** are members of a person's extended family. Relatives usually know where the other members of their family are.

   Relatives are _____ .

   Cousins are _____ .

3. **fictionalize**, **genre**

   It was necessary for Laurie to **fictionalize** her story; that is, she had to change details to make an interesting story.

   Of course, there are many different types, or **genres** (ZHAN-raz) of movies such as cowboy movies, detective or police stories, spy movies, historical movies, and comedies.

   To **fictionalize** means to _____ .

   A **genre** is a _____ .

4. **rejection letter**

   Laurie tried to sell her book of stories to publishers, and she collected **rejection letters**.

   Most story writers know that it is not easy to publish a book. They send the stories to publishing companies and get **rejection letters**. Some companies do not accept manuscripts at all. They simply send letters saying that they are not interested in the book.

   A **rejection letter** is a letter from _____ .

5. **nanny**

   Laurie got a job doing what she had always done–taking care of children. When Shirley and Ted's children grew up and no longer needed a **nanny**, Laurie left the best home she had ever had…

   A **nanny** is a person who _____ .

6. **jungle**

   Laurie was taken by one of her uncles to live with his family in the **jungle** in Nicaragua. For seven years, she lived in the hot, wet tropical forest with her aunt and uncle.

   Tarzan lived in a **jungle**.

   My room needs cleaning; it's like a **jungle**!

   A **jungle** is a _____ .

7. **mentally ill, unstable, mental illness**

   When she was still quite young, Laurie's mother became **mentally ill** and was taken to a hospital for treatment.

   Mental illness is a problem of lack of balance in one's ability to think clearly and understand what is happening around him or her.

   Laurie's story is about a child and a warm and loving woman who is also **mentally unstable**.

   If a person is **unstable**, he or she may need to see a doctor or a psychologist for help. There is help for most people with **mental illnesses**.

   A person who is **mentally ill** needs _____ .

   An **unstable** person cannot _____ .

   A **mental illness** is a problem of _____ .

8. **observant**

   The child watched everyone's actions; because she was **observant**, she knew who had left the house last.

   An **observant** person always knows what to buy for another person as a gift.

   An **observant** person is one who _____ .

9. **ranch**

   Thelma and her children lived on a poor **ranch** in Utah.

   The movie star has a cattle **ranch** in Montana.

   The land was too dry for a farm, but the grasses and other vegetation made it a good **ranch** for sheep or cattle.

   A **ranch** is a _____ .

10. **reduce**

    The woman went on a diet to **reduce** her weight.

    The salesperson **reduced** the price $10 because of the damage to the product.

    Laurie **reduced** the number of characters because a movie needs only a few characters.

    To **reduce** is to _____ .

11. **support**

    Thelma had to move to a community in northern Mexico because she couldn't **support** her children. There, among relatives, she and her large family were able to survive.

    It is true that a child needs **support** in the form of food, clothing, and love. The most important kind of **support** is love, respect, and security.

    Most parents want to **support** their children's education with money. Because going to school can be very difficult, most parents need to give emotional **support** like encouraging words, too.

    To **support** is to _____ .

    Emotional **support** or financial **support** means _____ .

12. **treatment**

When she was still quite young, Laurie's mother became mentally ill and was taken to a hospital for **treatment**.

The teacher gave the students in the writing class a sentence to begin to write with. Then she observed the different kinds of **treatment** each writer gave to the idea.

What do you think is proper **treatment** by parents for children who do not tell the truth? How should the parents act toward such children?

Treatment has several meanings. For a sick person, treatment is

_____ .

For a writer, a **treatment** of a topic is _____ .

How parents **treat** their children is how they _____
toward them.

13. **screenplay, script**

No one wanted to publish Laurie's book. Then, she decided to try to turn her story to a **screenplay**. For this purpose, she read **screenplay** after **screenplay** and then books about how to turn a story into a **script** for a movie.

The **screenplay** for an average movie is about 125 pages long.

The movie **script** was full of interesting dialogue for actors to speak.

A **screenplay** is a story that is _____ .

A **script** is also a _____ .

Strategy: Understanding the Audience

In movie-making, the audience is the group of people who sit in a theater and watch the movie. In teaching and in storytelling of any kind, the teacher or storyteller must know who is sitting out there. A movie is fiction, not a totally true story, but the moviemaker wants the audience to believe. What does the moviemaker do to create this willingness to believe on the part of the audience?

Related Reading 1

The Business of Magic: The Movie Industry

1   Movies are *illusion*. What we see is not real, but we react to it as if it were real. Movies are the best way (thus far) of telling a story because, like a slice of life, we see and hear the characters. We see and feel their emotions. We see what they see as the action of the story unfolds.

2   The success of a movie comes from its ability to *involve* the audience. We as the viewers are meant to feel the events of the movie as directly as possible, and not to understand that our emotions are being controlled by others. The moviemaker's ability to involve us, the audience, in the movie is his or her skill. This skill is the *art* of telling a story that is alive on the screen before us so that we feel as though we are part of the story.

3   Movies are the art form of the past century. Thomas Edison and his assistant William Dickson made the first film in the late nineteenth century. The instant success of the moving pictures encouraged others to develop the machinery and the technology for today's movies. Little more than one hundred years ago, in the late 1800s and the early 1900s, movies were silent (without sound) and black and white only. People in great crowds came to see the moving pictures, and the movie industry was born.

4   In a theater today, the action on the big screen and the sound absorb us as viewers. We surrender our disbelief and enter into the *magic* of a story. Think about the magic. Consider the psychology of creating *comedy*, *tragedy*, *action*, and *horror*. What makes people laugh? Why makes people cry? What *shocks* us, surprises us deeply? And what frightens us? These human emotional responses are the responses that moviemakers want to bring out in the audience. The craft (the work) of creating these responses is the art of the moviemaker.

Helping viewers forget the rest of the world—and about the people "behind the scenes"—is part of the craft of moviemaking.

5   The movie must remove the watchers from the rest of the world for the time they are in the theater. The movie must have the energy to make people think of nothing else while they watch. It is a kind of magic, but consider how *fragile* the *spell* is. For example, performers must not look directly into the camera because the actor would see us, the audience, and the make-believe environment would be destroyed. The fragile spell would be broken. Our presence (and the ruining effect of being watched) would destroy the film.

Strategy Focus: Scanning for Details

1. Who invented the first moving picture? (Look for capital letters.)

   _____

2. When were movies silent? (Look for numbers.) _____

3. Who was William Dickson? (Look for his name.) _____

4. What does craft mean? (Look for parentheses.) _____

Strategy Focus: Exploring the Ideas

Read the sentences below. Which ones tell why a movie is the best way of telling a story (until now, that is!)? Write a check (✓) in front of each correct answer.

_____ The audience can see the actors and hear their words.

_____ A person who is watching a movie believes in the realness of the movie.

_____ The audience is watching a slice of life.

_____ The audience experiences the whole story in a short period of time (about two hours).

_____ A movie is colorful and interesting.

_____ A movie puts a spell over the viewers.

_____ Every movie has a conflict which interests the audience.

_____ Famous people are on the screen.

Strategy Focus: Making Inferences

Do you think there is enough information to make these statements? Check (✓) *enough* or *not enough*.

1. If something stops the illusion of the movie, the audience loses interest.
   ☐ enough   ☐ not enough

2. The moviemaker controls the emotions of the people in the audience.
   ☐ enough   ☐ not enough

3. No one liked silent movies, so sound had to be added.
   ☐ enough   ☐ not enough

4. A story about a family losing a member and trying to deal with it is likely to be a tragedy.
   ☐ enough   ☐ not enough

5. Thomas Edison was a very clever, smart person.
   ☐ enough   ☐ not enough

6. Moviemakers need to know a lot about human psychology.
   ☐ enough   ☐ not enough

7. Actors who look into the camera don't become famous.

☐ enough   ☐ not enough

8. Some actions in a movie can destroy the make-believe environment of a movie.

☐ enough   ☐ not enough

Strategy Focus: Learning Vocabulary in Context

1. **art**

   The craft (the work) of creating these responses is the **art** of the moviemaker.

   Movies are the **art** form of the past century.

   The most popular **arts** are painting, architecture, design, and ceramics.

   She makes cooking an ordinary dinner seem like an **art**.

   Art refers to _____ .

   An **art** is something that _____ .

2. **comedy, tragedy**

   Consider the psychology of creating **comedy**, **tragedy**, action, and horror. What makes people laugh? What makes people cry?

   Everyone thought that the new **comedy** show on television was very funny, but they didn't think the **tragedy** was sad.

   The tragedy of the story was that the main character did not learn anything at all.

   A **comedy** show is one that _____ .

   Some people _____ when they see a play that is a **tragedy**.

3. **emotional response**

   These human **emotional responses** are the responses that moviemakers want to bring out in the audience.

   Her **emotional response** to getting flowers from her husband was to cry tears of happiness.

   An **emotional response** happens when _____ .

4. **horror, shock**

Consider the psychology of creating comedy, tragedy, action, and **horror**. What makes people laugh? What makes people cry? What **shocks** us and surprises us deeply?

It is common for people to scream in fear at a **horror** movie. Some people like being **shocked** by terrible things in movies.

When the truck left the road and hit the building, a **shock** went through the whole structure. The scene of the accident was a **horror** because many people were badly hurt.

A **horror** movie is one that _____ .

A **shock** or something that **shocks** is something that _____

_____ people.

5. **illusion, magic, spell**

Movies are **illusion**. What we see is not real, but we react to it as if it were real.

It is a kind of **magic**, but consider how fragile the **spell** is…the make-believe environment would be destroyed.

The show had a famous magician. His magic seemed to change the rules of nature. He pulled rabbits out of his hat and used mirrors to create an **illusion** of cutting a person in half. His show was very good. The audience watched with great interest, and the **spell** did not end until the curtain came down and the show ended.

An **illusion** is something that is _____ .

Magic refers to something that seems not to be _____ .

A **spell** is a _____ .

6. **fragile**

It is a kind of magic, but consider how **fragile** the spell is…the make-believe environment would be destroyed. The **fragile** spell would be broken.

There was glass in the package, but it was also marked **FRAGILE** so everyone was careful with it.

Something that is **fragile** is easily _____ .

7. **involve**

> The moviemaker's ability to **involve** us, the audience, in the movie is his or her skill. This skill is the art of telling a story that is alive on the screen before us so that we feel as though we are part of the story.
>
> My parents are **involved** in many activities, like a school board, a church choir, and a book study group.
>
> To be involved in something means that _____ .

Strategy Focus: Understanding Sequence

As you read the next related reading, pay attention to the order of events in making a movie. You will have some questions to answer about the sequence.

Strategy: Finding Meanings in the Reading

Note the words in *italics*. Look for meanings for those words in the reading.

 # Related Reading 2

How an Idea Becomes a Movie

1   The process of making a movie starts with an idea for a story. Some movie scripts come as fully written screenplays. However, the first step is usually a short summary of the story, with information about the plot or story line and the characters, but no information about the scenes or dialogue. This summary is called the treatment. In a treatment, the emotional appeal and the content must be clear. Most story treatments are just a few pages long, never more than thirty. The purpose of the treatment is to attract interest. First a producer must be interested. The producer is the businessperson who collects the money, the people, and the equipment to make the movie. It is for people like the producer to judge whether the *public* (the people who will come to see the movie) will like it and to attract *investors* (people whose money will pay the cost of production).

2   A treatment becomes a screenplay when the dialogue is added. The screenplay writer includes only necessary directions for action. The director will interpret the screenplay, so the screenplay writer gives *minimal instructions*. Directors like to make their own decisions.

3   The investor, the person with money for a movie production, wants to support a movie that will make money. The investor, therefore, might reject unusual plots or characters that are too unusual. Investors are taking a risk in any case. A movie must make a lot of money before it pays for itself and gives monetary rewards to the investors.

4   A *bankable star* is essential to a movie's success. If a movie does not have at least one big-name actor, like Brad Pitt or Julia Roberts, then a movie must have a big-name director or producer, like George Lucas or Steven Spielberg, or be a story by a big-name writer, like J. K. Rowling (who created the character Harry Potter). Moviegoers know that big-name stars act in good movies, so they choose movies to see based on the stars. Big-budget films require lots of special effects and large *casts*—many actors and extras, maybe a thousand people hired for one day's work in a movie. Small-budget movies have fewer numbers of actors and no scenes with many extras. Small-*budget* movie proposals have a greater chance of becoming films in movie theaters because they do not cost as much to make.

5   A movie is proposed to investors as a *package deal*. Usually, this "package" means a director, some specific actors, a budget, and a schedule for production. The producer of the movie tells the investors how much it will cost and what the profits should be. Investors buy into the package or decide not to. When there is enough money to make the movie, production can begin.

6   The first steps to making a movie require a time schedule and a budget. Before a movie can be made, people to make it are hired. It takes a large group to make a movie, even a low-budget movie. Casting (choosing the actors), hiring production crews, finding places to do the filming (*locations*), and arranging for lodging and food as well as transportation of the cast, the expert people, and equipment—these are all part of making a movie.

Strategy Focus: Determining the Sequence

Put the following phrases in order:

____ casting

____ putting together a package deal

____ the treatment

____ the time schedule and the budget

____ filming the movie

____ the screenplay

____ finding investors

Strategy Focus: Pulling Meaning out of Context

1. Some movie stars are **bankable stars**? What makes them *bank*-able?

2. What is a **budget**?

3. What is the **cast** of a movie?

4. What do **investors** provide?

5. What is a **location**?

6. A screenplay is very short and has **minimal instructions**. Is that a lot of directions or not many?

7. Who are the **public**? Why do moviemakers care about the public?

8. Describe a **package deal**. What must the package include?

Strategy Focus: Finding the Difference

What is the difference between...

1. a small-budget movie and a big-budget movie? (Name several differences.)
2. a treatment and a screenplay?
3. a cast and an actor?
4. any movie actor and a bankable star?
5. a producer and an investor?

Strategy Focus: Finding Details in the Reading

1. Who is J. K. Rowling?
2. What job does George Lucas do?
3. Name two big-name stars.

Strategy: Discussing Ideas

1. What kind of movies do you like?
2. How many genres of movies can you name? Write them here:

    _____ _____ _____

    _____ _____ _____

3. Are there any genres that you don't like?
4. Would you choose a movie based on the actors in it? Why or why not?
5. Do you care who the director of a movie is? Why or why not?
6. If you had fifty million dollars, and if you were interested in investing in a movie, what kind of package deal would you want? (Describe your ideal package deal.)
7. Do you think you would like to be involved in making a movie? In what job?
8. A movie budget must be able to pay for lodging for the cast and the moviemakers when they are on location. What do you think lodging is?
9. What do you think costs the most in making a movie? Why do you think so?

Related Reading 3

Who's Who in the Movie Credits

1   It takes a movie-making army to make a movie. As the movie begins, the credits roll. As the movie ends, more names are listed. The credits go to the people who did the labor of making the film. To moviemakers, the credits are an important part of the whole experience of the film because they made the film, using their expertise. Looking at the credits for a movie can tell one a great deal about the business.

2   The *producer's* name is probably the first one on the screen. The investors contract with the producer to oversee all the work of making the movie. The producer must bring together the materials and the people for the film project. Moreover, he or she must stay within a budget (a plan for spending the money).

3   Next the credits will list the *actors*. They are the players. Movie stars are well-known actors; people like Hugh Grant, Susan Sarandon, Pierce Brosnan, and Gwyneth Paltrow can make a movie a hit (a money-making movie that everyone wants to see). Customers for the product (in this case, people who are willing to pay to see the movie) often choose a movie based on the actors. Supporting players (actors with smaller roles and maybe less fame) come next on the credits.

4   The person who wrote the screenplay (the *screenwriter*) is usually listed next. If the story comes from a novel or short story and is an adaptation, the writer is usually also included in the credits.

5   The director of cinematography (moving picture photography) is responsible for how the film looks. He or she is in charge of the lighting crew, camera operators, and other technicians. This job involves working with light, with foreground (in front of the actors) and the background, with color. The *cinematographer* also works with the art director and the costume designers. Art direction involves set design. Costume design requires blending the clothing of the actors

with the background of the set. Movie making is an art, so harmony among the colors and lines makes the audience feel a sense of harmony among the people. When the colors clash, the audience senses that all is not peaceful in the story. The names of *art directors* and *costume designers* are always in the credits for a movie.

6   Next to be listed is usually the *musical director*. Today musical composers do not write symphonies like Mozart and Beethoven; they write movie scores. Every movie has a musical theme, and the music develops along with the story line, or plot. The musical theme is repeated throughout the movie; the audience associates the music with the feelings of the film. When action is exciting or dangerous, the music speeds up, and so do the heartbeats in the audience. During romantic scenes on the screen, the violins play soft music. All the music is adapted to the action of the script.

7   Before the movie actually begins, the last of the credits rolls. Usually the last name is the *director's* name. The last credit is the position of honor. And of all the production crew, the director has the biggest job. He or she works with all the people who are making the movie. The director is the one who creates a working plan from the screenplay, directs the performers and the camera crew during the filming, and also oversees the post-production of the film.

8   The people whose names are listed after the film is over are part of the movie-making army. These secondary credits usually begin with the *editor*. During the shooting of the movie, a director orders many "takes" of every scene. The camera moves in from different angles. The actors have slightly different expressions on their faces. The lighting may be different. Every evening the director and the editor watch all the film from that day. The final version of the movie will be made up of parts from many separate takes. The editor, with the director of the film, decides how the film becomes a single two to two-and-a-half-hour long story on film. Most film editing is done by an editor with a computer these days.

9   Next the credit for the sound and sound mixing appears on the screen. It is necessary for a *sound mixer* to coordinate and balance the actors' words, the sound effects (like a door closing, traffic sounds from outside a window, the sound of rain), and music. The names of the *camera operators* and the *grips* and *gaffers* (the people who do the physical work of moving lights, cables, camera tracks) may also be on the credits.

10   The names of the *property master* (or *manager*), the *makeup artists,* the *costume designers*, the *hairstylists*, and the *special effects* companies come next. There is also one person called *continuity*. Continuity keeps records of every scene, every actor, details of dress and props, and actors' places on the set. In one movie, continuity failed when actress Jodie Foster got into a car wearing one pair of earrings and got out of the car (supposedly fifteen minutes later) wearing a different pair of earrings. Few people in the audience noticed. The *casting* may be done by one person or by an agency. Casting is selecting actors for small parts and is an important part of the whole project.

11   Some movies require large numbers of extra actors. These people do not have speaking roles, but they make up a crowd or an army. Classic movies, like the movie called *Cleopatra* truly did have a cast of thousands, but most of them were extras. In any case, it does take a large number of people and some highly skilled experts to make a movie. Because the movie is the major art form of these times, moviemakers of all expertise try to become the best in their field. When movie studios had their own crews, movies were made using the people in the studio. Today, however, every movie-making expert prefers to work with a small group of people, people he or she knows well. A producer and maybe a director will look for the technical people who have the expertise that they need to make a successful movie.

Strategy Focus: Making Inferences

Do you think there is enough information in the reading to make these statements? Check (✓) *enough* or *not enough*.

1. A bankable star is a guarantee that people will come to see the movie.
   ☐ enough   ☐ not enough

2. Continuity is the most important job on a moviemaking project.
   ☐ enough   ☐ not enough

3. Brad Pitt is a bankable star.
   ☐ enough   ☐ not enough

4. A particular movie would never be made if the producer didn't like the treatment.
   ☐ enough   ☐ not enough

5. If a screenplay is adapted from a novel, the novelist is probably not the screenwriter.
   ☐ enough   ☐ not enough

6. No symphonies are composed by musical composers today.
   ☐ enough   ☐ not enough

7. Every movie needs extras.
   ☐ enough   ☐ not enough

8. Movies sometimes need more money than is in the budget.
   ☐ enough   ☐ not enough

9. Mozart and Beethoven wrote symphonies.
   ☐ enough   ☐ not enough

10. Pierce Brosnan is a well-known actor.
    ☐ enough   ☐ not enough

11. In some movies, the directors want the colors of the costumes to clash with everything else on the set.
    ☐ enough   ☐ not enough

12. Violin music is romantic.

☐ enough   ☐ not enough

Strategy Focus: Discussing the Ideas

1. Most people like to know that they will have steady jobs, jobs that continue. Think about moviemakers. How steady are their jobs? How do you think the off and on aspect of their employment affects them? What does it mean about their pay for a job?

2. There is a lot of risk in the movie business. Where do you think the uncertainty comes from?

3. What do you think makes a movie a hit?

Strategy Focus: Scanning for Definitions

Scan the reading to find these names of jobs. Who does what job? Use the alphabetized list of jobs in a movie-making crew to show that you know which person does which job. Write the word or phrase in the blank. Be careful! Some of the terms may be used more than once.

actor	art director	camera operator
casting	cinematographer	continuity
costume designer	director	editor
gaffer	grips	hairstylist
investor	makeup artist	musical director
producer	property master	screenwriter
special effects	sound mixer	

1. The _____ combines the music for the movie with sound effects and the actors' voices.

2. An _____ provides money to make the film.

3. The _____ is the person who prepares the screenplay from a story or a treatment.

4. A _____ agency (or a single person) has the job of selecting supporting actors to play in a movie.

5. _____ keeps records of what each person was wearing at the end of one day to make sure the person is wearing the same thing the next.

6. Some movies are science fiction, about topics that do not exist in truth, so many _____ are needed to make the movie and create imaginary things.

7. Like a librarian with rooms full of books to manage, a _____ keeps records about special objects that are needed for movies.

8. An _____ appears as a person in the story of a movie.

9. The _____ and _____ need to know how hairstyles and makeup have changed so to be sure that actors look right for any period in history.

10. The _____ of a movie is in charge of getting the package deal together and making the deals with investors and actors.

11. The _____ is in charge of pre-production, production, and post-production, working with every person on the technical staff and the cast.

12. A _____ designs or develops a musical theme and writes the music to achieve a specific effect.

13. The _____ creates a working plan from the screenplay, directs the performers and the camera crew during the filming, and also oversees the post-production of the film.

14. _____ chooses and hires the extras.

15. The _____ is responsible for how the film looks. He or she is in charge of the lighting crew, camera operators, and other technicians. This job involves working with light, with foreground (in front of the actors) and the background, with color.

16. The _____ is involved with set design.

17. The _____ blends or contrasts the clothing of the actors with the background of the set.

18. The physical labor of moving things around a movie is the work of _____ and _____ .

19. The _____ turns hours and hours of film into a movie by choosing the parts of the film and putting them together into a two-hour film.

20. The _____ sits behind a huge machine, looks through a small opening, and takes moving pictures of the action on the movie set.

Strategy Focus: Determining Meanings of Words and Phrases in Context

Select *a, b,* or *c* to best answer the question or finish the sentence.

1. What is the job of supporting actors?
   a. They have important parts, but not the main parts in a movie.
   b. They take the place of the main actors in some scenes.
   c. They hold up the other actors.

2. For a movie, what do extras need?
   a. They need to learn how to be actors.
   b. They need minimal instructions and costumes.
   c. They need to learn their lines of dialogue.

3. The skill of taking moving pictures for a film is the art of…
   a. investing.
   b. directing a movie.
   c. cinematography.

4. The person who keeps records of details like costumes, position of props, and people's places on a set is called…
   a. a director.   b. continuity.   c. producer.

5. If a person is in charge of casting, that person's job is…
   a. to select the people who will be actors or extras in the movie.
   b. to take care of the equipment that is necessary to make a movie.
   c. to find people with money who want to support the making of a movie.

6. The clothing that actors wear comes from which department?
   a. design   b. sound   c. costume

7. The job of the _____ is to review all the film that the camera people take, to select the best shots, and to arrange them into a movie.
   a. continuity   b. editor   c. property master

8. At the beginning and the end of the film, the list of actors, the producer, the director, and the technical people is shown. This is the list of…
   a. credits.   b. investors.   c. costumes.

9. Colors may blend together in pleasing harmony, or they might…
   a. agree   b. clash.   c. be good together.

10. A movie that many people come to see and therefore makes a lot of money is…
    a. a hit.   b. a big-budget film.   c. not a success.

11. Musical composers used to write symphonies, but now they write…
    a. movie themes.
    b. movie scores.
    c. musical responses.

12. Which is an example of a sound effect?

    a. props

    b. the sound of cars on a road outside

    c. a sound stage

Strategy Focus: Expanding the Meanings of Words

What so you think these sentences mean? Some of the new words in this unit are used in these sentences, but in somewhat different ways. Select *a* or *b*, whichever meaning seems closer to the meaning of the number item.

1. Don't wear that red skirt and red sweater together. The reds clash.

    a. Although both items of clothing are red, they are not the same red and do not look good together.

    b. That sweater and skirt have a special kind of harmony of color that is pleasing to the eye.

2. We are buying some new bedroom furniture—a bed, a dresser, a bedside lamp, and a comfortable chair. We can buy them separately, but as a package deal, the cost is $125 less than buying them individually.

    a. It is cheaper to buy a number of pieces of furniture individually, or one piece at a time.

    b. It is cheaper to buy a number of pieces of furniture in a group for one price.

3 We have invested our money in houses.

    a. We paid a lot of money for some houses.

    b. We put our money into houses, not the bank.

4. This house was designed for a large family.

    a. The plan for this house is suitable for a large family.

    b. A large family built this house.

5. I have finished writing a paper for my history class. Will you please edit it for me?

    a. Will you write my history paper for me?

    b. Will you read and check my history paper?

6. The designer created a room with white walls, white rugs on the floor, and all white furniture. The effect was shocking, but cool.

   a. The result of an all-white room was a feeling of coolness.

   b. No one likes the cold all-white room.

7. According to the family budget, we can spend $100 a week on food.

   a. The plan for spending money on food is $100 a week.

   b. We are spending $100 a week too much on food.

8. Her parents do not approve of her involvement with music and dance.

   a. She stays away from everything that is about music and dance.

   b. She enjoys music and dance, but her parents do not like it.

9. Look at this photograph. It is a picture of my family with our house in the background.

   a. Look at this nice picture of my family's home!

   b. You can see our home behind the family in this picture.

10. The children went to the dentist for a special treatment on their teeth to prevent tooth problems in the future.

    a. The dentist did something to make the children's teeth stronger.

    b. The children needed to have the dentist's help with some tooth problems.

11. The inside walls and supporting structures in the ceiling hold up the second floor of the building.

    a. A house with two floors must have strong walls and ceilings so that a second floor can be built on top of the first floor.

    b. A house cannot have a second floor because walls are not usually strong enough to hold it up.

12. Everyone in the community is asked to donate food for the poor by bringing food in cans to the concert.

    a. There is not enough food to continue the Food for the Poor program.

    b. The Food for the Poor program can continue another year because of the food donations.

Strategy: Writing About the Ideas

1. A slice of someone's life can be a good story. Write about a slice of your life that you think others might enjoy knowing about.

2. If you could be in the movie business, which of the many roles would you want to play? Would you want to be an actor or a director? Would you like to work with props or costumes? Do you think you would like screenwriting, operating a camera, or editing? Or would you prefer to work in advertising the movie? The only role that you may not choose is "investor," because investors don't do anything except spend lots of money. Choose one role and list what you think you would do in that job. Then write a paragraph about this part of the movie industry.

3. In the film, two people are sitting on a park bench. The fog is rolling in from the ocean, and they are cold. Half a yard (about 1.5 meters) from the park bench is an ugly machine. It is making fog for the movie scene. A technician is holding a large piece of cardboard and slowing waving it in front of the fog machine. The fog moves over the two actors on the park bench. Movies are illusions. What is your opinion?

Strategy Focus: Keeping a Vocabulary Journal

Choose five words from the new words in this unit to be your target words.

Write the words here: _____ _____

_____ _____ _____

Now write them into your vocabulary journal. Remember to include the following parts:
- your target word
- the sentence from the unit in which your target word appears
- a definition, including the part of speech.
- some sentences of your own

Strategy: Increasing Reading Speed

 Timed Reading

The Studio System

Movie-making factories were called studios. Like all other businesses in a free enterprise system, they had to follow the rules of good business. There was a person in charge, usually someone with a powerful personality. The strength of character was necessary so that the "boss" could deal with famous stars and rich investors. The top man in a studio (there was never a woman in this job) ran the studio. Some movie stars had exclusive contracts with one studio. They could not work for another. Big studios like Columbia, Fox, Metro-Goldwyn-Mayer, Paramount, RKO, United Artists, and Warner Brothers were the most important film-making companies in Hollywood, and at the time, in the world.

Studios had lots of workers and overhead costs. Overhead refers to the money for everyday operations. The studio had to make enough money to pay everyone. For example, studios had their own screenwriters. They had production crews, filming and sound equipment, offices, and marketing staff. A studio had warehouses full of props. Props (or properties) are items and objects that might be needed for a movie. Old cars, furniture of all kinds, everything from old-fashioned schoolbooks to streetlights, and costumes were all property of the studio. Like a librarian, the studio property manager had to be able to find any needed prop fast.

In the studio system, a movie was under the control of the studio manager, usually a producer. A studio employee (or a group of employees) wrote the scripts for the movies. A director was chosen to coordinate the parts. Art directors and camera experts worked with the director to imagine the finished film. Studio costume designers and set designers worked with the director to plan the work for the carpenters and seamstresses. The huge buildings that held sound stages changed into the setting for the movie. Sometimes the stage was a street, sometimes a desert, sometimes a field of flowers. The director of filming planned how to "shoot" the movie with cameras and film. A plan for sequencing the parts of the movie and a schedule for the actors completed the planning. With makeup artists and hairdressers, cameras and sound experts, everything was ready for the big day. The actors and actresses memorized lines, and all the parts of the great production came together. All was ready for the filming to begin. The post-production crew waited to do their part of the job.

Time: _____

Now answer these questions as quickly as you can.

1. The personality of a studio manager (or producer) had to be strong because…

    a. he had to deal with powerful people.

    b. he had a great amount of work to do.

    c. he had to be creative and able to do all the jobs in the studio.

2. The job of the _____ is to work with all the camera people, costume designers, property managers, and actors.

   a. producer

   b. investor

   c. director

3. The person who keeps records of items that a movie set might need is a...

   a. librarian.

   b. screenwriter.

   c. property manager.

4. Overhead refers to...

   a. the sound stage

   b. the cost of running a business

   c. the huge warehouses

5. What is the main idea of the reading?

   a. A studio was a movie-making factory; ideas went in and a movie came out.

   b. There are a lot of people for a movie director to work with.

   c. Many people work in a studio because a movie is a big production.

SECRETS IN THE STONES

Preparation

Strategies for Anticipation

1. First survey this unit. What kinds of secrets are in the stones?

   _____

   Take a careful look at the pictures. What clues do you get?

   _____

2. Next read the first sentence of each reading. What could the unit be about?

   _____

3. What happens to any building over time? What happens to ancient cities? We know that organic material, like wood, decays and that clay slowly turns to dust. The stones, however, remain. Archaeologists look for the stones of old cities. They try to make the stones give up their secrets. How can broken-down walls of ancient cities tell stories? What else will they find in these old cities?

4. Read this list of ideas. Write a check (✓) in front of each one that could be part of this unit.

   a. _____ the study of stones and rocks

   b. _____ scientists who study the past

   c. _____ ancient disasters

   d. _____ the time before history was written

   e. _____ the cities and societies of prehistory

   f. _____ methods of agriculture

   g. _____ stories about great people

   h. _____ how history affects us today

   i. _____ interesting people

   j. _____ medicines and how they help people

5. Archaeology is the study of civilizations of the past. Think about how long society and culture have existed. Consider how little information we have about ancient cities. How do we learn more about the people who lived there?

Strategy: Activating Background Knowledge

Write the names of some very old cities that you know about. Are these cities "alive" today? Or are they in ruins? Have archaeologists uncovered the cities and studied them? Write the names of these cities here:

_____ _____ _____

_____ _____ _____

If the cities are in ruins today, what caused the people to leave?

 ## Main Reading

The Mystery of the Mayans

1   Deep in the rain forests of Central America, huge pyramids rise high above the trees. Now heavy tropical vines, trees, roots, and grass cover silent long-lost cities. A thousand years ago mighty Mayan kings and powerful priests stood there, powerful over their people. Today archaeologists are excavating the site; they are uncovering the detailed stone structures. Gradually the culture and daily lives of this ancient civilization are becoming clearer. Every day, tourists climb among the ruins. They find themselves wondering about this lost culture. Whose cities were these? Who were these people? What did they live for? How did they live in these cities? Most important, why did they abandon their cities? Where did they go? No one has answers to all of these questions. However, archaeologists in Mexico, Guatemala, Honduras, Belize, and El Salvador are coming closer to understanding this culture. They have been working for 150 years to find answers to the Mayan mystery.

2   In a real sense, archaeologists are looking for history. Their job is to study the remains of lost human societies, slowly buried by the sands of time. Natural activities over long periods of time cover everything. Even the houses, towns, and cities where ancient people

lived sink back into the earth. The goal is to find them again. So they dig through the debris (de-BREE) of the site. They go through layers of sand, mud, and ancient garbage to find clues about life in past societies. Their first task is to locate places where people once lived.

3   Archaeologists search for sites all over the world. Some site are difficult to find—earthquakes have covered some of the sites with rock and soil. Others were abandoned because of war, fire, flood, or epidemics (widespread disease). Whatever the reason, cities were left to be found centuries or even millennia later. Archaeologists work to uncover these cities. Their goal in an excavation is to understand the unknown culture. They examine the artifacts (things that people made and left there). They try to figure out what the lives of the inhabitants were like. Beneath the surface of each archaeological site there is a story—the tale of the people who once lived there.

The Mayans, people of an ancient culture of more than 4,000 years ago, built structures such as this pyramid without the benefit of even the simplest tools. This is the Maya ruins of Palenque in Chiapas, Mexico.

4   Archaeologists are always looking for new sites. Finding a new site is an exciting discovery, and they work for years to uncover the remains. They work for years to uncover remains. Sometimes they use aerial photographs (photographs taken from airplanes or satellites). Archaeologists can see unusual land features, such as long ditches or evenly placed hills. Still other sites are found because everyone knows they are there. Stories pass from generation to generation, and eventually someone looks to see what is there. Travelers in the nineteenth and twentieth centuries explored Central America and found some of the Mayan cities. The sight of cities in ruins was certainly a surprise. Study began almost at once.

5   Mayan society began coming together in farming communities by 2600 B.C. At that time they were growing corn in great fields and developing an organized society. By 188 B.C., there was enough food to sustain, or support, cities. In the ruins of Mayan cities, there is evidence of trade, record keeping, and government. Much of the early Mayan civilization no longer exists. However, archaeologists know that before 600 A.D., the Mayans had a writing system. It was the only writing system in the Americas before the Spanish came. They used pictographs, much like the Egyptians. These stylized pictures tell stories of the people and their activities. Writing on tombs reveals some Mayan history. For example, there are details about the royal family, wars with other cities, and new kings. We know that there were several classes in the society. At the top, a royal family ruled with great power. Next came a powerful class of priests. There were also artists, merchants, craftsmen, and farmers. The Mayans had a great civilization. They made an accurate calendar. They designed a mathematical system with a zero as a number. In addition, they made many precise astronomical observations. They built pyramids, palaces, observatories, plazas, temples, public buildings, and ball courts. Amazingly, the Mayans created these structures without the wheel, metal tools, or beasts of burden. There were no horses, no camels, and no donkeys.

6   Palenque, Tikal, Copan, Uxmal, Calakmul, Caracol, and Tazumal are names of some of the major Mayan city-states. Some cities were as large as 60,000 people. Trade with other city-states supported the growth of the cities. Skilled farmers cleared away large portions of tropical rain forests as well as the ground for trade routes. They even stored water underground. With surplus corn and other goods, they traded with neighboring cities, and the merchants and crafts people prospered. Merchants traded salt, honey, cotton, flint, jade, and feathers. Cacao, the bean that makes chocolate, was often the currency. The common people, primarily the farmers, became increasingly separated from the ruling elite classes.

7   This powerful city-state civilization was at its peak between 250 and 600 A.D. when the society and religion were the most developed. Royal families, the nobility, ruled each city, and a large and powerful priest class supported the royal family. The rulers used the religion to gain power and control. The religion was structured around gods of all kinds. There was a god for scribes, a sun god, an earth god, a water god, a god for the underworld, and so on. The Mayan priests thought the gods caused events to repeat themselves in predictable cycles. They would contact the gods through rituals determined by their written calendar. Ceremonies were performed to satisfy the gods, and the supreme ritual was human sacrifice. A victim's life was offered to the gods as a blessing for the community. Sometimes the sacrificial victim would be a captured leader from another city.

8   The royal family and the priests also used their writing system as a tool of power. The secrets of writing were closely guarded, and they were taught only to the upper classes. Writing was magical and powerful. Also, it further elevated the upper classes above the commoners. The writing system was pictographic; it was made up of symbols that represent words or parts of words. It also had syllables of consonant-vowel pairs.

A sample of what the stone writing looks like is below:

9   In the example above, the pictograph represents the woman's name "Nancy." The face means the word is the name of a woman, and the next two symbols sound like "na," becoming "nan" when two of them are placed together. The last symbol is pronounced "sih." The Mayan writing system was finally deciphered in the mid 20th century. Archeologists had been trying to figure it out for many years, and they continue to discover new meanings and symbols.

10   Architecture in the different cities was created with perfection and great variety. The pyramids were actually temples representing mountains and caves. One pyramid is 175 feet high and covers 5 acres at its base. The architecture was carefully laid out to please their gods. Usually buildings were in line with stars and other bodies in space. The balance and harmony of the large structures around the central plaza in most sites are impressive to all modern-day visitors.

11   By 900 A.D., however, something caused the social structure to break down. The people abandoned their cities. Scientists are still not completely certain why it happened. They do not believe that there was an epidemic, a sickness, that caused many people to die. They believe that a number of factors caused the society to decline. First, the population had become too large. It could no longer live off the land. There was not enough food and water to support the cities. In particular, the priest class had become too large for the people to support. Many trees were cut down for agriculture and construction. The loss of the rain forest eventually caused a drought. And finally, wars between the city-states had become more violent. A careful study of rock at the bottom of lakes in the area indicated that the climate

had changed. As the city-states grew, the climate gradually became drier and drier. The Mayans themselves may have caused the severe drought conditions that existed in 862 A.D., the driest year in the area for the last three millennia. This date coincides with the abandonment of the cities. Misuse of land may have been the fatal error for the society.

12   Mayan civilization and culture flourished between 188 B.C. and 900 A.D. Where did the Mayan people go? Their descendants still live in Central America. They are productive citizens of their countries: Mexico, Guatemala, Belize, Honduras, and El Salvador. They can be proud of their Mayan heritage.

-- ■

Strategy Focus: Learning Vocabulary in Context

Here are some sentences from the reading. Can you figure out the meaning of the bold type words from the context clues?

1. **Archaeology** is the study of civilizations of the past. Think about how long society and culture have existed. Today **archaeologists** are uncovering the detailed stone structures of long-lost cities.

   Archaeology is _____ .

   An **archaeologist** is a person who _____ .

2. Beneath the surface of each archaeological **site** there is a story—the tale of the people who once lived there.

   A **site** is a _____ .

3. They do not believe that there was an **epidemic**, a sickness that caused many people to die.

   An **epidemic** _____ .

4. Sometimes they use **aerial** photographs (photographs taken from airplanes or satellites). Archaeologists can see unusual land features, such as long ditches or evenly placed hills.

   A photographer takes an **aerial** photograph from _____

5. Archaeologists uncover these cities. They examine the **artifacts** (things that people made and left there).

   Which of these groups are **artifacts**? Circle the correct answer.

   a. ancient cities like Rome

   b. stone jars, pottery, and mosaics

   c. public places, gardens, buildings

6. So they dig through the **debris** (de-BREE) of the site. They go through layers of sand, mud, and ancient garbage to find clues about life in past societies.

   The **debris** of a long-lost city is like to be…

   a. broken walls, pieces of pottery, bones.

   b. jewelry, clothing, and pictures.

   c. houses and animals.

   d. temples and large structures.

   The **debris** of a windstorm in a forest is likely to be…

   a. cinders, ash, and stone.

   b. buildings and paintings.

   c. fruits and nuts.

   d. leaves and broken branches.

7. Today archaeologists are **excavating**; they are uncovering the detailed stone structures. The goal of the excavation is to understand the unknown culture.

   When a site is **excavated**, it is _____ by people who remove the sand, the mud, and the stones. An ancient city that was once covered and now is open is an _____ .

8. They were growing corn in great fields and developing an organized society. By 188 B.C., there was enough food to **sustain**, or support, cities.

   If there is enough food to **sustain** a city, then the people in the city have enough…

   a. money.   c. food to eat.

   b. space.   d. room to live in.

9. "Mayan civilization and culture **flourished** between 200 B.C. and 900 A.D." means that...

   a. the city was destroyed in 200 B.C.

   b. the time that the city was most important was between 200 B.C. and 900 A.D.

   c. the city was not important until after the years 200 B.C. and 900 A.D.

   d. the city had been important until before 200 B.C. and after and 900 A.D.

10. Amazingly, the Mayans created these structures without the wheel, metal tools, or **beasts of burden**. There were no horses, no camels, and no donkeys.

    A **beast of burden** must be _____ .

Strategy Focus: Reading for Details

Skim and scan the main reading for the missing words. Fill in the blanks.

1. The Mayan culture flourished about _____ years ago.

2. The Mayan people lived in _____ _____ .

3. Archaeologists use _____ photographs to locate possible archaeological _____ .

4. Three of the most important cities of Mayan civilization are

   _____ , _____ , and _____ .

5. _____ activities over a period of time cover cities with sand and mud.

6. The first agricultural communities of the Mayan people started in about _____ B.C.

7. Pictographs are _____ pictures of activities or things.

8. The Mayans developed a system of mathematics that included the

   _____ .

9. The population of some Mayan city-states was about _____ people.

10. The descendants of the Mayan people of today live in

_____ , _____ , _____ ,

and _____ in _____ America.

Strategy Focus: Analyzing the Reading

Read carefully for the answers to these questions. Discuss your answers with classmates.

1. What must the farms of a region produce before a city can develop there?
2. How is archaeology like history?
3. What is the task of an archaeologist?
4. What are some signs that show archaeologists a possible site that can be excavated?
5. What is the importance of writing?
6. Why did the royal class keep writing from the common people?
7. When were the Mayan ruins "discovered" in modern times?
8. What caused the Mayan civilization to disappear?

Strategy: Scanning for Key Words

Before reading the next related reading, think about the title and look at the photograph on page 260. Then make a list of key words you expect to find in the reading. Next, scan each paragraph to see which of these words you find. As you scan, note other words and expressions that seem important. What does your list tell you about the content of the reading?

Related Reading 1

The Mystery of Stonehenge

1   People from all over the world come to the Salisbury Plain in England at the summer solstice—the time when the day is the longest and the night is the shortest. They come because Stonehenge is a mysterious monument from prehistory. No one knows who put up the great megaliths of Stonehenge. No one knows why Stonehenge was important to those people. Yet the mystery of Stonehenge interests many people.

The formation of the megaliths of Stonehenge may show that the people who built it almost 5,000 years ago knew more about the solar system than historians had previously thought.

2   Monuments like Stonehenge are made of great stones, called megaliths. Such monuments can be found all over the world—from England to Easter Island. There are also megalithic monuments in Algeria, the Caucasus, Ethiopia, India, Iran, Japan, Palestine, the Sudan, and Turkey. And all of these monuments date from prehistory. Unknown groups of people placed these enormous stones upright in the ground, sometimes in configurations—such as two large vertical stones with a third lying horizontally on top of the standing two— like at Stonehenge.

3   Some of these megaliths were actually tombs, marked burial places. Although many of these ancient monuments around the world are similar, most archaeologists believe that they were constructed in isolation. That is, they believe that each one was built by a different group of people and that each group did not know about the other groups. However, some people today think that the megaliths were built by a race of wise people who somehow influenced the entire world about 4,000 years ago. Most people now believe that the similarities exist only because the megaliths in each culture and each period of history were built of similar material (stone) and in a similar manner. However, people always ask the same questions about Stonehenge and other megalithic monuments: Who labored to transport and build these massive rock structures, and why did they build them?

4   Stonehenge was constructed in stages, starting around 2800 B.C. It consists of a ring of megaliths surrounded by a bank of dirt and a ditch. Inside the bank of dirt there are many holes. They, too, were dug in a circle. At dawn on Midsummer's Day (usually June 20, 21, or 22), the sun shines directly though a row of stone monuments. This particular row of megaliths divides the circle of stones in half — it is the central axis of Stonehenge. The fact intrigues archaeologists because it may show that these early builders knew more about the solar system than historians had previously thought. For them the important question remains: How did people of prehistory get so much exact information about the movement of the sun?

5   The peculiar spacing of the megaliths in the circle also fascinates scholars. Some think that the builders of Stonehenge used the spacing in the circle to predict solar and lunar eclipses by calculating the angles of the light. Other scientists theorize that Stonehenge was used as an observatory of sorts, to observe the phases of the moon. Is it possible that such wise and knowledgeable people lived 5,000 years ago? Were they the first true astronomers? If they knew so much about the stars and planets, why were their building techniques so primitive, so simple?

What did they use to move the stones to Salisbury Plain from the quarry? What did they use as tools to build these structures? The answers to these questions keep scientists searching. Perhaps there is much more for modern society to learn from these seemingly crude and simple structures.

Strategy Focus: Finding Word Meanings in Context

Find the meanings to these words in the reading.

1. A **megalith** is _____ .

2. The **summer solstice** is _____ .

3. A **central axis** is _____ .

4. A **tomb** is _____ .

Strategy Focus: Reading Critically

Indicate which of the following statements are facts by writing *F* for FACT in the blank, and which are the judgments of the author, the author's implications, or your own inferences, by writing *NF* for NOT A FACT in the blank. Be sure that you refer to the reading for the proof of your answers. Also remember that statements that seem wrong to you are likely to be someone else's judgments.

1. _____ Because we have no explanation for how megaliths were built, we can conclude that voyagers from outer space built them.

2. _____ Stonehenge was an important place for the prehistoric people of southern England.

3. _____ The builders of Stonehenge knew something about astronomy.

4. _____ About 4,000 years ago, a race of wise people built megaliths all over the world.

5. _____ The people who lived near Stonehenge used it to observe phases of the moon.

6. _____ Archaeologists have a clear explanation of why Stonehenge was built.

7. _____ The construction of Stonehenge began around 2800 B.C.

8. _____ Archaeologists will probably continue to study Stonehenge.

9. _____ The builders of Stonehenge were the first true astronomers.

10. _____ Stonehenge is made of megaliths in a circle and a circle of holes with an earthen bank and a ditch around it.

11. _____ During the longest day of the year, the sun shines directly through a row of megaliths at dawn.

12. _____ The stones of Stonehenge come from a quarry.

Strategy Focus: Making Inferences

Read each of these sentences. If the first part of the statement (the *if* clause) is true, is the second part (the *then* clause) also true? Look at this example:

> If megaliths are made of stone, then there are many megaliths on a beach.

The *if* clause is true: All megaliths are made of stone. However, all stones are not megaliths. A megalith is a very large stone. It is also put into a special position for a particular purpose. Beach stones are only stones, not megaliths.

Now look at the following sentences. Write *Yes* if the inference can be made or *No* if the inference cannot be made.

1. _____ If megaliths are found in Algeria, Ethiopia, England, and Iran, then the same group of people must have lived in all of those places.

2. _____ If archaeology includes the study of ancient megaliths, then archaeologists probably study old burial places, temples, and stadiums.

3. _____ If *mega-* means "great" and *-lith* refers to stone, then all megaliths are made of the same material.

4. _____ If *mega-* means "great" and *-lith* refers to stone, then all megaliths have a similar form.

5. _____ If Stonehenge is a calendar, then the people who built it must have known quite a bit about astronomy.

6. _____ If Stonehenge was built in England starting in 2800 B.C., then it was built by prehistoric people.

7. _____ If the sun shines from the same direction every Midsummer's Day, then a stone calendar can be built.

8. _____ If a ray of sunshine hits a particular place on a particular stone on the longest day of the year, then changes from that point can be measured to form an accurate calendar.

Strategy: Making and Checking Inferences

Use the information you have gained from the readings to make inferences about the science of archaeology—its content, subject matter, and methods. Then skim the next related reading to see which of your inferences are correct or incorrect.

 Related Reading 2

The Science of Archaeology

1   How do archaeologists open up the secrets in the stones? What do they do to analyze the things they find in a "dig" (as most excavations are called)? How do they determine how old the artifacts are? The ways and means of archaeologists form the science of archaeology, an exact science.

2   Finding a site and getting permission to excavate it is the first step in the archaeological process. Archaeological sites are protected by most governments. Once the site is defined and permission is received, the work of the dig begins, and it can go on for a long time. As a result, it is typical for one archaeologist to spend his or her entire career in one site. Excavation of a site like Pompeii in Italy, for example, has been going on for several centuries already, and it is likely to continue for years to come.

3   One of the first things to do in a dig is to make a map of the whole area, in which each section is numbered and named. Everything that is found in a section is *cataloged* (marked with the section number so that archaeologists know exactly where each artifact was found). At the beginning of an excavation, one narrow shaft is usually dug to get an idea of what is under the ground. Then, the painstaking work of removing the dirt begins — with small shovels, garden tools, even spoons and toothbrushes.

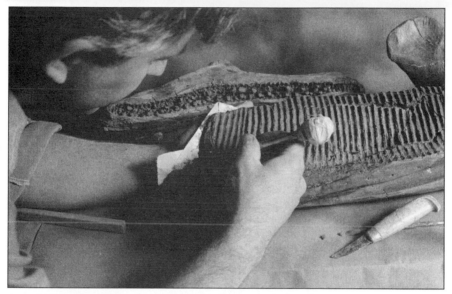

An archaeologist at work

4   When an important aritifact of the ancient culture is found (a group of artifacts that is found together is called "a find"), the archaeologist meticulously analyzes the remains, describing each in detail. After these relics are labeled with numbers and entered into a *catalog*, the archaeologist needs to determine how old they are. Archaeological dating is a highly developed aspect of the analysis of a relic. Basically, the methods of dating fall into two categories: methods of *chronometric dating* and methods of *relative dating*. The results of both types are necessary for most artifacts because each type provides important and distinct information.

5   Chronometric dating methods, as the name implies, measure time (*chronos* is Greek for time, and *meter* is Greek for measure). Archaeologists use these methods to establish the date of a relic (some relics are as ancient as 3,500,000 B.C.). One of the methods of chronometric dating is called *dendrochronology*. This method uses the careful study of tree rings to establish the age of a relic. (*Dendron* is Greek for tree.)

6   The science of dendrochronology is based on the fact that trees produce a new layer, a ring of growth, on their trunks or main stems every year. Dendrochronologists can count these rings to tell the age of a tree. Because of variations in climate, some of the rings will be distinctive. For example, during a year with an unusually large amount of rain, a tree will grow more than in other years and produce a wider ring. Conversely, during an exceptionally dry year, a tree will produce a distinctively narrow ring. The rings of trees in any particular area form recognizable patterns because the trees experience the same weather. Therefore, it is possible for dendrochronologists to match the rings of one tree with the rings of another. By matching parts of the ring pattern of a younger tree with parts of the pattern of an older one, archaeologists can extend their knowledge of weather further into

The rings on a tree trunk can reveal important information about the history of weather.

the past. In some parts of the world, knowledge of tree-ring patterns extends over a period of time from the present back thousands of years. Because the scientific knowledge of tree-ring history spans such a long time, when an ancient wooden tool is found, dendrochronology can often be used to determine its age.

7   Another type of chronometric dating is based on the law of *radioactive decay*. According to this law, the atoms of certain elements decompose in predictable ways. Three of the methods used to date relics this way are *radiocarbon* (carbon 14) dating, *potassium-argon* dating, and *fission-track* dating. All are based on the predictable rate of decomposition of the elements carbon, potassium, and uranium. If archaeologists can measure the amount of decay, then they can actually measure age. Thus, they can date both important ancient objects and the areas where they were found.

8   Obviously, chronometric dating is essential to archaeologists, but it is not suffficient. Archaeologists need to know not only how old an artifact is, but also how it fits into human history. By using methods of relative dating, archaeologists can determine when an object was invented by a group of people and how it was improved or replaced in the years after its invention. Thus, relative dating methods add a historical aspect to archaeological dating.

9   *Stratigraphic* analysis is one method of relative dating. When a site (such as Ebla) is occupied (either continuously or periodically) over a length of time, its history can be read backward, with the most recent history on or near the surface of the ground, and older and older history in each deeper layer. Many Middle Eastern cities are perfect places to practice stratigraphic dating. In the modern archaeological site of Chanakkale in Turkey, for example, nine layers of the city of Troy have been uncovered. On the other hand, caves near the Hudson River in New York have been occupied periodically. Sometimes many years passed between occupations of these hollow places in the rock cliffs above the river. However, whether a site was inhabited continuously

or periodically, the method of getting the raw material for stratigraphic analysis remains the same. Archaeologists carefully excavate the site, noting the *strata* (the layers). Generally, the deeper the stratum, the older that layer is. Because each stratum yields remains, archaeologists can analyze the remains and discover the sequence of events at a site.

10   *Cross-dating*, another method of relative dating, establishes time links between groups of people. For example, when archaeologists began to study the culture of the people of Sri Lanka, they found both Chinese and Arabic pottery on this island in the Indian Ocean. Both types of pottery had some distinctive aspects. By examining the unusual characteristics of these containers, archaeologists were able to date them chronometrically. The presence of the containers also showed that the Sri Lankans were linked to both Arabia and China, most likely through trade. Then, because these vessels were found in one stratum together with Sri Lankan containers, the archaeologists were able to establish the age of the Sri Lankan vessels because they knew the age of the Chinese and Arab vessels.

11   By using a combination of chronometric and relative dating, archaeologists can construct a description of a site and its inhabitants. The completeness of their description depends on the type and quantity of artifacts. With proper evidence, they can determine when a site or a layer was occupied and by whom. With enough evidence, they can also learn about the history of the site. For example, through stratigraphic analysis, they can figure out the economy of the site, and they can determine such important changes as when a society went from an agricultural economy to a *commercial* (business) economy. By cross-dating, archaeologists can figure out when the inhabitants of one area traded with another and thus come to understand the trade patterns of the area. In these ways, the work of the archaeologist can truly help write the human history of the distant past.

Strategy Focus: Learning Vocabulary in Context

The words in Column A are defined in Column B. The number to the right of the word in Column A tells you the paragraph in the reading where that word appears. Write each word in the correct blank for its definition.

Column A   Column B

1. relic (4)   (a) main stem of a tree _____

2. meticulously (4)   (to) decay _____

3. span (6)   remains _____

4. chronometric (4)   in an opposite way _____

5. trunk (6)   connection _____

6. conversely (6)   (a) hollow place in rock _____

7. decompose (7)   (a) business _____

8. link (10)   (a) layer _____

9. cave (9)   (a) container _____

10. vessel (10)   time measuring _____

11. commercial (11)   carefully noting every detail _____

12. stratum (9)   (to) extend over _____

Strategy: Analyzing Information

The reading refers to several types of archaeological dating. There are at least two types of chronometric dating: dendrochronological dating and radioactive decay dating (using carbon 14, potassium-argon, and fission-track). There are also methods of relative dating: stratigraphic and cross-dating. In this activity, several archaeological situations are described. In each situation, one or more methods of dating are used. Identify the methods.

1. In the Chanakkale dig—the site of the ancient city of Troy—the archaeologist Heinrich Schliemann was able to identify nine separate layers. Each layer was one distinct settlement, ranging from the Neolithic era (the New Stone Age) to Roman times.

   His method of dating was _____ .

2. Schliemann found objects in the lowest level that indicated that the people of the village at the Troy site had made objects of stone like those that were found in a nearby settlement and had been dated to 4500 B.C.

   This method of dating was _____ .

3. Schliemann found something organic in some pieces of pottery in a layer of ashes. The material was sent to a laboratory for chemical analysis.

   The methods of dating that were used in this situation are

   _____ and _____ .

4. Another archaeologist, Wilhelm Dorpfeld, did more excavations on the site of Troy. He meticulously collected shards from the pottery of the different layers. He paid special attention to the shards from the third layer, which had been identified at first as the Troy of Greek stories. He realized that the pottery shards from the third layer did not show Greek designs. The first pieces that showed Greek designs on them were found in the seventh layer. From this evidence, Dorpfeld concluded that the seventh layer was Greek Troy, not the third.

   The method of dating in this case was _____ .

5. During a dig near an amphitheater in Aphrodisias, an excavation in southern Turkey, art historian Charles Walker White found dozens of broken marble statues. It seemed strange at first that there were so many statues; however, the carving on the statues was somewhat unskilled. The quality of most of the work did not look like the work of true artists. Yet there were many examples of a particular style of marble carving, a style that had been dated in fine statues that were found elsewhere. White was able to determine that he had found a school where artists were trained to carve marble. Furthermore, by analyzing the style of carving (how the hair was carved, the way the eyes were carved, how the folds of cloth were carved into the marble), White was able to date the statues.

   The method that he used was _____ .

6. An explorer on Mount Ararat brought back an old piece of wood. He believed that it was a piece of Noah's ark. Two separate kinds of tests were performed on the wood. For one test, a chemical analysis was necessary. The other test required taking a thin, pencil-like sample of the wood.

The two methods of dating were probably _____

and _____

Strategy: Organizing Information for Writing

One good way to study and learn new information is to list and organize the information that comes from the reading. It works the other way too: to write well, make a list of ideas, put them into a logical order, and then expand the ideas. Understanding the organization of ideas in a context is like cataloging: it is understanding the most general categories and the specific types or examples. Look at the reading again, and look for the general topic and the information that supports each general topic.

1. What are the two general types of archaeological dating?

   _____   _____

2. What are two examples of the first type of archaeological dating?

   _____   _____

3. What are two examples of the second type of archaeological dating?

   _____   _____

4. What are the three types of radioactive-decay dating?

   _____   _____   _____

The organization of ideas should be fairly clear now. This reading has strong internal logic. That is, the parts fit together so that the writer's thoughts are clear.

Strategy: Making Questions

Use your new knowledge of the unit theme (and your imagination) to write a series of questions based on the title of the next related reading. For example, you could write: "What is a lost continent?" or "Where was Atlantis?" Read through the text quickly to find the answers to your questions.

Related Reading 3

The Lost Continent of Atlantis

1   Can archaeologists use the stories of ordinary people to find evidence of lost cultures? Perhaps the greatest of all stories about past societies, past civilizations, is the story of Atlantis. The challenge for archaeologists has been the difficult task of finding Atlantis, the lost continent.

2   Stories of Atlantis have interested people for *millennia*—since the lost continent was first mentioned in the stories of the Greek philosopher Plato, who lived from 428 to 347 B.C. (approximately). Plato told the legend of Atlantis in two of his writings. His description of the "lost continent" still excites the modern mind. Plato's Atlantis— a vast island "larger than Libya and Asia Minor put together"—was a paradise, with magnificent mountain ranges, green plains that were full of every variety of animal, and luxuriant gardens where the fruit was "fair and wondrous and in infinite abundance." The earth was rich with precious metals, especially the one prized most highly by the ancients, *orichaic* [or-i-KAYik], an *alloy* (metallic mixture) of copper and something else, perhaps iron.

3   According to Plato, the capital city of Atlantis was beautiful; it was constructed in black, white, and red stone. The city was carefully planned, with five zones built in perfect concentric circles. Each circular zone was built inside a larger one. According to Plato, the capital had canals and its nearby port was "full of vessels (ships) and merchants coming from all parts, who…kept up…din and clatter …night and day." The city was full of life and culture.

4   Aristotle, who lived between 384 and 322 B.C. and who was Plato's student, assumed that the story of Atlantis was a myth or an allegory. He believed that Plato was using the idea of a lost continent to explain his own political theories. Some scholars today do not think that

Aristotle was right in this assessment of Plato's stories of Atlantis, for several reasons. The most important is that Plato was a brilliant scholar; if he had meant to create Atlantis to illustrate his principles, he would have done a better job. The story of Atlantis that he told is full of curious detail. It is unlike a political allegory, and more like a historical report. In two of Plato's *dialogs*, his characters discuss the lost continent of Atlantis; they find the story puzzling, but they react to it as if it were fact.

5   Plato described Atlantis in clear terms. He said that the continent lay beyond the Pillars of Hercules, the Greek name for the Straits of Gibraltar. He described Atlantis as rich and fertile, with rich plains for farms and mountains full of trees. The people of Atlantis were technologically advanced: they understood metal-working, had written laws, and were fine engineers and architects. He said Atlantis was a great sea power, and that it launched an attack on Athens and on Egypt. During the war that followed, a natural disaster occurred which "swallowed" the entire Atlantean culture in the time of one day and one night. The effect on the Athenian army was equally devastating. All of this could possibly have happened, but the date is a problem: In Plato's account, the continent disappeared in 9600 B.C., long before there was an Athens to fight against.

6   Efforts to figure out whether there was truth in Plato's accounts continue to this day. A satisfactory explanation of Atlantis must be scientific; it must answer the questions of archaeologists, historians, anthropologists, and geophysicists. Archaeologists have pointed out what Plato described was not unlike the high Bronze Age civilizations around the Aegean Sea and in the Middle East. The Minoan culture on the island of Crete, for example, was quite advanced. The Hittites of Asia Minor had a flourishing civilization. The Egyptian culture was very advanced, and so was the Babylonian civilization. In fact, all of these groups flourished between 2500 and 1200 B.C. Because of the oddness of the date he mentions for the disappearance of Atlantis,

people have wondered whether Plato's date was misinterpreted. If the date had been 1500 B.C., instead of 9600 B.C., then some of the theories would seem possible.

7   They seem possible because Minoan culture on Crete disappeared about 1500 B.C. Because the Minoans were in contact with both the Athenians and the Egyptians, the story seems to fit. What if the powerful Minoans were actually the Atlanteans? What if present-day Crete and the three islands of Thira are all that remain of a great civilization? It is a fact that there is a group of islands about 70 miles north of Crete. This island group (called Thira or Santorini today) has two volcanoes, and the islands are situated around a giant *caldera*— the kind of crater that a huge volcanic eruption causes. This kind of crater is the result of long volcanic activity; the volcano actually falls in on itself and the sea rushes in. The largest part of a volcanic island disappears when this collapse occurs. The collapse of an island in this way usually causes a huge tidal wave that spreads great destruction in all directions.

8   There was such a disaster in modern times. In 1883, there was an explosion on the island volcano of Krakatoa in the Sunda Strait between the heavily populated islands of Sumatra and Java. Thirty-six thousand people were killed as nearly three hundred villages were destroyed by the explosion, the shock waves, and the tidal wave. The sound of the explosion was heard three thousand miles away. Volcanic ash went fifty miles into the sky, and it rained mud in Japan, Europe, and Africa—wherever the air currents carried it. The size of a caldera shows the strength of a volcanic explosion. The Krakatoa caldera is one-fifth the size of the Thira crater, so scientists estimate that the Thira explosion was five times greater than the Krakatoa explosion. Such an explosion would have destroyed much of the civilization of Crete and killed thousands of people. Archaeologists and geophysicists agree that the great Minoan civilization died due to natural disasters (earthquakes, floods, and fires) in the late 1600s B.C. According to a

separate account, in the 1500s B.C. an island north of Crete blew up and caused widespread destruction in the Aegean and Mediterranean areas. This seemed too much of a coincidence to a Greek professor of archaeology by the name of Marinatos. He wasn't willing to believe that both events occurred at almost the same time. Therefore, he investigated the island of Thira in 1967; as a result of his excavations, he found Minoan remains under the volcanic rocks on Thira.

Strategy Focus: Scanning for Details

1. The Greek name for the Straits of Gibraltar (and the Rock of Gibraltar) is probably…

   a. Thira.   c. the Pillars of Hercules.

   b. Egypt.   d. Atlantis.

2. Aristotle…

   a. was older than Plato.

   b. was killed in an explosion.

   c. was Plato's student.

   d. was a famous Greek archaeologist.

3. *Orichaic* is a…

   a. famous person.

   b. Greek philosopher.

   c. city from ancient times.

   d. a mixture of metals.

4. How large did Plato say Atlantis was?

   a. as large as a vast island

   b. as large as a continent

   c. smaller than Athens

   d. larger than Libya and Asia Minor put together

5. The city of Atlantis was _____ , according to Plato.

    a. well planned

    b. built of red, white, and black stone

    c. built in five zones

    d. All of the above are correct.

6. A *caldera* is...

    a. a volcanic crater.

    b. a dead volcano.

    c. a lake.

    d. an island.

7. Krakatoa blew up in...

    a. 1996.   c. 1967.

    b. 1880 B.C.   d. 1883.

8. The caldera of Thira is _____ the caldera of Krakatoa.

    a. one fifth the size of

    b. 20 percent larger than

    c. twice the size of

    d. five times greater than

9. The civilization of Atlantis was probably...

    a. Greek.   c. American.

    b. Egyptian.   d. Minoan.

10. The Sunda Strait is between...

    a. Europe and North America.

    b. Sumatra and Asia.

    c. Krakatoa and Thira.

    d. Java and Sumatra.

Strategy Focus: Learning Vocabulary in Context

1. The city was carefully planned, with five zones built in perfect concentric circles. Each circular zone was built inside a larger one.

   Concentric circles have…

   a. the same center.   c. the same size.

   b. the same color.   d. different shapes.

2. The **challenge** for archaeologists has been the difficult task of finding Atlantis, the lost continent.

   A **challenge** is a _____ .

3. Stories of Atlantis have interested people for millennia—since the lost continent was first mentioned in the stories of the Greek philosopher Plato, who lived from 428 to 347 B.C. (approximately). Plato told the legend of Atlantis in two of his writings.

   A **legend** is a kind of…

   a. story.   c. philosophy.

   b. city.   d. land mass.

4. Because of the **oddness** of the date he mentions for the disappearance of Atlantis, people have wondered whether Plato's date was misinterpreted. **Oddness** is the quality of strangeness.

   If something is **odd**, it is…

   a. unusual.   c. painful.

   b. normal.   d. different.

5. He described Atlantis as rich and **fertile**, with rich plains for farms and mountains full of trees.

   Fertile land…

   a. is mountainous.   c. has farms.

   b. is fruitful.   d. is flat.

6. Archaeologists and geophysicists agree that the great Minoan civilization died because of **natural disasters** (earthquakes, floods, and fires) in the late 1600s B.C.

   Natural disasters are things like _____ .

7. Aristotle, who lived between 384 and 322 B.C. and who was Plato's student, assumed that the story of Atlantis was a myth or an allegory. He believed that Plato was using the idea of a lost continent to explain his own political theories.

   A **myth** is like...

   a. a story   c. an allegory.

   b. a legend.   d. All of the above are correct.

8. During the war that followed, a natural disaster occurred which "swallowed" the entire Atlantean culture in the time of one day and one night. The effect on the Athenian army was equally **devastating**.

   If something is **devastating**, it...

   a. helps a lot.   c. costs a lot.

   b. destroys a lot.   d. changes a lot.

9. This kind of crater is the result of long volcanic activity; the volcano actually falls in on itself and the sea rushes in. The largest part of a volcanic island disappears when this **collapse** occurs.

   A **collapse** occurs when one thing _____ another.

   a. falls in on   c. changes to look like

   b. becomes   d. appears as

10. This seemed too much of a **coincidence** to a Greek professor of archaeology by the name of Marinatos. He wasn't willing to believe that both events occurred at almost the same time.

    A **coincidence** is the result of _____ .

    a. an explosion

    b. two things happening at the same time

    c. being Greek

    d. geophysics

Strategy Focus: Understanding the Reading

1. Why did it rain mud in Europe after Krakatoa erupted?

2. Do you think Plato had traveled to Asia Minor and Libya? Why or why not?

3. In Plato's mind, what made a land a paradise? Do you have the same opinion?

4. What are some of the things that make a place seem "vast"?

5. Do you think that Professor Marinatos found Atlantis? What proof would you need?

6. Which of the following events do you think was the most important in the development of civilization? Explain your answer.

   a. the discovery of ways that fire could be used

   b. the invention of writing

   c. the invention of the wheel

   d. domestication of grains and animals

Strategy: Recognizing Organization

Sometimes in academic English a student needs to understand the structure of a paragraph—how it is organized. Reading well requires understanding more than just the words, sentences, and ideas. Learning to read well is also learning how to think critically about organization and support. A good reader can use this skill to become a good writer because of the links between reading and writing. In other words, being a good reader is the first step to becoming a good writer.

Every good paragraph has a main idea; every good article has a main idea. Writers choose how they want to support, develop, or prove the main idea. The way a writer chooses to support the main idea is an organization-of-thought decision. The following list is a review of the basic kinds of thought organization in English. These are the choices a writer has; they are also the kinds of development that a reader should anticipate.

1. **Time Order**. Ideas and information in time order are organized according to time: what happened first, second, third, and so on. History books are usually written in time order.

2. **Process**. This special kind of time order is used to explain how something is done. The information is arranged in a fixed and definite order. For example, instructions like recipes or how to put a bicycle together are written in process order.

3. **Example**. Whenever specific examples of a fact are known, the examples can be used to show or prove that the main idea is true. Words like *for example, for instance, like, as in,* and *also* are frequently used in this kind of development.

4. **Cause and Effect**. This type of organization gives a reason for something happening. The paragraph or article usually answers the question of why something occurred.

5. **Description**. Organization by description gives a specific and accurate picture of something, someone, or someplace. Usually there are a lot of details in description, and these details are arranged to create a word picture for the reader.

6. **Definition**. The purpose of this type of organization is to define or to clarify the meaning of something.

7. **Comparison and Contrast**. There are times when the similarities or the differences of two or more things (people, places, things, ideas) are in focus. At these times, the appropriate organization is usually comparison and contrast. Words like *in contrast, on the other hand,* and *similarly* are often used.

Now stop to think about appropriate topics. What topics can you think of, for each of these seven types of organization?

_____

_____

_____

_____

_____

_____

Strategy Focus: Analyzing the Paragraph Organization

Read the following paragraphs for specific purposes: to find the main idea, the kind of support, and the organizational development. Do not try to understand every word, but rather read for general meaning and organizational patterns.

1. A number of theories exist to explain the origins of the city of Tiahuanaco, high in the Andes Mountains of South America. For example, some people have credited the city with a rich and interesting history. It has even been credited with giving birth to "the American man." Several writers have described it as the capital of an empire which may have equaled the civilization of the Incas of Peru. Others have called it the capital of the lost continent of Atlantis, or a city built millions of years ago by space travelers from Venus. For many years, there has been no solution to this early-American puzzle. It is a fact, however, that very few archaeological sites have created as many questions as Tiahuanaco. And still, the questions about this site remain unsolved.

   The main idea of this paragraph is…

   a. that some people believe that the city gave birth to "the American Man."

   b. that some people have described it as the capital of an empire which may have equaled the civilization of the Incas of Peru.

   c. that some people have wondered whether the city is the capital of Atlantis, the lost continent.

   d. that there may be many theories about the city, but there still is no real explanation of the origin of Tiahuanaco.

   The primary method of organization is…

   a. definition.

   b. example.

   c. process.

   d. comparison and contrast.

2. Prehistoric builders in Western Europe were challenged to build enormous stone megaliths such as those at Stonehenge. The builders probably dug deep trenches to begin with. If one side of the hole was slanted, the heavy stones could be slid down into the hole with ropes and smooth logs used as rollers. Then the top part of the stone could be pulled into place with ropes and levers. The final step, of course, was to straighten the megalith, which could also be done with ropes. Thus the great stones of Stonehenge, which weighed as much as 45 tons, could be put into place even 4,000 years ago.

    The main idea of this paragraph is…

    a. that the stones were put into place with ropes.

    b. that the great stones were put into place 4,000 years ago.

    c. the method that prehistoric builders used to erect the megaliths of Stonehenge.

    d. that some of the stones at Stonehenge weighed 45 tons.

    The primary method of organization is…

    a. reasons.

    b. process.

    c. comparison and contrast.

    d. examples.

3. Easter Island is one of the most isolated spots on Earth. It is more than a thousand miles from Pitcairn Island—the closest neighbor in the Polynesian chain of islands. It is 2,300 miles west of the coast of South America. The island owes its triangular shape to three volcanoes that formed it: Rano Kau, Maunga Terevaka, and Katiki. These three mountains are its three corners, and the middle of the island is grass-covered volcanic soil. There is evidence that rich vegetation and forests may once have grown on Easter Island, but today there is little plant or animal life. Trees are sparse, and there are no running streams, although there are crater lakes in the mountains. The coast is rocky and steep. The fresh, soft air that is typical of the more tropical Pacific islands is missing, because Easter Island is on the northern edge of the southern temperate zone. Therefore, the island has four seasons and a pleasant, moderate climate. The average temperature is 72 degrees Fahrenheit. The average rainfall is about 50 inches a year. The ancient inhabitants of

Easter Island called it "the navel of the world." It is an appropriate name for a remote and dramatic place of strong waves, steep cliffs, high volcanoes, and open, wide-swept slopes. Dominating the treeless landscape are the island's famous megaliths.

The main idea of this paragraph is...

a. that Easter Island is one of the most isolated spots in the Pacific.

b. a picture of Easter Island and some of the important aspects of the place.

c. a picture of the statues that dominate the island.

d. an explanation that Easter Island was formed by volcanoes.

The main method of organization is...

a. time order.   c. definition.

b. reasons and result.   d description.

4. Archaeologists do not agree on what makes a city. There have been many attempts to define a city, but the results haven't been totally satisfactory. However, archaeologists have been able to list a number of characteristics that mark "urbanization," which is part of city-making. Those attributes are permanent settlement, specialization of skills and jobs among the city-dwellers, the development and spread of a particular type of architecture, the construction of public facilities (like buildings, parks, and gardens), and growth of a stable population size. However, archaeologists admit that all of these factors do not need to be there for a community to be considered a city.

The main idea of this paragraph is that...

a. archaeologists do not agree on what makes a city.

b. a city needs a population of a certain size before it is considered a city.

c. certain characteristics mark urbanization.

d. a city must include permanent settlement.

The principal method of organization is...

a. process.   c. definition.

b. comparison and contrast.   d. time order.

5. The Spanish conquistador Francisco Pizarro arrived in Peru with 180 soldiers in the middle of a struggle for power among the Incas. One son of the emperor, Atahualpa, won, but he did not stay in power very long. In 1532, Pizarro and his men moved inland from the coast and defeated Atahualpa. The people were terrified by the guns and the horses, so they surrendered. Atahualpa bargained for his freedom and agreed to pay Pizarro the greatest amount of ransom in history. Atahualpa filled one room with gold objects and two others with silver artifacts, pots, and fancy ornaments. Pizarro collected the treasure, melted it down, distributed it among his men, and then killed Atahualpa. This betrayal ended good relations between the Incas and the Spaniards.

The main idea of this paragraph is…

a. that Pizarro and his soldiers arrived in Peru in the middle of a power struggle among the Incas.

b. that the Incas did not resist the Spanish horses and guns.

c. that Atahualpa offered gold and silver to Pizarro for his freedom.

d. the retelling of the story about Pizarro and the Incas in Peru.

The main method of development is…

a. time order.

b. description.

c. examples.

d. cause and effect.

6. The concept of zero as a number was essential to the development of mathematics. The mathematics of the Mayas of Mexico was superior when compared to that of other cultures. They were familiar with the idea of zero nearly 1,000 years before anyone in Europe had it. Arab traders opened up caravan routes across the desert of the Middle East and brought with them to Europe the concept of zero as a number. The Greeks wrote numbers by using letters of the alphabet, and with the Roman number system, it was difficult to add or subtract because sometimes four figures (for example, VIII) were needed to express one number (for example, 8). Neither the Greeks nor the Romans could deal with large numbers. In contrast, the Mayas could express any number by using three symbols: the dot, the bar, and the dash. For zero, they used a shell shape.

The main idea of this paragraph is that...

a. the Mayas were familiar with the concept of zero before any other culture.

b. the science of mathematics required the concept of zero as a number to develop.

c. the Mayas could express any number by using only three symbols.

d. the Greeks wrote numbers by using letters of the alphabet.

The principal method of organization is...

a. definition.

b. reasons.

c. comparison and contrast.

d. process.

7. Priceless ancient artifacts have been destroyed because fashion changed or because an item went from one person to another. What was once a treasure to a whole culture became a treasure for one person when a thief looted a temple or stole from a tomb. What was once a prized decoration on a wall became old-fashioned, to be replaced by paint and new decorations. Furthermore, new religious ideas replaced old religions, and the new values resulted in the destruction of ancient, beautiful, and artistic statues, paintings, and buildings.

The main idea of this paragraph is that...

a. not all cultures share the idea of beauty.

b. the changes in people's attitudes have resulted in the loss of valuable cultural items.

c. valuable artifacts must not be stolen.

d. religions need beautiful statues, paintings, and buildings.

The primary method of development is...

a. definition.

b. cause and effect.

c. comparison and contrast.

d. process.

Strategy: Writing Your Own Ideas

1. Think about the concept of "power" and the concept of "strength" in a society. In what ways do people today measure the power of a society? What other ways are there to measure "success" in a society?

2. Think about your own society. What influences affect daily life? Are any influences from outside the community? How might information from one society have spread to another society?

Strategy Focus: Keeping a Vocabulary Journal

Choose five words from the new words in this unit to be your target words.

Write the words here: _____ _____

_____ _____ _____

Now write them into your vocabulary journal. Remember to include the following parts:
- your target word
- the sentence from the unit in which your target word appears
- a definition, including the part of speech.
- some sentences of your own

Strategy: Increasing Reading Speed

 Timed Reading

The Clay Armies of China

Wang Xueli, a site director of the Shaanxi Institute of Archaeology, explained: "In March of 1990, workers were building a highway from Xian [SHYAN] to the new airport. The road passed Jing Di's tomb. The road builder noticed abnormalities in the soil and called us."

Something, it seemed, was there. Soon archaeologists began their work. First they surveyed the whole area, recognized the patterns in the soil, and made a map and an excavation plan. Then they began to dig—not into the tomb of the emperor, but into the fields around it. They unearthed an army of clay soldiers in twenty-four separate pits. These soldiers, each about two feet tall, were like soldier dolls. They were once dressed in silken robes and had once had movable wooden arms, but the cloth had decayed and the wooden arms had, too. So now they stand like armless guards, still loyal to their emperor after 2,100 years. Also buried were doll-sized horsemen, cooks, servants, food supplies, and kitchen utensils. The old Chinese saying "Treat death as life" means that archaeologists have learned a great deal from the fields around the tomb of Emperor Jing.

Wang's discovery is the second clay army found in China. The first discovery, in 1974, was an army of 10,000 life-sized clay soldiers with weapons and horses. They were found inside the tomb of Qin Shi Huang Di (*Di* means emperor). Qin Shi Huang was the emperor who built the Great Wall of China, the leader who united all of China. His reign lasted from 221 to 210 B.C. He was against learning, however, and burned books and killed scholars.

There are many differences between the soldiers of Qin Shi Huang and the soldiers of Jing. For example, the faces on the soldiers in Qin Shi Huang's clay army are all the same. They show no feelings. Their clothing is painted on them.

The tiny soldiers of Jing Di's army have beautiful, individual faces. They show all kinds of feelings, as if each had a different personality. It is known that Jing was a Taoist. Qin Shi Huang followed Confucius; the Confucian philosophy taught strong discipline, ceremony, public service, and, therefore, so did Qin Shi Huang. Jing, however, in following Taoism, believed in looking inward to the soul, seeking harmony with nature. Why such a difference in the soldiers? Perhaps the emperors' personalities affected the artists who made the statues.

Time: _____

Now answer these questions as quickly as you can.

1. In 1990, the site of the buried army was found by…
   a. workers.   b. farmers.   c. Qin Si Huang.

2. Jing Di was emperor _____ Qin Shi Huang.
   a. at the same time as
   b. of a different area than
   c. after

3. *Clay* is…
   a. a place.   b. like dirt.   c. a person.

4. "The road builders noticed abnormalities in the soil" means…
   a. something was strange about the fields.
   b. the fields looked different from other fields.
   c. Both of the above answers are correct.

5. The main idea of this reading is that…
   a. Wang is a good archaeologist.
   b. there is history in the ground which archaeologists can write after they dig.
   c. the Chinese Emperor Jing was buried with a clay army which archaeologists have unearthed.

ALL KINDS OF INTELLIGENCE

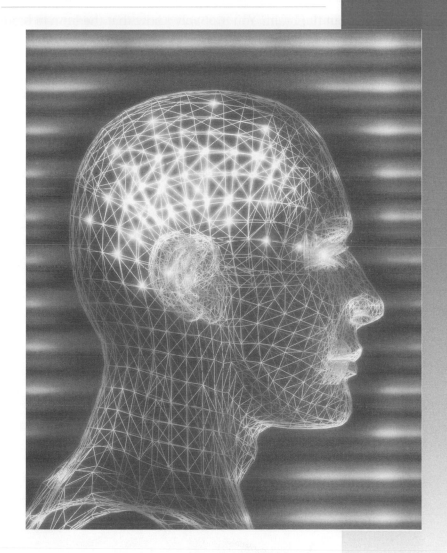

Steps to academic Reading 5,

 **Preparation**

Strategies for Anticipation

Brain activity is proof that a person is alive. We know that all human brains are different, that each person is unique. For example, some people are talented in one discipline and others are good at completely different things. What is it that makes each person the unique individual that he or she really is? A scientist would answer these questions with one phrase: the brain.

What do you know about the brain? You probably know that the human brain is in the head. People say, "Use your head! Just think!" When someone "thinks," that person is considering the evidence, judging whether something is right or wrong, and making inferences. The brain processes information. The brain produces "ideas" and "thoughts." Each person's brain is what makes that person unique—different from all other people. However, the brain is more than a thinking device. It truly controls everything that the body is and everything it does.

Survey this unit, and consider the parts. Every part is connected to thinking and to intelligence. Some of the intelligence is natural (human intelligence), and some may be artificial (machine intelligence). Brainstorm ideas with your classmates. Write down some ideas that you expect in this unit:

_____

_____

_____

_____

_____

_____

_____

Strategy: Reading Critically

As you read the following, think about its structure. How are the ideas put together?

Monday
11-28.

 Main Reading

"It's on the Tip of My Tongue"

1   The human brain is vulnerable to problems of memory. How many times have you tried to remember someone's name and not been able to? How many times have you looked for your keys? How often do you have to return home to get something that you need for the day? These lapses of memory (failures to remember) are part of human experience. As people get older, they become fearful of losing their memories. However, most people, even young people, experience some problems with memory. That's one reason why there are studies on the topic. It is also why we are learning so much about how we think and how we remember.

2   Psychologists tell us, for example, that our brains "fill in the gaps." If we see a picture of a fallen tree on a road, we wonder what happened. If someone tells us that the tree was hit by a big truck, then it is human to "see" a truck hitting the tree and causing it to fall. The action all happens in the mind's eye, that is, in the imagination. The tree might have actually been struck by lightning, but the accident with the truck will be remembered. Furthermore, the memory of the accident will be so "real" that a person will insist that it actually happened.

3   Psychologists Mark Reinitz and Sharon Hannigan have shown that the mind has a need to understand cause-and-effect relationships. This need makes people "remember" things that have not happened. Therefore, some of our memories can be illusions, mental pictures that are not real! This research and many other studies are helping us understand why we can't remember important (and unimportant)

things like neighbors' names and where we left our keys. People tend to worry about forgetting things. Absentmindedness may be part of getting older, but it is also part of the brain's way of cleaning away unneeded information.

4   Being distracted (thinking about something else) is a primary reason why some people are forgetful. There is even a stereotype of forgetfulness: the absent-minded professor. She is thinking about teaching her morning class, and she doesn't notice that she has put her sweater on inside out. He is thinking about a question a student asked, and he puts his cold cup of coffee into the office refrigerator instead of the microwave oven. Are these people mentally ill? Are they dangerous? No, they are distracted.

5   Some new studies show many interesting aspects of how our brains work. Harvard University psychologist and author Daniel Schacter believes that in our minds we change our reality. He has written a book about the topic, *The Seven Sins of Memory*. According to Schacter, here are some of the ways we affect our memories:

6   **We block some memories.** When we block some memories, we "forget" them or remember only part of the memory. For instance, many people forget names—or remember only that the name starts with an A or a P. Schacter calls this phenomenon blocking. Can you always remember the names of streets or the name of a book that you have recently read? This information is in your mind, but sometimes something else gets in the way, and you cannot bring the name to the surface. It stays on the tip of your tongue.

7   **We create composite memories by combining pieces of many memories into one memory.** Schacter says that we combine memories and create composite memories (grouped ideas). Schacter uses people's memories of an airplane accident as an example. A cargo plane (carrying packages, not people) hit an apartment house. A number of people were killed, and many others were injured. There was a lot of discussion about the accident. There were reports on the radio, and

stories about it in the newspaper. However, there was nothing about the accident on a television video. Even so, months after the accident, a group of psychologists were asked about the videos of the accident. They described "what they had seen." In truth they could not have seen anything, for there was no video. Yet, they had combined what they heard and read to "make" a memory. Schacter calls this phenomenon misattribution. It is incorrectly connecting the content of a memory with the context.

8   **We are suggestible, ready to take ideas from others and make them our own.** Suggestibility describes why people believe something that never happened. They become convinced because they are told about an event. They see it in movies, and they hear about it. So they combine these thoughts into false memories—but not real ones. Psychologists believe that many childhood memories are created by parents for their children. They tell the child that something happened: "Remember when we went to the seashore?" And the child collects beach and vacation ideas into a memory. *Propaganda* is deliberately telling people ideas that you want them to believe. Advertising is another form of suggesting to people, and people of all ages tend to believe advertising. All of us are suggestible; children are particularly so.

9   **We filter our memories according to our emotions about the topic.** Schacter calls it bias. To be biased is to have a strong opinion, positive or negative. Schacter says that we tend to discard as untrue those memories that don't fit the opinion. That's why, he says, married couples who divorce tend to remember only the bad times of their marriage and not the fact that there were also good times. They throw away the memories that do not fit their present feelings.

10   **We hold onto painful memories.** Schacter also mentions the fact that the brain holds onto some memories, particularly emotional situations that are painful. All emotions (*joy, anger, regret, trauma*) strengthen memories, but the negative emotions seem stronger in

making unforgettable memories. An embarrassing moment, a terrible accident, a feeling of rejection–these memories stay with us longer than happy memories. Schacter calls this phenomenon persistence. A persistent thought is one that will not disappear. A child remembers unkind words from an adult for years.

11   As researchers learn more about how our brains work, we begin to understand more about how education works as well. We know that there is a great deal of information in the mind, but we don't always know how to access it. On a computer, when you want to find something, you type in key words and search the database. With your own mind, that technique doesn't always work with trying to remember a name or a fact. However, there is one rather unusual way to stimulate your memory. When you are searching for a name, roll your eyes. It sounds strange, but start with your eyes looking straight up, and then focus slowly to the right, around to the bottom, and then to the far left, and back to the top. Roll your eyes several times. Chances are, odd though it sounds, that within a short time, minutes or days, you will remember the name. This technique stimulates parts of the brain that hold memories.

Strategy Focus: Understanding Internal Structure

There are eleven paragraphs in the main reading. Each of these paragraphs has a main idea. These ideas are restated in the list below. Write the paragraph number that matches each of these ideas. You will be arranging these main ideas to reflect the structure of the reading.

_____ Because we have biased opinions about some memories, we tend to remember the parts of reality that match our feelings.

_____ Memories that are very negative stay with us longer than other, happy, memories.

_____ Some people are easily distracted and forget things because of it.

_____ When we can't remember all of a person's name, it is because we are blocking it.

_____ Two researchers have discovered that many of our memories are illusions.

_____ Research about memory can help us understand more about education.

_____ Sometimes we incorrectly connect content of a memory with how we learned the information, creating a misattribution.

_____ All people, young and old, sometimes forget important things.

_____ A Harvard psychologist has published some of his research findings in a book.

_____ People are likely to believe what others suggest is true.

_____ We seem to make full pictures in our minds, even when we don't have all the information.

strategy focus:

Strategy Focus: Learning Vocabulary in Context

1. **one's mind's eye**

   The action all happens in the **mind's eye**, that is, in the imagination.

   I have enjoyed your story about the house on the edge of the forest. In my **mind's eye**, I can see the little house and the garden. I'm sure it is just as I imagine it.

   When I see something in my **mind's eye**, I am _____.

2. **to block on, blocking**

   When we **block** some memories, we "forget" them or remember only part.

   I know the name of the writer very well. I have read three of her books, but all I can remember is that her first name is Barbara and her last name starts with K. I must be **blocking** on her name. **Blocking** happens more often when I am tired.

   When I **block** on something, I ___*forget*_____.

3. **gap, lapse**

   Psychologists tell us, for example, that our brains "fill in the **gaps**."

   I don't remember anything about my first day in school. I also have a **gap** in my memory of when I was a teenager. For example, I don't remember my sixteenth birthday.

   These **lapses** of memory (failures to remember) are part of human experience.

   There are no **gaps** in my grandfather's memories of his childhood on the farm. However, some days he has **lapses** of memory about current events.

   A **gap** occurs when _____ an emty space _____.

   A **lapse** of memory happens if a person _____ pause _____.

4. **to distract, to be distracted**

   Being **distracted** (thinking about something else) is a primary reason why some people are forgetful.

   Gloria was trying to watch a movie and talk on the phone at the same time. The movie was **distracting** her, and the person on the other end knew she was **distracted** by television. So he decided to call her back later when he could have her full attention.

   If a person is **distracted**, then he or she is _____ took your attention _____.

   If two things are interesting and therefore attracting the attention of a person, those two things are _____.

5. **stereotype**

   There is even a **stereotype** of forgetfulness: the absent-minded professor.

   He was the **stereotype** of the tourist in Hawaii. He was wearing a brightly colored shirt, short pants, and a lot of camera equipment.

   I think it's wrong to **stereotype** people. All blondes are not silly, and all people with glasses are not intelligent.

   Mrs. Donohue fits the **stereotype** of the Irish grandmother. She loves to sing, dance, tell stories, and boss other people around.

   A **stereotype** is _____ when you judge a person for hole groups.

6. **composite**

Schacter says that we combine memories and create **composite** memories (grouped ideas).

Here is a photograph of all the members of my family. It's really a **composite** of five different family photos, but I put them together so that I could have one picture with all the family members on it.

A **composite** is made up of _memories._

7. **cargo**

A **cargo** plane (carrying packages, not people) hit an apartment house.

Experienced travelers know that they can sometimes travel cheaply on a **cargo** ship. There are no special activities for passengers, but the cost is much less. Passenger ships, on the other hand, sometimes carry small amounts of **cargo**, usually for their passengers. A person's car, for example, might be carried as **cargo**.

Some airplane companies, such as those belonging to package delivery companies, carry only **cargo**, no people.

Cargo is _Carrying packages._

8. **attribute, misattribution**

Schacter calls this phenomenon **misattribution**. It is incorrectly connecting the content of a memory with the context.

I heard a great story on the radio yesterday. I was surprised when the story-teller **attributed** the story to the artist Pablo Picasso. Picasso gets credit for many works of art, but not many stories.

I thought Jerry told me the news last week, but now I know it couldn't have been Jerry. He was out of town, so I am guilty of **misattribution**. I wonder if Sue told me. I'd like to be able to **attribute** the information to someone.

To **attribute** information to someone means to _____.

Misattribution occurs when one thinks that person X said it, but in reality _____.

أفعال،

9. **suggest, suggestible, propaganda, deliberately**

We are **suggestible**, ready to take ideas from others and make them our own.

Propaganda is **deliberately** telling people ideas that you want them to believe.

Let me give you some ideas for gifts this year. I can **suggest** some good books for your brother.

Children are vulnerable to advertising because they believe everything. Advertisers **deliberately** use the fact that young people are **suggestible**. Advertisers' job is to increase sales. So they plan how to attract children to their products. They make children believe that they want things that they might not really want.

Propaganda is a special kind of advertising. If you tell a person twenty or a hundred times that he is thirsty, he begins to want something to drink. If you tell a person that X is true enough times, he will believe it. People are **suggestible**! Propaganda can be used **deliberately** to change people's opinions.

If a person does something **deliberately**, has he or she thought about it? Is he or she doing it for a purpose?

If I **suggest** something to you, I am ___advise___ .

The fact that people are **suggestible** means that their opinions

_____ .

Propaganda is a special type of ___advertising___ , which is used to change ___people's opinions.___ .

To do something **deliberately** is to do it because _____ .

10. **bias, to be biased**

To be **biased** is to have a strong opinion, positive or negative.

Is it possible for a parent not to be **biased** about his or her children? Most parents admit that they have feelings of **bias** because it is natural for a parent to be proud of the child.

The people of the town wanted to have an opinion of the park plans from a person without **bias**. They asked five people from different parts of the country. These opinions were honest and not affected by local issues.

It's not easy to avoid making an early decision, but a good judge has no **bias**.

A person who is **biased** is ___to have a strong opinion___ .

A person with a **bias** has ___parents be ploud of the child___ .

11. **persistent, persistence**

Schacter calls this phenomenon **persistence**. A **persistent** thought is one that will not disappear.

That child has a **persistent** cough. It just won't go away.

Tom asked Mr. Wagoner for a job at Wagoner's Store every Saturday for two months. Finally, Tom's **persistence** had results. Mr. Wagoner hired him. Tom was **persistent** in his asking for a job.

The quality of **persistence** is good in a child because children face many disappointments.

Something or someone that is **persistent** doesn't ___disappear___ .

Persistence is ___good in a child___

12. **access, to access**

We know that there is a great deal of information in the mind, but we don't always know how to **access** it.

I don't have **access** to that building. I don't have a key.

You can use my computer to **access** your e-mail. Just log on and use your own password. Your messages will come up.

Access to that building is through the front door, the side door, and the back door. There is also roof **access**.

If you have **access** to something, then you can ___enter or get in___

To **access** information is to ___find.___ .

Strategy Focus: Discussing the Issues

1. Why do you think many people have trouble remembering where they put their glasses or their keys?

2. Think about an advertisement that you have seen. What does the advertisement suggest?

3. Many magazine advertisements have beautiful women and handsome men in the pictures. Why do advertisers use good looks to sell products? What aspect of the human brain is the focus?

4. Do you believe that emotional response has anything to do with how clearly you remember something? Why or why not?

5. Some opinions are *objective*. Others are *subjective*. An *objective* opinion is like a photograph because it gives a clear picture with all the details. A *subjective* opinion is like a painting of the same scene. It gives the artist's interpretation. The reading says that many of our memories are not as objective as we believe. People can be objective about topics that are not interesting or threatening to them. What things are you likely to be *objective* about? When are you likely to be *subjective*? Why?

Strategy: Reading Scientific Material

The next related reading is written in the language of science. To understand the new words that you read, write each one down on a long strip of paper. As you find definitions for the medical words, record the meanings. Nearly all of these scientific words are useful words for you, and you can use your list of definitions to help you read efficiently.

 ## Related Reading 1

The Human Brain

1　　　It is common to compare the human brain and the computer. The human brain is the central processing unit (CPU) of a living body. It directs all the body's functions. The brain sends signals for the body's *respiration* (breathing), *digestion* (the breaking down of foods into substances that the body can use), and the *circulation* (blood and other fluids through the body). In human beings, the brain regulates the ability to move muscles to walk, talk, and also maintain balance. The brain receives and interprets information from the *senses*: it not only allows us to see, hear, feel, smell, and taste, but it also enables the body to react to *sensory* input. The brain recognizes danger and sends messages about how to escape from a dangerous situation.

2   The human brain is adaptive to some specific function, or tasks. It can recognize patterns; that's why people can express their understanding of the world by such means as language and mathematics. The brain makes possible experiencing emotions such as sadness and happiness. The brain is also responsible for the human ability to think—to form ideas, to remember, to predict, to judge, and to create imaginary pictures. Indeed, there is no life without the brain. Babies that are born without a fully formed brain die soon after birth, usually within a few hours. It is surprising, therefore, that less is known about the brain than about any other organ of the body. Scientists and doctors understand the heart, liver, stomach, and lungs much better than the brain.

3   The adult human brain is made up of about one hundred billion cells. All of these cells and more are present when a person is born, but some brain cells die naturally every day. There are so many brain cells, however, that their loss is not noticed. However, it is important to remember that the brain never gets any new brain cells; if they are destroyed, they are gone forever. It is also important to remember that some activities like smoking and some chemical substances, like drugs, increase brain cell death dramatically, and that great loss of brain cells damages a person *irreversibly*.

4   The brain cells that do the thinking are called *neurons*; they come in many different sizes, some less than a millimeter in length, some more than a meter (about a yard). Each brain cell generally consists of a central cell body with a set of dendrites and an axon, both of which extend from the cell body. The thin, threadlike dendrites are branches like long thin hairlike roots that they go out from the central cell body, sometimes forming as many as a thousand branches. Each branch sends and receives messages to and from other neurons, thus forming a *network* of brain connections.

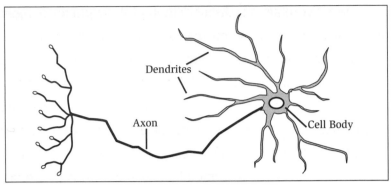

A neuron

5   Although one neuron may have thousands of dendrites, it has only one axon extending from the central cell body. The axon is a long *filament* (rather like a thread) that is surrounded by protective insulation. Axons transmit (send) information from one neuron to another; so, together with dendrites, axons make communication among neurons possible. Surprisingly, neurons almost never touch one another; they are separated by an extremely small space, a *synapse*. One or more specific chemicals called neurotransmitters (or "senders") are released from the axon of one neuron and travel across the synapses (small space or gap) between the axon and the connecting dendrites from other neurons. It is through these neurotransmitters that neurons communicate with one another.

6   Although nearly one hundred distinct (different) neurotransmitters have already been identified, most experts think that more of these chemical communicators will be discovered. Each of the roughly one hundred chemicals causes a distinct reaction in the receiving dendrite. Sometimes the reaction tells the neuron to ignore the message. However, at other times, the reaction produces a distinct electrical current. The electrical impulse (a signal) travels through the dendrites to the cell body, where tiny amounts of energy begin to collect. When a large enough charge has accumulated in the cell body, the cell body transmits an electrical charge (the impulse) down its axon

to a synapse. The charge crosses the synapse and enters another cell. How does the energy get from the axon to the other cell? Inside the axon, very near the synapse, there are hundreds of tiny containers or pockets (they are called *vesicles*), all full of neurotransmitters. When an electrical impulse reaches these vesicles, it may cause some of them to release their chemical contents. The chemicals jump across the synapse, carrying the message.

7   Communication among the neurons is an electrochemical process; it involves interrelated electrical and chemical signals. The human brain supports an amazingly complex electrochemical communication system. It consists of about 100 billion neurons; each one is capable of receiving chemical information from 100 to 1,000 other neurons, transforming the chemical information into an electrical impulse, and finally transmitting this information by using various combinations of at least one hundred distinct neurotransmitters. The number of cell connections and the amount of information that can be received and transmitted are staggering! Most people do not understand such large numbers because they are far too large for the human mind to imagine. Moreover, as experts learn more about the brain, the statistics (the numbers that show the results of a research project) from their research will undoubtedly be even more difficult to understand.

8   Some of the most important and interesting research on the brain focuses on the connections among neurons. This research shows that neurotransmitters nourish (feed) the dendrites in the neuron. Without these nourishing chemicals, dendrites become weak and may even die and decay. If the neurotransmitting chemicals are produced, the brain remains healthy and develops its abilities. In order to produce neurotransmitters, neurons must be stimulated (exercised by receiving information). Most of this stimulation must come from outside, from the environment. Therefore, the role of stimulation must also be studied.

9   A striking example of the effects of outside stimulation on brain development comes from some recent research projects on vision. The research demonstrated that without *visual* stimulation (without interesting things to see) to cause the release of neurotransmitters, the ability to see and understand visual information does not develop. For example, one research project involved the study of children born with severe *cataracts*. Cataracts are cloudy places on the lens inside the eye, which can prevent the eye from seeing. Scientists now know that what actually happens is that the cataracts prevent light from reaching the neurons' dendrites. Researchers have found that if the neurons in a newborn baby's eye are not stimulated within a specified amount of time, they react in predictable ways. Some of the dendrites seem to "look for" connections with neurons that are not genetically programmed to receive and process visual stimuli. For example, the dendrites might connect with neurons that process *tactile* information (information that is received through the process of touch) or *auditory* information (information that is received as sound, through hearing). If only one eye has a cataract, the dendrites of the affected eye's neurons often connect with the neurons of the unaffected eye. These connections strengthen that eye's ability to respond to visual stimuli. If the dendrites fail to connect with another neuron, they *atrophy* (become smaller and weaker) and die. After some time, there are no neurons left that can interpret information from the eye with the cataract.

10   This damage seems to be permanent and irreversible. Even if removing the cloudiness of the cataract surgically results in a perfectly healthy eye, the eye does not "see" because it has already lost its connecting network of dendrites. Those neurons that could have done the connecting and interpreting have either made other connections or atrophied. Because of this research, doctors today remove cataracts from babies' eyes as soon as possible to prevent blindness. If the cataracts are removed early, the child's eyes will receive the necessary visual stimulation to develop normal sight.

11   Medical research supports the idea that stimulation of all kinds is necessary for a healthy brain, especially for children (whose brains are developing), but also throughout life. Stimulation produces the neurotransmitters which in turn nourish the neurons that make up the brain. There might actually be a connection between the amount and kind of stimulation and the kind of intelligence a child develops as an adult. For this reason, medical experts suggest that people keep their brains working by working their brains. Reading challenging ideas, doing puzzles, and focusing one's attention on interesting topics are some suggestions.

12   Another important finding from the research on vision and similar brain functions is that the brain is constantly changing. Neurons can change functions; they can release new neurotransmitters in response to new stimuli. They can learn to recognize new relationships. In other words, the brain can continue to learn, and there is no age limit on learning. In some cases, when the cells in one part of the brain are damaged, neurons in another part of the brain can take over the functions of the damaged neurons.

13   As people learn more about the brain, their appreciation of this remarkable organ increases. There is much in the research that applies to ordinary people leading ordinary lives—on everything from the effects of not enough sleep or poor nutrition to the damage that smoking or drug use causes to brain cells. One thing is certain: the brain needs exercise just like all other parts of the body. All people need to use their brains to think; those who do not "use their heads" will lose some of the unique power of their incredible brains.

Strategy Focus: Finding the Main Idea

There are thirteen sentences in the list that follows. One is a general statement that summarizes the reading; first look for the most general statement and write *thesis* (main idea of a reading) in the blank before it. The others are main idea statements for the numbered paragraphs. Check these sentences to match them with individual paragraphs. Write the matching paragraph number in the blank.

1. _____ The brain has a lot of brain cells but once lost, they do not grow back.

2. _____ Researchers are studying the role of stimulation in brain development.

3. _____ The brain is always changing and learning.

4. _____ Messages are transferred within the brain by an electrochemical process.

5. _____ The brain is a complex organ that scientists are learning more about daily.

6. _____ Research on cataracts in babies has shown the importance of timely stimulation.

7. _____ The brain needs to be exercised in order to work well.

8. _____ Brain cells with a complex structure are neurons.

9. _____ The brain is capable of critical thinking.

10. _____ Neurotransmitting chemicals are essential for a healthy brain.

11. _____ Once brain connections for vision are made, these connections do not move.

12. _____ The brain runs the whole body.

13. _____ Over a hundred different chemicals cause the brain to work as it does.

Strategy Focus: Scanning for Details

Read quickly to find the answers to these questions.

1. Find the names of five body organs in the reading.

   _____ _____ _____

   _____ _____

2. How many brain cells does a newborn baby have? _____

3. What is the scientific name for thinking cells? _____

4. What two reasons are there for brain cells to die?

   _____ _____

5. What is the space between neurons called? _____

6. What brain structure is like a center with threads branching out?

   _____

7. What is a *vesicle*? _____

8. What is a *cataract*? Why do doctors remove cataracts as soon as possible in babies? _____

9. What is the *visual* sense? _____

10. What is the *tactile* sense? _____

11. What is the name of the sense of hearing? _____

12. What other senses are there? (There are five senses in all.)

    _____ _____ _____

    _____

Strategy Focus: Understanding Scientific Style

In a report on research, the writer's focus is on what information researchers have learned, not the person or people who did the research and experimentation. That is why there are many passive verbs. The main reading is written in scientific style, and it contains many passive verb forms.

Here are some passive phrases from the reading. Can you change them to active voice?

Example:

Passive: [The] brain does not ever get any new brain cells; once they *are destroyed*, they *are gone* forever.

Active: *The brain does not ever get any new brain cells; once something destroys them, nothing makes them return.*

1. Passive: There are so many brain cells, however, that their loss is *not noticed*.

   Active: _____

2. Passive: [Less] *is known* about the brain than about any other organ of the body.

   Active: _____

3. Passive: Therefore, the role of stimulation *must also be studied*.

   Active: _____

4. Passive: In order to produce neurotransmitters, neurons *must be stimulated* (exercised by receiving information).

   Active: _____

5. Passive: …tactile information (that is, information that *is received* through the process of touch).

   Active: _____

6. Passive: If the cataracts *are removed* quickly, the child's eyes will receive the necessary visual stimulation to develop normal sight.

   Active: _____

Strategy Focus: Learning About Word Families

The main reading is full of scientific kinds of words (verbs and related nouns) that are used in everyday speech. Here are some pairs or sets of words that you will find useful. Write the letter of the meaning in front of the pair or set of scientific words.

a. to stop (from happening)

b. to control, as with a law

c. to give shape to

d. to join, to link

e. to protect from outside forces

f. to excite, to interest

g. to build up, to collect

h. to value, to know the worth

i. to add together, to mix

j. to go around in a circle

k. to send and receive messages

l. to give an answer, to act after a stimulus

m. to see in one's mind, to make a mental picture

n. to understand what a new thing is

o. to use food appropriately for nourishment

1. _____ to connect – connector – connection

2. _____ to imagine – imaginary – imagination

3. _____ to digest – digestion

4. _____ to stimulate – stimulus/stimuli – stimulation

5. _____ to insulate – insulation

6. _____ to prevent – prevention

7. _____ to combine – combination

8. _____ to communicate – communicator – communication

9. _____ to regulate – regulation

10. _____ to circulate – circulation

11. _____ to appreciate – appreciation

12. _____ to accumulate – accumulation

13. _____ to react – reaction

14. _____ to recognize – recognition

15. _____ to form – formation

Strategy Focus: Learning Vocabulary in Context

Here are some of the other words in the reading. Read them in context and figure out the meanings.

1. **synapse**

   Surprisingly, neurons almost never touch one another; they are separated by an extremely small space, a **synapse**. One or more specific chemicals called neurotransmitters (or "senders") are released from the axon of one neuron and travel across the **synapses** (breaks or gaps) between the axon and connecting dendrites from other neurons.

   A **synapse** is a _____ .

2. **filament**

   The axon is a long **filament** (rather like a thread) that is surrounded by protective insulation.

   There is a **filament** in most electrical lightbulbs. It is the thin metal wire that glows.

   Scientists can learn a great deal from one **filament** of hair.

   A **filament** is like _____ .

3. **atrophy**

   If the dendrites fail to connect with another neuron, they **atrophy** (grow smaller and weaker) and die.

   Studies show that if person doesn't speak his or her native language for several years, the native language **atrophies** although it does not disappear.

   When a body part **atrophies**, it _____ .

4. **tactile, auditory, the senses, sensory**

   [Dendrites] might connect with neurons that process **tactile** information (that is, information that is received through the process of touch) or **auditory** information (information that is received as sound, through hearing).

   The five senses are visual, **tactile**, **auditory**, olfactory, and gustatory. They are the **senses** of sight, touch, hearing, smelling, and tasting.

The brain receives and interprets information from the **senses**: it not only allows us to see, feel, hear, smell, and taste, but it also enables the body to react to the **sensory** input.

Tactile information is information that is received through the

process of _____ , and **auditory** information

is received as _____ .

Sight and hearing are two of the five _____ .

The eyes, ears, nose, skin, and mouth receive _____ input.

5. **respiration, digestion, circulation**

   The brain is the central processing unit of a living body. It directs all the body's functions, such as **respiration** (breathing), **digestion** (the breaking down of foods into substances that the body can use), and the **circulation** (blood and other fluids through the body).

   If you have too much acid in your stomach, you might have **digestion** troubles.

   If your hands are cold, rub them together to increase blood **circulation**.

   Respiration refers to _____ .

   Digestion refers to _____ .

   Circulation refers to _____ .

6. **irreversible**

   Sensory input refers to receiving information from one's senses like eyesight and hearing. That damage seems to be permanent and **irreversible**.

   The company president's decision to sell cannot be undone. It is **irreversible**.

   If something is **irreversible**, it is _____ .

7. Each branch sends and receives messages to and from other neurons, thus forming a **network** of brain connections.

   A **network** involves...

   a. thinking.

   b. connections.

   c. branching.

Strategy Focus: Discussing the Reading

1. The writer compares the human brain with a computer. How is the human brain like the central processing unit of a computer? Which is more powerful? Why do you think so? What do computers do better than a human brain can? What are some of the things that a human brain does better?

2. *Myelin* is the natural insulation around nerves. It is like rubber or plastic around electrical wires. Some nerves do not have myelin around them when a child is born. For example, a newborn child does not have the myelin insulation around the neural (nerve) connections that are necessary to walk. That's why a human baby cannot walk. Likewise, baby cats (lions, tigers, cheetahs) and baby dogs (wolves, jackals, foxes) cannot walk at birth. However, newborn horses, baby cows, and many wild animals can walk soon after birth. What does this fact tell you about survival?

3. *Use it or lose it*: What does this saying mean in regard to brain stimulation? How can you exercise your brain?

4. What kind of electricity does the brain use?

Strategy Focus: Making Inferences

Do we have enough information to make each of these statements? Check (✓) *enough* or *not enough*.

1. A person dies when all of his or her brain cells die, a few each day.

☐ enough   ☐ not enough

2. The use of chemical substances (like drugs) kills brain cells.

☐ enough   ☐ not enough

3. Cataracts affect vision.

☐ enough   ☐ not enough

4. A baby has to learn how to see.

☐ enough   ☐ not enough

5. Scientists find it easy to study the human brain.

☐ enough   ☐ not enough

6. The brain tries to help the body survive, no matter what problems the body has.

    ☐ enough   ☐ not enough

7. All brain cells are nearly like all other brain cells.

    ☐ enough   ☐ not enough

8. Children have brain cells, and these cells are open to the connections made in learning.

    ☐ enough   ☐ not enough

9. Thinking is good for the human brain.

    ☐ enough   ☐ not enough

10. Brain cells must receive food (nourishment) to work well.

    ☐ enough   ☐ not enough

Strategy: Using a Matrix to Solve a Puzzle

Look at the matrices (one matrix, two matrices) or charts in the next related reading and try to figure out what they mean. Then check your understanding by carefully reading the explanations. As you try to solve the puzzles, make charts and diagrams of your own. When is a matrix more useful than a paragraph?

 # Relating Reading 2

Exercising the Brain Through Riddles

1   Some of the oldest forms of entertainment in the world are word games, riddles, and puzzles. For example: *What walks on four legs in the morning, on two at midday, and three in the evening?* This old riddle has entertained many people for years. And when morning, noon, and evening are seen as times of life, the answer is clear. A baby crawls on hands and knees, an adult walks on two legs, and an old person needs a cane. Finding the answer requires a flexible mind,

but some riddles require only careful listening. Other riddles require the thinker to go through the process step-by-step. Meanwhile, here are some puzzles that require only following a *methodology*, an organized way of discovering the answer. They can be a lot of fun, but sometimes the answer is not as simple as it seems.

2 **Careful listening riddle**

In the St. Ives riddle you need to know that a *kit* is a kitten:
  As I was going to St. Ives,
  I met a man with seven wives.
  Each wife had seven sacks.
  Each sack held seven cats,
  Each cat had seven kits.
  Cats, kits, man, and wives,
  How many were going to St. Ives?

3 **Solution:** The answer to this one is not difficult at all, and it requires no mathematics. If you don't understand, read each line carefully and think about it. What does the riddle say? "I" was going to St. Ives. Everyone else was leaving St. Ives.

4 **Careful reading and figuring out the riddle**

To solve this riddle, you need to think before you answer; what seems like the answer at first glance is NOT.

  Arthur bought his wife a gift of a beautiful
  bottle of skin lotion.
  He paid $10.
  He intends to recycle the bottle,
  so he asked about the price of the bottle.
  The shopkeeper told him, "The lotion is
  worth $9 more than the bottle."
  How much is the bottle worth?

5 **Solution:** Most people will look at this little question and not recognize that it is a puzzle at all. They will say, "If the bottle of lotion costs $10, and if the lotion is worth $9 more than the bottle, then subtract 9 from 10. The bottle is worth one dollar." However, that is not the correct answer, and the interpretation of the story is also incorrect.

Read again what the shopkeeper said. The shopkeeper did not say that the lotion was worth $9. She said that it was worth $9 more than the bottle. In fact, the one dollar that is left is twice the value of the bottle.

This problem can be written as an equation: $2x + 9 = 10$.

To solve for x, you subtract 9 from both sides: $2x + 9 - 9 = 10 - 9$. That reduces to $2x = 1$.

To solve for x, divide both sides of the equation by 2.

That reduces to $x = .5$ (or ½) Half of one dollar is fifty cents. Therefore, the bottle is worth 50 cents, and the lotion is worth $9 more than the bottle, or $9.50.

6 Puzzles like this one are popular because they keep the mind sharp and ready to think clearly. It has been proved that people who work puzzles are less likely to lose their mental abilities; perhaps that accounts for the large number of puzzle books that are sold every day. Or perhaps people simply enjoy working the puzzles.

7 **Step-by-step riddle**

Solve this kind of riddle by following the directions one at a time.

Joshua has two kinds of socks,
black ones and brown ones.
He has ten pairs of each color. (40 socks!)
Joshua is rather lazy, and he doesn't wash his
socks very often. When he does wash his socks,
he doesn't take the time to pair them (put two black
ones or two brown ones together). He just throws
them all into a box in the bottom of his dark closet.
How many socks must Joshua take out of the box
to be sure that he has a matching pair?

8 **Solution:** With this puzzle, just follow the action. First Joshua takes out one sock. It is either black or brown. Then he takes out another sock; this one is either black or brown. If the first sock is black and the second sock is brown (or if the reverse is true), then the third sock must be either black or brown. It will match one of the two socks that Joshua took out of the box already. The answer is that Joshua will need to take out three socks to be sure. He might have a matching pair with only two socks, but we can't be certain.

9 **Step-by-step riddle:**

A frog falls into a well.
The well is ten yards deep.
The well has a rope.
The frog can climb up the rope, but slowly.
The frog can climb up three yards a day.
At night, the frog rests. As he rests, he slides down two yards.
How many days will it take the frog to climb out of the well?

10 **Solution:** The first calculation is to figure out how much progress the frog makes each day. He climbs three yards and slides back two yards. Therefore, he makes a yard of progress each day. (But don't be fooled! Don't think that if the frog makes a gain of one yard each 24 hours that it will take him ten whole days. It isn't that easy!) Use the step-by-step methodology and follow it through.

- The first day, the frog climbs three yards and slides back two yards, making one yard of progress.
- The second whole day, the frog makes a gain of another yard for a two-yard progress.
- The third day, the frog climbs up three more yards and slides down two yards, but the frog is now three yards from the bottom.
- At the end of the fourth whole day, he is four yards from the bottom.
- At the end of the fifth day, he is five yards from the bottom and the top—halfway there!
- At the end of the sixth day, the frog is six yards from the bottom and four yards from the top.
- At the end of the seventh day, the frog is seven yards from the water at the bottom of the well and three yards from the top.
- During the eighth day, the frog climbs up those three yards, and he doesn't need to rest! Because he is at the top of the well, he jumps out of the well. It didn't take him ten days at all!

11   **Step-by-step and "thinking outside the box"**

To solve this kind of riddle, you will use the step-by-step method, but you will also have to notice what rules there are and what rules there are not.

An explorer needs to cross the desert, starting from the town of Palm Spring and going to Oasis.
It is a six-day hike. However, one person can carry only enough food and water for four days. How can he cross the desert?

(Hint: Can he do it all alone? Or does he need help?)

12   **Solution:** To solve this puzzle, follow the methodology and talk the story out. Draw a map for the explorer. On one side write *Palm Spring*. On the other side write *Oasis*. Draw 5 dots between Palm Spring and Oasis to represent the stopping points for each day of travel. Label them Camp #1, Camp #2, Camp #3, Camp #4, and Camp #5. If the explorer goes alone, he will eat one day's worth of food and drink one day's worth of water the first day. He will have three days' worth left.

13   If two people go, both carrying four days' worth of food and water, they would have eight days' worth of food between them. They could walk one day and each consume one day's worth and have six days' worth left, walk a second day and have consumed two days' worth (for a total of four days' worth). That would leave four days' worth of food and water. Then the second man would have to turn around and go back, and he would need to take two days' worth of food with him. That would leave two days' worth of food and water for the explorer, which is not enough.

14   If three people start out with twelve days' worth of food and water, by the end of the first day there is nine days' worth left. One person could take one day's worth and travel back to the beginning point. Four days' worth of food and water (three consumed and one for the return trip) would be used and eight would be left. The next day, the two remaining people consume two more *allotments* of food and water $(8 - 2 = 6)$, and one person takes two of the remaining six and returns to the starting point. That leaves four days' worth of food and water for the explorer to complete the hike.

15 Note that there is another possible answer. For this solution you can use the map. The one person could do it all alone, but it will take the same number of allotments of food and water (12) and more time. He could start out from Palm Spring with four days' worth of food. At the end of the first day's hike, he could consume one and leave two allotments at a camp there (put a *2* at Camp #1). He would consume the fourth allotment that he had started with on the walk back to Palm Spring. At Palm Spring he would pick up four more allotments. This time he would walk two days toward Oasis (consuming two days' worth on the way) and leave one allotment at the stopping place for the second day (at Camp #2). Then he would return with one allotment to stopping Camp #1, consume the allotment he had carried back from Camp #2, and take one of the two allotments left there earlier (and leaving one) for the day of return to Palm Spring. The next day, carrying four allotments, he would travel to Camp #1, consume the food and water there from his first trip out, continue the next day to Camp #2 and consume what he left there his second time out, and he would still be carrying four days' supplies with him for the four remaining days of his hike to Oasis.

Logic Riddle

This kind of puzzle is is really a test of a person's ability to make inferences. To solve a logic puzzle all you need is a piece of paper and a pencil. It also helps to solve a few of these puzzles for practice because there is a method for solving them. Hint: It is best for one person to read this part while the rest of the class follows directions:

Each of four people (Mr. Smith, Mr. Glover, Mr. Brown, and Mr. Hill) owns a different kind of car. From the following clues, you can figure out each man's full name and what kind of car he owns. The kinds of cars are Porsche, Mustang, Miata, and Mercedes.

1. Mr. Smith (who lives in a condominium), Alan, and Mr. Brown all belong to a club for sports car owners.
2. The Porsche isn't owned by either Cary or David.
3. Neither the Mustang nor the Mercedes is owned by Mr. Brown.
4. The Miata doesn't belong to David (who lives in a small apartment).

5. Alan, who doesn't own the Mercedes, isn't Mr. Glover.

6. John and Mr. Brown are neighbors.

7. Mr. Hill is afraid to drive a Porsche.

17 **Solution:** Set up two kinds of *grids*. On these grids, you will write the results of the inferences that you make. The first is a *fill-in-the-blank* grid.

First name	_____	_____	_____	_____
Last name	_____	_____	_____	_____
Type of car	_____	_____	_____	_____

The second kind of grid is a *crosshatch* grid with the variables written across both axes (An *axis* is either the up and down or the across direction on a graph; the plural of axis is *axes*). There are three variables in this puzzle (first name, last name, and type of car). The horizontal (across) axis is a *row*; the vertical (up and down) axis is a *column*.

	Smith	Brown	Glover	Hill	Porsche	Mustang	Mercedes	Miata
Alan								
Cary								
John								
David								
Porsche								
Mustang								
Mercedes								
Miata								

18 Now, you read each clue and make *X*s where a first name, a last name, or a type of car won't fit. In this case, you are *eliminating* possibilities. This part of the process is called the *process of elimination*. The first clue says that Mr. Smith, Alan, and Mr. Brown are members of a club. Therefore, you can make an inference: you know that Alan is not Mr. Smith or Mr. Brown. Put *X*s after Alan in the crosshatch grid under *Smith* and *Brown*.

	Smith	Brown	Glover	Hill	Porsche	Mustang	Mercedes	Miata
Alan	X	X						
Cary								
John								
David								
Porsche								
Mustang								
Mercedes								
Miata								

In the fill-in-the-blank grid, write in the name *Alan* on the first name line, and the names *Smith* and *Brown* on the last name line.

First name	_Alan_	_____	_____	_____
Last name	_____	_Smith_	_Brown_	_____
Type of car	_____	_____	_____	_____

19 Read the second clue and below *Porsche*, cross out *David* and *Cary*. (Now you see why the names of the cars need to be listed on both axes. You may know something about a person through his last name and not through his first name.) Read clue 3 and put an *X* after *Mustang* and *Mercedes* for Mr. Brown. Clue 4 tells you to put an *X* after David's name in the Miata column. The fourth clue also tells you that David lives in a small apartment; looking back at clue l, you see that Mr. Smith lives in a condo. Therefore, you can make another inference. A person can only live in one place; therefore, you know that David is not Mr. Smith. The fifth clue tells you to make an *X* after Alan's name, under *Mercedes* and under *Glover*. That means that now you know Alan's full name: Alan Hill. Therefore, you can make another inference: none of the other men is Hill, so you can cross out *Hill* for *Cary, David,* and *John*. Make a big *O* under *Hill* in Alan's row.

Go to your fill-in-the-blank grid and add the names *Hill* (under *Alan*) and *Glover*, in the fourth set of blanks.

First name	_Alan_			
Last name	_Hill_	_Smith_	_Brown_	_Glover_
Type of car				

20   The sixth clue tells you that John isn't Mr. Brown (one lives next door to the other), so cross out *Brown* in John's row in the crosshatch grid. The last clue tells you that Mr. Hill doesn't have a Porsche. You know that Alan is Mr. Hill, so you can cross out *Porsche* on the grid after Alan's name and also under *Hill*. That means that John must own the Porsche because Porsche is crossed out after Alan, Cary, and David. Draw a big *O* in John's row under *Porsche*. Make *X*s in the other car columns because if John owns a Porsche, he doesn't own a Mustang, a Miata, or a Mercedes. There is nothing certain yet to add to the fill-in-the-blank grid. Now go back to clue 6. You know that John owns the Porsche and that John isn't Mr. Brown; therefore, Mr. Brown doesn't own the Porsche. Now you have three *X*s under *Brown* in the car column, so Mr. Brown owns the Miata. Now put *X*s in the other three spaces in the Miata row, cross out *Miata* in Alan's row (Alan isn't Mr. Brown), and now there is only one space left: the owner of the Miata is Cary. Draw a big *O* under *Miata* in Cary's row. Add *X*s to Cary's row because he doesn't own the other cars if he owns a Miata. Therefore, Cary is Mr. Brown (draw an *O* under *Brown* in Cary's row) because Mr. Brown owns the Miata. Draw *X*s in the blanks of Cary's row and under *Brown* in David's row. That means David is Mr. Glover. Let's stop and fill in some blanks in the other grid:

First name	_Alan_		_Cary_	_David_
Last name	_Hill_	_Smith_	_Brown_	_Glover_
Type of car			_Miata_	

21   Now there are several other places that have three *X*s: Alan Hill must own a Mustang, so draw the big *O* there and fill in *Mustang* in the fill-in-the-blank grid. Remember to cross out Mustang in David's row. Now you know that David doesn't own the Porsche, the Mustang, or the Miata; therefore, he owns the Mercedes. Add that information to the grid.

Looking at the Smith column, there are three *X*s; therefore, John must be Mr. Smith, and we know that he owns the Porsche. Add that information to the fill-in-the-blank grid to complete it.

First name	Alan	John	Cary	David
Last name	Hill	Smith	Brown	Glover
Type of car	Mustang	Smith	Miata	Mercedes

One of the hints in figuring out puzzles like this one is to use the two kinds of grids. The second hint is that when you have gone through all the obvious hints, look for a row or a column that has two *X*s. Try to figure out how you can find a third box to put an *X* in by reviewing everything you know about the people or the elements in that row or column.

22 Logic Puzzle

Note that in this riddle *F* means a woman, a female; *M* means a man, a male.

Linda (F), Terry (F), Martin (M), and John (M) all went out on Friday night. One went to a restaurant, one to see a movie, one to a coffeehouse to hear some folk singing, and the other to a play. Each one went with a friend—Betty (F), Lance (M), Sally (F), or Tim (M). Two went out with members of the same sex, and two went out with members of the opposite sex. Can you figure out the name of the person each one went out with and where they went? Use the clues that follow. The solution to this one is not given to you. You are on your own!

1. One of the four went for coffee with a woman named Betty.
2. Martin went out with a friend named Lance.
3. The pair who went to a restaurant were a man and a woman.
4. Linda and a friend, who wasn't Tim, went to a see a play.
5. One pair of friends went to a movie.

Make a fill-in-the-blank grid with columns for *Name, Guest,* and *Event.*

Make a grid with nine horizontal lines (eight rows) with these directions:

Write the names of the first four people (*John, Linda, Teresa,* and *Martin*) down the left side on the horizontal lines; then write the names of the entertainment possibilities (*restaurant, movie, coffee,* and *play*) below these names also on the vertical axis.

Draw nine vertical lines and write *Betty, Lance, Sally,* and *Tim; restaurant, movie, coffee,* and *play* as column names. See the grid that follows. And good luck!

	Betty	Lance	Sally	Tim	Restaurant	Movie	Coffee	Play
John								
Linda								
Teresa								
Martin								
Restaurant								
Movie								
Coffee								
PlaXy								

Strategy Focus: Learning Vocabulary in Context

The new words in this reading are used in a number of sentences to help you understand their full meaning. Read the sentences and then decide on the meaning.

1. **grid, crosshatch, vertical, horizontal**

   The **grid** was a box that was made up of eleven **horizontal** lines and eleven **vertical** lines, creating a **crosshatch** pattern of one hundred squares.

   The students were told that answers to the examination were to be recorded on a special piece of paper; it had a **grid** to be read by computer. The numbers for the questions were arranged **vertically**, and the choices (a, b, c, and d) were arranged **horizontally**.

   The symbol for "number" is a **crosshatch** (#).

   During the race, the speeds of the vehicles in the race were recorded on a large **grid**.

The speeds were noted across the **horizontal** axis, and the names of the drivers were written along the **vertical** axis.

A **grid** is a picture made of _____ .

A **crosshatch** is a symbol made of _____ .

A **vertical** line goes in a/an _____ direction.

A **horizontal** line goes in a/an _____ direction.

2. **row, column, calculate, calculation, subtract, axis**

The arithmetic test contained fifteen questions for the students to **calculate**. The first five were columns of numbers to be added, then there was a row of five sets of numbers to be **subtracted**.

During the race, the speeds of the vehicles in the race were recorded on a large grid. The speeds were noted across the horizontal **axis**, and the names of the car drivers were written along the vertical **axis**. By reading the two **axes**, a person could **calculate** the relative speeds at different times in the race. Speed **calculations** are made in miles per hour (mph) or kilometers per hour (kph). The average speeds were noted in a **column** at the end of each row.

Nine **subtracted** from ten leaves one.

The soldiers marched in straight **columns** and perfect **rows**.

In setting up a graph, two variables are placed, one on each **axis**.

A **row** is a line that goes _____ .

A **column** is a line that goes _____ .

To **calculate** requires _____ .

A **calculation** is an _____ .

To **subtract** one number from another is to find the…

    a. total of the two.

    b. difference between them.

    c. increase in them.

An **axis** is most like a _____ .

3. **closet, condominium, condo, to be worth**

The **closet** in the **condominium** was remodeled, and now there are shelves for shoes, drawers for socks and underwear, and poles for clothes to hang on. A well-planned **closet** is worth a lot to a homeowner. The school has a large supply **closet** where paper, pencils, and the like are stored.

There is a difference between the cost of a house and the cost of a **condominium**.

Because **condos** are attached houses, there is less land; therefore, a **condo** costs less than a house with a yard. Land is worth a lot of money.

An old car may **be worth** much more to the owner than its market value.

A **closet** is a place to _____ .

A **condominium** is a _____ , and a condo is _____ .

If something **is worth** a lot of money, then you _____ to buy it.

4. **to eliminate, the process of elimination, to reduce**

Only five people could enter the contest from each school. The judges had to **eliminate** ten of the fifteen students who wanted to participate. It was the only way to **reduce** the number to five.

Improvements in automobile manufacturing are, one by one, **eliminating** many of the old dangers of driving and **reducing** the number of deaths in automobile accidents.

I didn't know the right answer to the questions, but I realized that I knew some of the wrong answers. I could **reduce** the number of choices, so I **eliminated** the answers that were obviously wrong. By the **process of elimination**, I decreased my choices to two per question. Then I studied the questions and gave my best guess.

To **reduce** the number of things is to _____ the number.

To **eliminate** is to _____ the number of choices.

In the **process of elimination**, a person decreases the number of choices by _____ .

5. **to consume**

The paper mill **consumes** ten railroad cars of wood every day.

The fire **consumed** everything in its path.

She has an all-**consuming** interest in Shakespeare and won't even look at other writers' works.

The average teenager **consumes** eight fast-food meals a week.

To **consume** is to _____ .

Strategy: Analyzing Your Own Intelligence

A psychologist and educator, Howard Gardner, says that intelligence is the ability to solve problems or make things that are valued in one or more cultural situations. To achieve this goal, he says, one needs more than verbal and computational skills. These two skills, verbal and computational, are the traditional "intelligences," the aspects of a person's intelligence that schools use and teachers teach.

According to his original theory introduced in 1983, Gardner says that there are seven kinds of intelligences.

- the ability to see patterns, to reason, to solve logic puzzles and do mathematics (logical-mathematical intelligence)

- the ability to master language, to manipulate language to express thoughts in speech and in writing, to use language as a tool for memory (linguistic intelligence)

- the ability to judge size, to work with mental images to solve problems, to know how things will fit together (spatial intelligence)

- the ability to understand and create musical pitches, tones, and rhythms as an auditory skill (musical intelligence)

- the ability to coordinate one's own bodily movements, to make one's body move as one wants (bodily-kinesthetic intelligence)

- the ability to understand and respond appropriately to others' feeling and intentions (interpersonal intelligence)

- the ability to know one's own feelings and motivations (intrapersonal intelligence)

As you answer these questions, you can help yourself understand these difference intelligences. Circle *yes* or *no*.

Logical-Mathematical Intelligence ____

1. Were you able to understand the logic puzzles   yes   no
   in this unit?
2. Do you like mathematics?
3. Are you good at math?   yes   no
4. Do you look for cause-effect relationships?   yes   no
5. In puzzle pictures in which there are hidden objects,   yes   no
   can you find the hidden objects?

Linguistic Intelligence ____

1. Do you speak more than one language?   yes   no
2. Do others consider you a good writer?   yes   no
3. Do you enjoy writing long letters to   yes   no
   family and friends?
4. Do you like to look things up in a dictionary?   yes   no
5. Do you read and sometimes write poetry?   yes   no

Spatial Intelligence ____

1. Can you figure out what size box you need for a   yes   no
   pile of books?
2. Can you imagine a box inside a box inside a box?   yes   no
3. Do you always know what size suitcase you will   yes   no
   need for the things you need to pack?
4. Do you like to put together jigsaw puzzles?   yes   no
5. Can you imagine the steps that you will have to   yes   no
   take to bake a cake before you begin?

Musical Intelligence ____

1. Do you sing songs in your head (no sound)?   yes   no
2. Can you feel the rhythm of a dance without the   yes   no
   sound of a drum?
3. Can you sing the scale, from the lowest note to   yes   no
   the highest?
4. Do you play a musical instrument?   yes   no
5. Can you recognize singers' voices even if you   yes   no
   haven't heard a song before?

Bodily-Kinesthetic Intelligence ____

1.	Can you dance well?	yes	no
2.	Can you pat your head and rub your stomach at the same time?	yes	no
3.	Do you play a sport well?	yes	no
4.	Can you close your eyes while you are standing and then lift one foot and keep your balance?	yes	no
5.	Can you estimate (guess) how high you can reach without trying to reach?	yes	no

Interpersonal Intelligence ____

1.	Can you tell when another person is sad?	yes	no
2.	Do you talk to strangers in the supermarket or on an elevator?	yes	no
3.	Do your friends ask you for advice?	yes	no
4.	Do you know exactly what to write on a postcard to a friend?	yes	no
5.	Have you ever been able to read another person's mind?	yes	no

Intrapersonal Intelligence ____

1.	Do you have personal goals and a plan for how to achieve them?	yes	no
2.	Do you try to figure out ways of getting what you want?	yes	no
3.	Do you ask others for help in accomplishing your goals?	yes	no
4.	Do you know why you feel happy or sad on any particular day?	yes	no
5.	Do you like yourself?	yes	no

Now count the number of *yes* answers in each category and write the number in the blank after the name of the intelligence. The higher the number of *yes* answers, the more likely you are to have that kind of intelligence. Compare your scores. If one score is higher, that is probably your most developed intelligence. If all your scores are equal, you are likely to be balanced in all things.

Strategy: Writing About the Ideas

1. As you read this unit, what did you learn about yourself as a thinking person? What talents do you probably have that you do not use? What could you do to use those talents? Do you think your talents need to be "exercised" to become useful? Choose one talent that you have and write about how to develop it.

2. What areas of intelligence do you probably lack? Do you think that practicing those areas will help you develop that kind of intelligence? The brain is a learning machine, and you can learn. Write a plan for increasing your intelligence.

3. How do you feel about puzzles? Write three sentences about your responses to the puzzles. Show your three sentences to a classmate, and read your classmate's three sentences. Many people will not try puzzles because they are afraid that they will fail. Write about how different people respond to the challenge of puzzles.

Strategy Focus: Keeping a Vocabulary Journal

Choose five words from the new words in this unit to be your target words.

Write the words here: _____   _____

_____   _____   _____

Now write them into your vocabulary journal. Remember to include the following parts:
- your target word
- the sentence from the unit in which your target word appears
- a definition, including the part of speech.
- some sentences of your own

Strategy: Increasing Reading Speed

 # Timed Reading

Acupuncture as a Method of Healing

An *acupuncturist* is a kind of healer. Acupuncturists use knowledge of the body's electrical impulse system to ease pain and heal. There are pathways through the body that are similar to the circulatory system, which supplies oxygen and nutrients to the body by pumping blood through the body. The electrochemical system is a separate system with pulses just like those that the heart causes in the body. (However, these electrochemical pulses are much harder to feel.) The system works something like the brain's neural transmitters, along the *meridians* (the pathways) of the body. Stimulating one part of the body with an extremely fine needle stimulates the acupuncture point that is connected to it.

The practice of acupuncture has its origins in the Chinese medical tradition. The "barefoot doctors" of Chinese history practiced acupuncture, but only recently has the practice come to be common in the Western world. The stimulation caused by twirling a needle that has been placed into a meridian seems to trigger the nervous system to create and send out chemicals that reduce inflammation and pain.

Researchers have studied the effects of acupuncture on patients. They have found that acupuncture causes the release of *endorphins*, natural body chemicals that act like painkillers. Researchers also believe a hormone called ACTH—a natural chemical that fights inflammation—is released. That's why injuries heal more quickly with acupuncture.

An added benefit is that acupuncture causes no negative side effects. Prescribed drugs, like all medicines, can have some serious side effects. *Aspirin*, perhaps the most common of all medicines in the world, has many strong points in its favor; however, even one tablet causes a small amount of bleeding in the stomach. Acupuncture causes no negative things to happen in the body. Acupuncture has been used to treat headaches, *arthritis*, and serious breathing problems (such as the ones associated with *asthma*). People who suffer from arthritis (inflammation of bones at joints like knees and elbows) and strokes have used acupuncture to improve their quality of life. They can do more with less discomfort. No one is absolutely sure why it works, but the theory is this: the acupuncture needle stimulates a sensory nerves which sends an electrical impulse to the brain. That impulse signals the release of brain chemicals which stop the *nocioceptors* (pain receivers) and send out endorphins (the "feel-good" chemicals). In any case, acupuncture helps many people who are suffering.

Time: _____

Now answer these questions as quickly as you can.

1. Asthma causes…
   a. skin problems.
   b. breathing problems.
   c. bleeding in the stomach.

2. Knees and elbows are called…
   a. joints.
   b. points.
   c. meridians.

3. Acupuncture is ____ medical practice.

   a. a dangerous

   b. a new

   c. an ancient Chinese

4. Meridians are...

   a. doctors.

   b. pathways.

   c. needles and techniques.

5. Which of these is a good title for this reading?

   a. Chinese Medical Practices

   b. Modern Application, Ancient Practice

   c. How Arthritis Patients Can Be Helped

TIMED READING CHART

After completing each timed reading, mark your time and comprehension score on the chart. By keeping a written record, you will be able to see the progress you are making. You should try to get your comprehension at 8 or above. Also, notice the number of words per minute you are reading.

- If you are reading below 100 words per minute, you are reading every word very carefully. This speed is good if you need to analyze something in detail.

- If you are reading between 101 and 250 words per minute, you are reading at a speed that is good for studying textbooks and for learning. This is careful reading.

- If you are reading between 251 and 400 words per minute, you are reading at a good speed for casual or informal reading, such as the reading of magazines or newspapers.

- If you are reading above 400 words per minute, you are reading at an accelerated speed. This speed can be used if you need to read something important very quickly. In some cases, this speed actually can help comprehension; it can help you learn information.

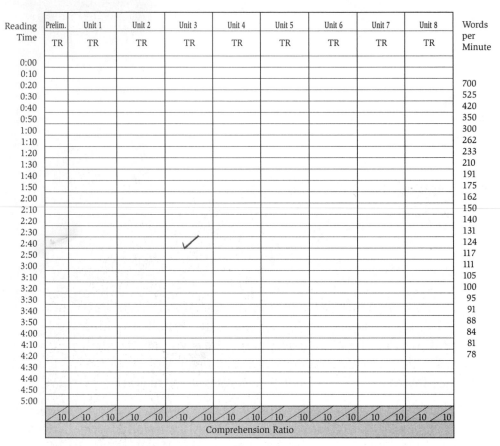

Reading Time	Prelim. TR	Unit 1 TR	Unit 2 TR	Unit 3 TR	Unit 4 TR	Unit 5 TR	Unit 6 TR	Unit 7 TR	Unit 8 TR	Words per Minute
0:00										
0:10										
0:20										700
0:30										525
0:40										420
0:50										350
1:00										300
1:10										262
1:20										233
1:30										210
1:40										191
1:50										175
2:00										162
2:10										150
2:20										140
2:30										131
2:40				✓						124
2:50										117
3:00										111
3:10										105
3:20										100
3:30										95
3:40										91
3:50										88
4:00										84
4:10										81
4:20										78
4:30										
4:40										
4:50										
5:00										
Comprehension Ratio	10	10	10	10	10	10	10	10	10	10

Note: TR = Timed Reading

INDEX

Target vocabulary items, foreign terms, and titles of works are in italic print. The page numbers provided can be used to locate each vocabulary item in an explanatory context. Various topics and activity types are in roman print.